THE JUMBO BOOK OF MAGIC

THE JUMBO BOOK OF MAGIC

by Magic Magazine Editorial Board

DRAKE PUBLISHERS INC.   NEW YORK   LONDON

Published in 1976 by
Drake Publishers, Inc.
801 Second Avenue
New York, N.Y. 10017

Library of Congress Catalog Card Number: 76-21174
Main entry under title:

The Jumbo Book of Magic.

Drake Publ.   New York

June 16, 1976   6'76

ISBN: 0-8473-1194-5

Printed in the United States of America.

Table of Contents

WHILE SEATED AT THE TABLE

INDISPENSABLE SLEIGHTS

IMPROBABILITIES

CALCULATION TRICKS WITH ORDINARY CARDS

BE SURPRISED

MYSTERIES OF A PREARRANGED PACK OF CARDS

DO IT AGAIN

IMPROMPTU CARD TRICKS

MAGIC WITH A SVENGALI PACK OF CARDS

Introduction

When you get right down to it, a magician is supposed to be skilled in creating illusion. He's supposed to be able to stand up before an audience and perform seemingly impossible effects that will leave his audience spellbound and wondering how the tricks were performed.

How does a magician learn all these skills? He can buy the effects one at a time in his local magic shop, and study and practice each one. He can watch more-experienced magicians, and if he watches closely enough, often enough, he might learn a new effect that way too.

Another, better way, is to read and study the many books on magic that are available in bookshops. That's why this book was created, to jam-pack as much new and different magic between the covers as they could. It was not an easy task, for the selected material was gone over again and again, tricks and effects were accepted and then later rejected as they weren't as good as some others. Up until the very last minute, changes were made so that you, the reader, could gain the greatest benefit. Rest assured that there were sufficient illusions left over to form another three books just like this one!

Now, before you get started, let's talk about magic for a moment.

A great magician once said that "Presentation is everything." If you simply do tricks, you're just fooling your friends. If you can add some of your own personality, change the words a bit, inject a little humor where it's called for, then you're performing magic. And you know? That's precisely the point! The magic is YOU and what you bring to the performance of a trick.

Before you can do an effect successfully, you have to know the effect, how it works, and how to wrap your fingers around it comfortably. This requires much practice, and any magician can tell you that to do an illusion correctly will require a great deal of practice. But do not sit there working the trick and looking down at your hands while you practice! If you do, you'll find that when you're performing in front of an audience, you can't do the trick without looking at your hands, and that's the worst form of misdirection you can come by!

Instead, stand in front of a mirror so that as you practice, you are forced to look toward where your audience will be. Then practice so you can do the trick without even thinking about what your hands are doing. You say you can't do that? Then you need much more practice!

In this book, the world's top magicians are exposing their secrets to you. As a magician yourself, you are obligated to keep those secrets and not even tell them to your best friends! Maybe you think it makes you look smart to show that you know how a trick works, but remember that somebody else is trying to make a living doing those tricks!

When you turn the next page, you'll be on your way to becoming a real magician. Remember always to look like one, and to act like one. Always be sure that what you say and do will reflect well on our craft, and honorably upon yourself.

Now that we have shown you that the road to success is through constant, arduous practice, and that you are honor-bound to keep the secrets of the craft, let's not allow another moment to pass. You're about to become a master magician. Turn the page, and let's get started.

BYRON G. WELS
Editor/Publisher
The Magic Magazine

THE JUMBO BOOK OF MAGIC

THE CURIOUS FOLD

I have never seen this in print, but I believe it is rather old. However, it is not well known, and it always provides good entertainment for a dinner table audience.

The bill is held upright as shown in Fig. 1, then folded down from the top as in Fig. 2, and twice to the left as in Figs. 3 and 4. These moves are now reversed, but when the bill is open once more, it is upside down!

The secret is to make the second fold *backward* as shown in Fig. 3, and the third fold *forward* as shown in Fig. 4. When the bill is opened, however, these two folds are both opened from the *front*. This automatically turns the bill upside down.

Unless the spectators have observed you very carefully, they will be unable to duplicate the moves.

In making the folds, the bill should be held at the left side by the left thumb and fingers, the right hand doing the folding. Make the folds rapidly and the moves will be more difficult for the spectators to follow

Do not repeat the trick too often. A good presentation is to cause the bill to turn upside down, then repeat, bring it right side up and hand it to the spectators to see if they can do it.

NAMING THE DATE ON A BORROWED BILL

Few people know that all dollar bills now in circulation bear the date 1935. The date will be found in the lower right hand corner.

You can make use of this fact in a mystifying and little known mind reading trick.

Ask for the loan of a dollar bill. Tell the person not to look at the date, but to wad the bill into a ball. Place the ball against your forehead and appear to be concentrating. Very slowly call out the date 1-9-3-6, and start to return the bill. Then look puzzled and place it to your forehead once more. Say, "No, that's not correct. I'm sorry I spoke so soon. It's a 1935 bill." This line of patter helps suggest that bills are differently dated.

Hand back the bill for verification.

My friend Dave Price, who cuts a mean deck of cards in Nashville, pointed out to me that most five dollar bills now in circulation are dated 1934, and the few that are dated 1928 have the date in red, which is easy to spot at a distance. He also called my attention to the fact that it is possible to secure 1928 dollar bills. You can carry one in your pocket, and when you perform the trick, use your bill to make clear to the spectator where he will find the date on *his* bill. The fact that the two dates are different will throw him off the track in trying to solve the trick—a neat little presentation touch.

FOUR PILES AND A DOLLAR BILL

The previous trick, *Naming the Date on a Borrowed Bill,* can be combined very neatly with a card effect.

Previous to showing, place an ace, nine, three, and five on the bottom of the deck. False shuffle, and have a spectator cut off about two-thirds of the cards. Discard these cards, handing the lower third to the spectator with the request that he deal them into four piles.

The reasons for the cut are that it takes too long to deal an entire pack into four piles, the deal from a cut makes things seem fairer, and when the cards do not come out even at the end of the deal (as is often the case) it also makes things seem more on the up-and-up.

After the piles are formed, borrow a bill, have the date called out, then turn up the top cards of each pile to reveal the four figures of the date.

CIGARETTES

THE UNREVERSED WORD

The well known trick of holding a pack of Camel cigarettes to a mirror, causing the word "choice" on the side of the pack to remain unreversed in the reflection, first appeared in print in a little manuscript by Dr. Harlan Tarbell

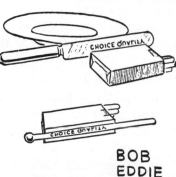

called "Ten After Dinner Tricks." The stunt is still an excellent one for dinner table purposes.

The simplest way of presenting it is to lean a table knife against a plate, so that the shiny side of the knife acts as a mirror when the pack is placed flat on the table in front of it. First place the pack on the table with the words "choice quality" right side up. Call attention to the fact that both words are reversed in the knife. Then take the pack in hand, casually turning it over as you do so, and pretend to manipulate something on the side of the pack. Replace it in front of the knife, this time with the words upside down. In the reflection, the word "quality" will appear reversed, but the word "choice" is unchanged. This is due, of course, to the curious construction of the letters in the word "choice."

If glass stirring rods are available, a more effective way of presenting the trick is made possible. Place the rod over various words on the pack, calling attention to the fact that when you read the words through the rod, they are reversed by the refracting power of the glass. Shine the rod briskly with a napkin, stating that static electricity causes a peculiar change in portions of the glass. Hold the rod over the words "choice quality". The word "choice" is unchanged, although "quality" is reversed!

An interesting variation of this trick can be performed with the names of people whose first name are Bob, Eddie, or Joe. Merely print their full names on a piece of paper, printing the first names in the manner shown. Through the stirring rod (or in a mirror) the first names will not be changed, although the last name will be reversed.

Also note that Spud cigarettes carry the phrase "choice tobaccos" on the side, and therefore can be used as conveniently as Camels.

BITING THE CIGARETTE

A startling bit of hokum, easy enough for anyone familiar with the art of "tonguing" a cigarette.

Light a cigarette and take a few puffs. Then turn it around so that the lit end goes into your mouth. Light the other end. Take a few more puffs.

Now bite the cigarette in half. The half that remains in your mouth will lie on the tongue, the lit end projecting into the mouth cavity.

Remove the half that projects from the mouth. The spectators, unaware that the cigarette has been divided in half, will think that you merely removed the cigarette from your mouth.

Open your mouth slightly, and with your tongue quickly reverse the half, popping it out through your lips. Puff on it a few times to prove that it is lit.

Sam Berman, Chicago's ace ball manipulator, showed me this novelty years ago.

THE MAGIC INHALE

The magician inhales on his cigarette, but when he breathes out, there is no smoke in his lungs!

Secret: blow gently through the cigarette instead of inhaling. This causes the end to flare up as though you had inhaled. Take the cigarette from your lips and breathe out slowly and vigorously.

Try it, and you'll be surprised at the number of people who fall for it!

COINS

COIN THROUGH THE PLATE

For this trick you need a small piece of wax, about half the size of a pea. You can carry it behind a vest button. before showing the trick, secretly transfer this piece of wax to the underside of a saucer. The center of the underside is usually concave, so the saucer may rest on the table without the wax sticking to the table cloth.

Borrow a coin, preferably a half dollar, and a small square of paper. Have the spectator mark the coin for later identification. Wrap the coin in the paper, using the well-known fold which permits the coin to slide into the hand.

Tap the paper on the edge of the plate to prove the coin is still inside, then permit the coin to slide into the left hand. Lower this hand to your lap as your right hand takes the paper and places it on the saucer.

Ask someone to strike a match. While this is being done, hold it to the edge of the table. The left hand comes up from beneath and presses the coin against the wax, causing it to stick to the underside of the saucer.

Place the saucer on top of a glass of water. The spectator sets fire to the paper. As it burns, the heat melts the wax and the coin falls visibly into the glass below.

Retrieve the coin, and dry it with a napkin (this also serves to remove the wax that may have adhered). Return it to the owner for identification.

VANISHING COIN

To perform this subtle vanish (first shown to me by Joe Berg of Chicago) you must be resting your chin on your left hand as shown in the drawing.

Hold the coin in your right hand and place it in front of you on the table.

Ask the person opposite you to cover it with his hand. As he reaches forward say, "No—I mean the *other* hand." As you say this draw back your hand (it is a perfectly natural gesture) in such a way that your fingers bring the coin just above the opening of your left sleeve. The person is confused about the changing of hands, so it is a simple matter to drop the coin, unobserved, down the left sleeve!

Place your right hand on the table once more as though it still held the coin. Have him cover your hand with his. Then ask him to remove his hand. Slowly open your fingers to show that the coin has vanished.

The vanish can, of course, be used for any small object that can be dropped down the sleeve without difficulty.

TESTING A HALF DOLLAR

This is more of a gag than a trick, but it never fails to get a laugh.

Ask your audience if they have seen the new method of testing half dollars to determine if they are genuine.

Place the half on the table, then grasp an empty tumbler in the manner shown. Strike the half several times using the tumbler as a hammer. The "X" in the drawing labels the portion of the glass which strikes the coin. It makes a terrific racket, but the tumbler never breaks.

Pick up the half dollar saying, "And if the half doesn't break, you know it's not a counterfeit."

Matt Schulien, of Schulien's north side German restaurant and bar, was the first person I saw present this stunt. The gag line at the finish comes from Dorny.

MATCHES
LIGHTING A MATCH TWICE

From time to time various methods of making a match burn twice have been devised. One method is to strike the match, blow it out, then dip the head in water. Under pretense of drying the match, you stroke it through your hair, and in doing so, exchange it for a match previously placed there. This second match is then struck.

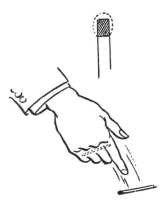

A method employing paper matches appeared recently in one of the Magic magazines. With a razor, trim off the sides and top of the head. If this prepared head is struck on the side, and quickly blown out, you will discover that the other side of the head will ignite. Consequently the match may be struck a second time.

To my mind, however, the most effective method for this effect consists of preparing a handful of wooden matches in advance by covering the heads and a small portion of the stick beneath the head with black ink. You can do this by merely dipping the heads into the ink. Let the matches dry and carry them in your pocket until you wish to use them.

When you find yourself seated at the table, secretly drop several of these matches into the ash tray. The heads will pick up ash and look exactly like burned matches.

In presenting the effect, first take a genuinely burned match from the tray and attempt to strike it. You are, of course, unsuccessful. Then take one of the prepared matches, and with appropriate patter and hokum, strike it triumphantly.

If you are adept at switching small objects you can present it this way. Have one of the prepared matches finger palmed in the right hand. Light another match, quickly shake it out, and toss it on the table. Needless to say, as you toss it to the table you retain the match just struck and throw down the faked one. State that as soon as the match cools, you will strike it again. Feel the head of the match gingerly, jerking your fingers away as though it were still warm. Blow on it to cool it more rapidly, then strike it with a flourish.

COLOR CHANGING HEADS

This sleight, which I worked out several years ago, has since become a popular impromptu stunt with a number of night club performers who work tables. Le Paul, I think, was the first to start using it. A description of the effect appeared in the winter issue of the *Jinx* 1938.

At the beginning of the trick, the left hand holds two matches with *blue* heads. The right hand has palmed two matches with *red* heads, concealing them in the manner indicated in Fig. 1.

State that you intend to pull the heads from the matches in the left hand. The fingers and thumb of the right hand grasp the heads and make an attempt to pull them off. Do this twice. The third time, the fingers of the left hand take the matches from the right hand and the right fingers carry away the two matches previously held in the left hand. The exchange is a very natural one, and no one is expecting a switch.

After the switch, the matches in the left hand will be upside down. It appears as if the heads have been pulled away. The right hand pretends to toss the heads under the table or to place them in the coat pocket. This enables you to dispose of the two matches in the right hand.

The rest of the trick is patter and build-up. State that you are going to expose how you did the trick. Of course you didn't really pull off the heads, you explain. Under cover of the right hand you merely turned the matches upside down, so the lower ends would be brought to view. But—you continue— you have never been able to understand why the trick always causes the heads to change their color. With the right forefinger, rotate the matches around to reveal the red heads. Toss the matches on the table for inspection.

Emphasize at the outset that the heads are blue, otherwise the audience may forget the original color.

FOLDER MATHEMATICS

I think this clever trick first appeared in print in an issue of Ted Annemann's *Jinx*.

Hand a full folder of matches to someone with the request that while your back is turned he tear out a few matches and place them in his pocket. The number must be less than ten. After doing this, he is to count the number of matches that remain in the folder, and to tear from the folder a sufficient number of matches to be able to form that number on the *table*.

For example, he first tears out five matches and pockets them. This leaves fifteen matches. He then tears out enough matches to form the number fifteen on the table. The number is formed by placing one match to the left, then enough matches in a pile on the right to represent the last digit of the number (1 — 1111). These matches are also to be placed in the pocket. Once again the spectator tears out some matches. These he holds in his closed fist.

At this point you turn and face the table. One look at the folder and you are able to state the number of matches in his hand.

Secret: substract the number in the folder from nine.

MATCH FOLDER WAGER

Challenge anyone to strike, one at a time, all twenty matches in a folder. Only one striking attempt is allowed for each match.

The odds are enormously in your favor because of the chemical on the striking surface quickly wears off, making it difficult to strike the last few matches.

It can be done by striking the first ten matches on the *right* side only of the striking surface, then the remaining matches on the *left* side.

SHOOTING THE MATCH

J. B. Ward, of Dewsbury, England, sent me this effect shortly after the publication of my book *Match-ic* in 1936. I have never seen it performed by American magicians.

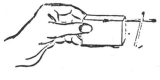

A match box is placed on its edge, with one match inserted into the top, and a second leaning against the first as shown. The left hand graps the box, the thumb pressing against the side nearest you.

Patter about the vertical match representing a soldier behind a trench. With the right hand, take a third match. This represents the gun of an enemy soldier. Place the right hand in front of the match box and pretend to "shoot" the soldier in the trench. As you say "bang" the left thumb slides a trifle forward. If the thumb is pressing against the box, this slight and indetectable motion will cause the leaning match to fly suddenly backward! It is the same principle as that which produces "spirit raps" from a pencil.

The effect can be heightened by having the spectator place his forefinger on top of the box to steady it. He will feel a slight tremor as the match flies backward, but the modus operandi will remain a mystery.

THE NAZI CROSS

This is an amusing gag that has been making the rounds in recent months. Place five matches on the table and ask if anyone knows how to make a Nazi cross with five matches. The answer: stick four of them in his ear and light them with fifth!

Stress the fact that the matches must not be broken, and that no more than five are permitted. This throws them off the gag and helps build up the punch line.

MISCELLANEOUS

JAPANESE PAPER BIRD

There are three reasons why I feel justified in including this item in the book.

One: It is the most ingenious and entertaining paper-folded toy ever invented.

Two: Very few people, including magicians, have seen it.

Three: It lends itself to one or two novel presentations.

Rather than repeat here the complex instructions necessary in order to explain how the bird is folded, let me refer the reader to Houdini's *Paper Magic,* page 117, where the method of folding is described. For those who are interested, I might add that the earliest description I have found of this item is in Tissandier's *Scientific Recreations,* a French work published in 1881 and later translated into English. Both Houdini and Tissandier ascribe the invention of the bird to the Japanese.

The bird itself is extremely lifelike. When the tail is pulled, it flaps its wings. It can be folded from any type of paper, and from a square of almost any size. It never fails to delight persons of all ages.

Carry some four-inch squares of flash paper with you. Fold the bird from one of them. Pass it around the table so that others can have the fun of operating it, then place it on top of an inverted glass. Patter about the bird's extreme fear of fire. To illustrate why—touch a lit cigarette to the bird's tail.

Another presentation angle is to conceal a dime in your hand, dropping it into the paper (in this case a larger piece of ordinary paper) while you are folding it, so that the dime will later be inside the bird's body. Refer to the bird as a "magpie" and patter about its love of coins. Often it swallows the money that it carries in its bill, you say. Tear open the body and shake out the dime.

Or better, have a borrowed dime marked, and fold it in a piece of paper, marking the usual fold so that the dime drops into the hand. Then fold the bird from another sheet of paper, leaving the dime inside. Fly the bird over to the folded paper, touching its bill to the place where the dime is supposed to be. Then tear up the paper to prove the dime has vanished and find it inside the body of the bird.

VANISHING COFFEE STEAM

The magician waves his hand over his coffee and the steam suddenly stops rising from the cup!

Secret: Either the magician or a confederate seated next to him blows gently at the cup. Waving the hands misdirects attention from your lips, which should appear as normal as possible.

TAPPING TABLE OBJECTS

I first ran across a version of this ingenious table effect in Walter B. Gibson's excellent volume, the *New Magician's Manual*.

The magician arranges seven objects in front of him on the table. A spectator is asked to think of one of the seven. The magician starts tapping the objects with his table knife. At each tap the spectator is to spell (to himself) a letter in the name of the object he has in mind. When he completes the spelling, he says "stop". This is done. When he says "stop" he discovers, to his surprise, that the magician is touching the chosen object with his knife.

The seven objects used are as follows:

1. Cup
2. Fork
3. Plate
4. Napkin
5. Ash tray
6. Match box
7. Cigarette

This list must be memorized. In presenting the trick it is necessary to make the first two taps on any objects you wish, then start tapping them in the order indicated by the list.

The trick is puzzling enough to withstand several repetitions.

TRAVELLING FOUNTAIN PEN

A borrowed fountain pen (or eversharp pencil) is caused to travel invisibly from your inner coat pocket to that of the gentleman on your right.

Yes, the gentleman on the right is tipped off in advance.

Borrow a fountain pen. Take it in the left hand and appear to place it in the inside coat pocket, saying "That's a fine looking pen, mind if I keep it?" Actually, drop it down the right coat sleeve, near the arm pit. The right arm hangs normally at the side so that the pen drops noiselessly into the fingers.

Remove the left hand from the coat, open the fingers wide, and look at the hand. While the attention of the audience is on this hand, the right hand drops the pen into the lap of the person on the right who quietly clips it to his coat pocket while everyone is watching you.

By this time the owner of the pen is asking to have it returned. "But," you protest, "I really haven't got the pen. However, I believe the gentleman on my right can return it to you." If your stooge is a convincing actor,, the trick can be built into a real piece of magic.

In the absence of a stooge, slip the pen under a napkin on the table, and produce it later by removing the napkin to expose it.

SILVERWARE
TABLE KNIFE THROUGH BODY

Hold a cloth napkin by the two upper corners, then swing it over the left arm as shown, as though you were about to produce a fish bowl. Exhibit a table knife in the right hand. Appear to place this knife behind the cloth, the point of the knife touching the center of the napkin; and with the knife, lift the cloth from the left arm so that your right hand holds the knife and cloth in the manner shown in Fig. 2.

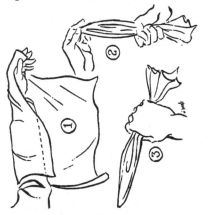

Actually, as soon as the knife is behind the napkin, it is pushed into the left sleeve. The right forefinger is extended, and with this finger the napkin is lifted from the arm. The illusion is perfect from the front.

With the left hand pretend to take the point of the knife through the cloth. The right hand comes out from under the napkin and grasps the cloth at the base. If the left hand pulls on the cloth, it can release its hold and the napkin will retain its shape as though the knife were still inside.

Hold the cloth horizontally (Fig. 3) then suddenly turn to the person on your left and stab him in the chest with the extended cloth. At the same time your left hand is lowered, permitting the knife to drop into your left palm. With the left hand reach behind the person's body, under his coat, and bring out the knife.

This last touch is a product of the nimble brain of Laurie Ireland.

BREAKING THE SPOON

"Everybody knows this old method of *bending* a spoon." As you say this, grasp the spoon and pretend to be bending it, using the familiar method of letting the handle slip through your fists. After having done this, show the spoon to be unharmed, and place it on the edge of the table.

Now look directly into the eyes of the person seated opposite you. This will cause him to look at you. At the same time, pretend to lift the spoon from the table by placing both hands over it. Actually, as soon as your hands cover the spoon, the fingers flip it backward into your lap. Raise your hands as though they held the spoon: keeping your fists next to each other and tightly closed. Lean forward so that your fists are almost under the nose of the person opposite you.

Ask him if he has seen the new method of *breaking* a spoon. When he says no, suddenly pretend to break the spoon in half, making a "pfffft" noise with your mouth. Immediately open both hands showing that the spoon has vanished. It never fails to create surprise and astonishment.

I must thank Bob Hummer, the vagabond magician, for the misdirection features involved in this sequence of moves.

BENDING THE SPOON

This is not recommended for privately-owned silverware, but in a public restaurant no harm is done and the gag always goes over. It's a favorite of Henry Gordiene's.

Take a spoon between your hands and go through the well-known moves of pretending to bend it, the head of the spoon resting on the table, the handle concealed by your fingers.

Instead of pretending, however, you actually do bend the spoon. A thumb beneath the end of the spoon makes this a simple matter. Bend the spoon until it is almost a right angle.

At this point look up and ask, "How does that look? Does it look as if the spoon is bending?" There will be a chorus of affirmations.

"Well, it should!" you say, as you take the spoon by the handle and hold it up to view.

The spoon can, without damage be easily straightened.

SWALLOWING THE KNIFE

An old favorite (described in 1885 in Sach's *Sleight of Hand*) but here are some new angles.

Place the knife near the endge of the able. Cover it with both hands as shown, and lift it to your mouth, actually taking the knife in your hands. Start to place the blade into your mouth, then change your mind and replace the knife on the table. State that you forgot to *salt* the knife. Take the shaker and sprinkle some salt over it. This is always good for a few chuckles. Pretend to lift the knife once more. This time your hands draw the knife to the edge of the table and permit it to drop into your lap. Keep your hands in the same position as before, as though they still held the knife. Raise them to your mouth, then suddenly pretend to drop the knife down your throat. Show your hands empty and smack your lips.

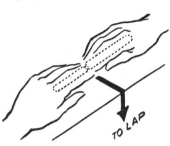

Someone is sure to ask where the knife went. Lower your hands to your lap and push the knife into your left sleeve. Raise the hands, and extract the knife. The audience will be convinced that the knife went into your sleeve, and they give you credit for some fancy manipulative work.

Another variation is to tip off a friend in advance so that when the audience asks where the knife went, your friend (who is preferably seated at the other end of the table) stands up and shakes a table knife out of *his* sleeve. (You can take advantage of this moment by replacing your knife, unobserved, on the table.)

SPOON TO KNIFE

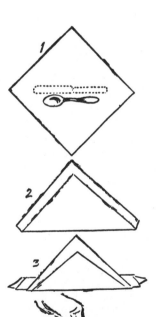

The effect is as follows. A spoon is wrapped in a cloth napkin. When the napkin is unrolled, the spoon has changed to a table knife.

Spread the napkin on the table as shown in Fig. 1 with the knife concealed beneath it. Place the spoon on the cloth just *behind* the knife. Now fold the corner nearest you over to meet the opposite corner. Note that the corner on top must be an inch or so *behind* the lower corner.

Start to roll the spoon in the napkin, making the rool *beneath* the napkin so that the knife is included in the roll. After rolling forward a few inches, turn the napkin over, bring the roll upward and continue rolling forward until you reach the far corners. As you complete the roll one end of the cloth is permitted to go around the roll once, so that it comes flush with the other corner. This is concealed by the hands which are held over the center of the roll as it is rolled forward on the table.

Place the fingers of the left hand on the *lower* corner, holding it against the table. The right hand takes the *upper* corner and pulls it toward you, unrolling the napkin. This automatically causes the spoon to drop into your lap (this is concealed by the cloth) and exposes the knife inside the napkin!

THE MUSICAL KNIFE

This is an old stunt, but one of the most entertaining when properly presented.

Hold a fork in the left hand so that the handle is almost touching the table. Take a table knife in the right, and with the blade, pluck one the the center prongs of the fork. Immediately hold the tip of the knife blade over an empty tumbler. At the instant the knife is above the glass, the left hand allows the handle of the fork to rest on the table. This will produce a musical note, easily heard unless you are in a very noisy restaurant. Do this several times, stating that the note occurs only when the knife is held over something *empty*. Place two empty glasses side by side and move the blade of the knife from one to the other. The left hand raises and lowers the handle of the fork so that the tone occurs only when the knife is directly over the brim of each glass.

Conclude the effect by holding the blade over the *head* of the person nearest to you!

I am indebted to Dorny for this routine and gag finish.

THE VANISHING SPOON

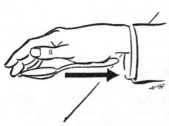

This requires a little practice until you get the knack. The spoon rests on the table, with the handle pointing toward you. Cover it with your right hand. The fingers touch the bowl of the spoon, tipping it slightly to raise the handle about one half-inch from the table. The fingers then flip the spoon backwards, into the sleeve. The hand is raised to show that the spoon has vanished. Performed rapidly, the vanish is very surprising.

NAPKIN

CHARACTER READING FROM THE TEETH

Tell your table companions that you have recently learned the art of reading character from the biting impressions of a person's teeth. To prove it, pass a cloth napkin around the table, asking each person to bite into the cloth to leave an impression. Take back the napkin and study the impressions carefully. Then put it down saying, "You folks certainly bit on that one."

IMPROVISED BRASSIERE

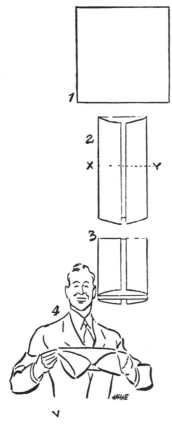

I have been unable to discover the source of this clever napkin stunt which began making the rounds recently.

The napkin is placed flat on the table as in Figure 1. The right and left sides are folded to the center as in Figure 2.

Grasp the napkin in each hand at points X and Y, lifting it so that it folds backward along line XY. Lay it on the table again in the position shown in Figure 3.

Take the two corners on the left between the thumb and fingers of the left hand, and the two on the right in the right hand. Bring the hands suddenly against the chest, as in figure 4, with surprising results.

There are so many patter versions which might accompany this stunt, that I have left them to the reader's imagination.

THE INVISIBLE HAIR

You must have a cloth napkin, well-starched for this amusing stunt.

Take the center of the cloth in the right and draw it up through the left fist. The napkin will retain its shape so that the hand can hold it as shown in the first drawing. With the right hand pretend to pluck a hair from the head of the nearest person, and tie one end of it around the tip of the napkin. Hold your right hand about a foot to the right, as though it held the free end of the hair. Move your right hand back and forth. At the same time, the thumb of the left hand moves up and down. This causes the napkin to bend over to the right and back up again. With a little practice you can harmonize the motions of the napkin and the hand so that it gives a perfect illusion of a hair attached to the tip of the cloth.

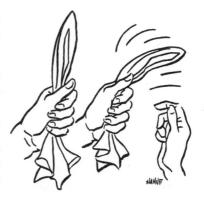

As a finish, pull the cloth over as far as you can to the right, then bend over and pretend to *bite* the hair in two. As you click your teeth together, the left thumb allows the cloth to spring upright.

SALT SHAKER

THE VANISHING SALT SHAKER

This is undoubtedly one of the most startling table tricks. Its success depends almost wholly upon the use of misdirection.

Place a coin (say a dime) on the table before you. On the coin, place a salt shaker. Cover the shaker with a cloth napkin (folded twice), pressing the cloth around the shaker so that it assumes the shape of the shaker. If paper napkins are available, so much the better. Use three or four of them together.

State that you intend to cause the dime to vanish. Make some passes over the shaker, mumble some double-talk, then lift the shaker and napkin, drawing them back toward the edge of the table. As you do this, lean forward and look intently at the dime. All eyes will be misdirected toward the coin. This permits you to let the shaker drop into your lap. The napkin retains the shape of the shaker. Shake your head as though the trick had failed and cover the dime once more. Repeat the passes and the double-talk. Remove the napkin, but the dime is still there. This is build-up to strengthen the belief of the audience that the shaker is still beneath the cloth.

Pretend to be thinking then say, "No wonder the trick isn't working. It's not the dime that's supposed to vanish, but the salt shaker." As you say this, smash the napkin to the table with your fist.

As a variation, start the trick with a *pepper* shaker on your lap. State that you intend to cause the dime to change to a penny. When you drop the salt shaker, your left hand comes up and pushes the pepper shaker into the napkin. After the trick has apparently failed, state that you had it all wrong. It's the salt shaker that changes, not the coin. Take away the napkin and show this to be the case.

INDISPENSABLE SLEIGHTS

Card tricks of any really entertaining value cannot be presented without the aid of a few simple sleights but with them, even a simple trick can be made to look like real magic. The word 'sleight' has a terrifying effect on most people who like to learn a few tricks, and is at once associated with the idea of hours of drudgery practicing intricate movements requiring intense application to master them. However I will guarantee that anybody of ordinary intelligence, with the ability to shuffle a deck of cards by the overhand method fairly neatly, can in a couple of hour's time gain a working knowledge of the simple sleights that follow and in a very short time he will, by using them, have them literally at his fingers' ends. The novice is advised to follow the directions given exactly. Later, as the simple principles underlying the various moves become clear, he will experience the fascination of devising his own methods and putting into practice variations and tricks of his own invention.

1. THE OVERHAND SHUFFLE

This is the term applied to the ordinary shuffle in which the cards are passed singly or in small packets from the right hand to the left, the cards being drawn off by the left thumb. It affords a means of keeping a card or several cards completely under control without arousing the least suspicion on the part of the onlookers. In the following exercises turn the top card face up so that you can follow the processes easily.

A. Take the deck face down in the left hand, holding it at an angle of about 45 degrees towards the right. Lift the deck with the right hand retaining the top card in the left by a slight pressure of the left thumb. Shuffle off all the cards on top of this one. Lift the whole deck with the right hand and shuffle off all the cards into the left to the

27

last card, dropping this on the top. Thus with two perfectly fair shuffles you have the top card back in its original position.

B. With the pack in the left hand lift it with the right but this time press lightly on the bottom card with the left fingers, retaining it and at the same time draw off the top card with the thumb as before. The top cards thus falls on the bottom card in the left hand while the right hand holds all the rest of the deck. Shuffle these cards freely on top of the two in the left hand. The card you are controlling is now second from the bottom and you can turn the pack over and show the bottom is an indifferent one; then turning the cards face down lift off and show several cards from the top, also indifferent cards. Shuffle again, this time retaining the bottom card and lifting all the others with the right hand. The special card will now be the last card of this portion and you have simply to shuffle freely until it alone remains in your hand and you drop it on the top of the pack.

C. To retain a card at the bottom of the deck you will have already noted that it is merely necessary to retain it in your left hand by pressing on it with the left fingers.

D. It is very often necessary to place a definite number of cards on top of another card. This is done by what is termed 'running', and means simply drawing cards off the top of the deck one by one with the left thumb in the course of a shuffle. If the cards are in good condition, and I take it for granted that only such cards will be used by you, a few minutes practice will enable you to run off any number of cards in this manner with the greatest of ease.

E. To make the best use of the overhand shuffle, it must be combined with a very simple move, so simple that I evolved it from my own inner consciousness as a schoolboy only to find in later years that it had been used by gamblers as far back as records go. It is called the jog, that is, a card pulled back a little over the inner end of the deck so that it becomes a marker indicating its own position or that of the card or cards immediately below it. To apply the idea take a few cards, say the four aces and put them on top of the pack. Hold the pack in the left hand ready for shuffling and lift the rear half with the right hand. In making the first movement of taking the cards off with the left thumb, move the right hand about half an inch inwards towards the body and draw off one card only, then move the right hand forward again and continue the shuffle as usual. At the end of the movement one card will protrude from the deck at the inner end marking the location of the four aces. To bring them back to the top seize all the cards below the protruding card, lift them and drop them on the top just as if you were making a simple cut. You have the four aces back on the top. (See illustration).

Any number of cards, up to about half the deck can be retained undisturbed by this simple expedient. After the first card has been

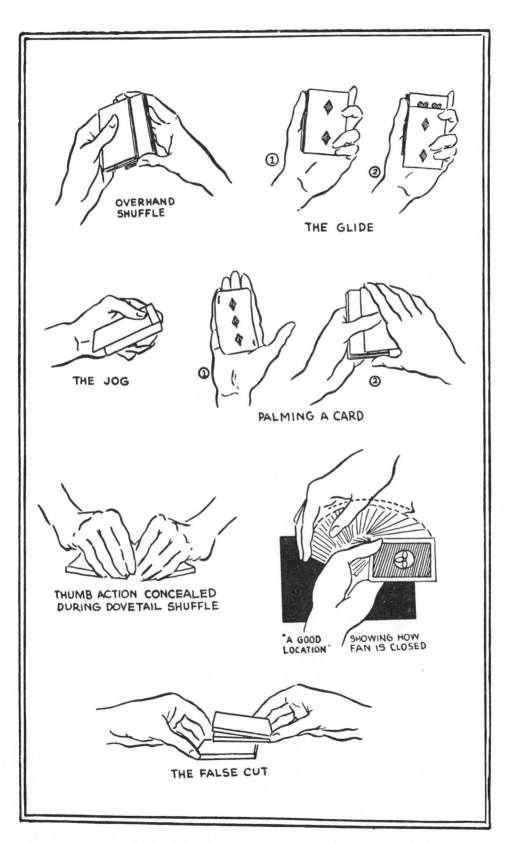

OVERHAND SHUFFLE

THE GLIDE

THE JOG

PALMING A CARD

THUMB ACTION CONCEALED DURING DOVETAIL SHUFFLE

"A GOOD LOCATION"

SHOWING HOW FAN IS CLOSED

THE FALSE CUT

jogged make the shuffle so that the cards fall irregularly and the projection of the jogged card from the rear end of the deck cannot be noticed. I cannot advise the reader too strongly to use this expedient until it becomes second nature. The whole action can be done without looking at the hands and while carrying on an animated conversation with your audience.

F.   To retain the whole deck in order.

Take the deck in the left hand as if about to deal, push off a small packet with the left thumb and take them in the right hand. From the bottom of the pack push off a few cards on top of the right hand packet. Again push a packet off with the left thumb receiving it below the cards in the right hand, and again with the left fingers push a packet taking it on top of the right hand packet. Continue in the same way until the whole pack is in the right hand. Do not attempt to make the movements quickly, this is the only sleight I know of that a rather rough execution rather enhances the effect.

The shuffle leaves the pack in the condition of having been cut once. If it is necessary to return it to its original order from the top card down, spread the faces to show the cards are well mixed and cut at the original bottom card which you noted before beginning.

The Riffle Shuffle

This is the term applied to the shuffle in which the deck is divided into two packets, the ends put together, the cards being bent upwards and released in such a way that they become interlaced. To retain a card or a small packet of cards on the top, you have simply to release it or them from the right hand portion last of all. If the bottom cards are to be retained then they are let fall from the left hand in the first movement of the shuffle. It will readily be noted that cards can be retained both at the top and the bottom at the same time.

A false cut

Hold the deck by the sides near the ends between the thumb and second finger of each hand. Now pull out about one third of the cards from the bottom and put them on the top but still hold them with the thumb and second finger. With the right third finger lift about half the lower packet, draw the hands quickly apart releasing the top packet which falls on the table resuming its original position. On it drop the packet from the left hand, and on that the right hand packet. The cards are in their original order. (See illustration).

2.   PALMING A CARD.

Contrary to the opinions of most magicians I maintain that palming a card is not a difficult operation. It simply requires confidence and a proper understanding of the right method. To get the right position hold your right hand palm upwards and on it lay a face up card so that the top index corner touches the top joint of the little finger and the lower index corner presses against the fleshy part at the base of the thumb. Bend the fingers naturally keeping the thumb near the side of the hand and the fingers close together. Now turn the hand over. The card will be retained in the hand with ease and as long as you keep the palm towards your body it will be safely hidden. (See illustration).

Now with a thorough understanding of the way the card is to be held in the hand, the next step is to learn how to get it secretly into that position from the top of the pack.

Take the pack face down in the left hand in position for dealing. Place the right hand over it, thumb at the inner end, the first joints of the four fingers resting on and covering the outer end of the pack. Run the fingers and thumb of the right hand over the edges and ends of the cards in the natural way of squaring the pack, and bring them back to the same position with fingers covering the outer ends. Then with the left thumb push the lower end of the top card to the right. The least contraction of the right hand will then secure the card in the exact palming position. Move the fingers and thumb of the right hand to the right hand corners of the pack and hold it between the forefinger and thumb while the left hand squares the sides. Remove the left hand and hold the pack in the right. (See illustration).

If these actions are followed exactly, the palming of the card will be imperceptible to the closest observer. Later when you put the pack down to be cut, or hand it to be shuffled by someone on your extreme left, the action is perfectly regular.

Do not hold your right hand and arm stiffly as if paralyzed or immediately put it behind your back. Keep your wrist relaxed and natural and forget about the card being in the hand.

To get the card back on the pack, hold out your left hand and have the pack placed on it and cut by the spectator. Pick up the lower portion with your right hand, adding the palmed card to the top, and assemble the pack.

3. THE SIMPLE PASS

A card having been chosen, cut the pack for its return. Have it replaced on the lower portion and replace the cut on top, slipping the tip of your left little finger on the card and between the two packets. Hold the outer ends of the pack tightly closed and riffle the ends of the cards a couple of times. Seize the upper portion between the right thumb at the rear and the fingers at the outer ends. Lift it off, and at the same moment drop the left thumb under the lower packet and turn it face upwards, and immediately shuffle the cards of the right hand packet onto the faces of the lower packet.

Do not be in a hurry and do not look at your hands. Look at your victim, ask him if he is sure he will know his card again and go straight into the shuffle. Turn the pack over and continue the shuffle. You have the card on the top to do with as you will.

It should be sufficient to say that the greatest of present day magicians use this pass only.

4. THE DOUBLE LIFT.

Many modern card tricks employ this sleight of lifting two cards as one. It is not difficult, the difficulty lies in making it naturally. With the pack well squared in the left hand face down, bring the right hand over it, thumb at the rear, fingers on the outer end. Make a motion of squaring the ends and at the same time press the fingers back a little making the ends of the deck slightly wedge shaped. With the ball of the thumb lift the rear ends of the two top cards and slip the tip of the left little finger under them.

With the right thumb tip on the back of the two cards and the tip of the right forefinger on the face, turn the two cards as one and lay them face up on top of the pack, the ends protruding over the inner end of the deck for about half an inch. Exhibit the card in this position, name it, and seize the cards again at the lower outer corner as before and turn them face down on the back of the pack.

The little finger tip should be inserted before attention is called to the card and the turn made naturally and without hesitation or fumbling. There are many uses for the sleight, for instance you apparently show the top card and put in the middle, it immediately returns to the top.

5. THE GLIDE

Hold the pack face up in the left hand between the first joint of the thumb on one side and the second joints of the four fingers on the other. Call attention to the bottom card, say it is the 2D. Turn the pack face downwards and with the tip of the left finger draw the bottom card, 2D, back towards the body about ¾ of an inch. Now with the tip of the right hand second finger draw out the next card, say it is the 8H and put it face downwards on the table.

The sleight is easy and deceptive. For instance, you may get a chosen card second from the bottom by means of the overhand shuffle as already explained. Show the bottom card, turn the pack face down and deal the bottom card face up; draw back the next card by the glide and deal cards from above it to a chosen number - then deal the chosen card face down. Have the card named and turn it up.

A GOOD LOCATION

Pack is held in the left hand and any card is freely selected. The selected card is now returned to the pack, but performer pinches the cards tightly so that the selected card will not go all the way into the pack. Immediately the other hand swings the cards around left to right closing the pack as in the illustration. It will be noted that the selected card is now protruding slightly. Right hand now picks up all of the cards underneath the protruding card and shuffles on to top of the pack. Next the protruding card is removed and placed on top of the pack. Thus your selected card is brought to the top of the pack in a simple manner.

With these few simple sleights at his command, it is hoped that the reader will find the pages of this book an open sesame to endless hours of entertainment.

FOR READY REFERENCE
SEVERAL METHODS OF FORCING CARDS
(from Annemann's "202 Methods of Forcing")

The pack having been shuffled by a spectator, is returned to performer who takes it in right hand, at the same time casually pulling up left sleeve followed by the left hand pulling up right sleeve. When right hand with deck pulled up left sleeve, the bottom card of deck was easily spotted. Asking the party if they are satisfied, a pass is made and card brought to about two-thirds down in pack. A slight break is held at this spot. The thumb of left hand now runs the cards of the upper portion, fanwise, over into the right hand, the person being, at the same time, invited to take one. When about half of the upper portion has been passed. a card, NOT THE ONE TO BE FORCED, is pushed temptingly forward. The person may be inclined to take it—whether he is so inclined or not, the performer draws it back, with the remark. "Oh! not necessarily that one." This gives him confidence, and the performer continues to pass the cards over to the right hand, spreading them nicely fanwise, until he reaches the one to be forced, which he exposes a little more than usual, then continues, "Just take any one you please." It will, of course, be understood that the action must be timed, as near as possible, to meet the hand, as it is raised to draw a card.

The card to be forced is on the bottom of deck. The cards are run from left to right in the usual manner, but the action is started while approaching the audience so as to give time for the following maneuvre: With the second and third fingers of the left and right hand work the bottom card over toward right side. The cards are still run from left to right passing above the chosen card. Ask someone in the audience to indicate his choice by touching the card desired. When it is indicated lift up this card with all the cards above it and as the pack is squared up the forced card slips in from below.

In this method a few top cards are prearranged. Three cards of one number (say five) are placed on the top of the deck and the card to be forced then placed at eight from the top. The pack is false shuffled, keeping the top eight cards in place. The three top cards are then dealt onto table in a row and one selected while face down. This one is turned over and the spectator handed deck to count down and remove the fifth card, which is the right one.

What is known as the "bridge" makes possible a neat cutting force. The card is on bottom of deck. Cutting same about center, the lower half, which is to be placed on top, is given a bend (concave) at the ends. Spectator is asked to cut deck somewhere and look at face card of cut. If cut is made at sides, this will work time after time, as the slight break at sides will cause upper half to be lifted off by a quick cut. By bending the sides, the bridge can be placed at ends for an end cut. Previous cutting by the spectator will give you this information. Most cuts are at sides.

Place a short card near center of the deck. Card to be forced mentally is above it. Hold deck straight up in front of spectator. With first or second right fingers riffle top of deck from face to back, smoothly and without a stop. Ask spectator to note cards and to think of one that he sees. Practice before a mirror to get speed. The short card will click by and the following card will register on the spectator when the rest of the deck is a slow blur. Don't try to stop at the card but let it work itself. It will seem impossible at times that a card will show up in this way but try it before several people before you judge.

THE KNIFE METHOD

In this method the card to be forced is placed about 15th from the top. Cards are held in the left hand. The little finger makes a break directly underneath the known card. A flat knife is handed to spectator who is asked to insert it anywhere he may please. Performer slowly riffles the pack. It is only necessary that the knife enter the pack below the chosen card and fairly near to it. The top fifteen cards are now pushed forward onto the blade, pack being tilted slightly downward. Performer grips the knife with right hand and the fifteen cards, the lowest of which is the known card, are pushed well forward and slightly raised. The spectator is asked to note this card, which appears to be the one he has cut.

MAGIC WITH CARDS

Reggie the Rattlesnake

P RIOR to the advent of this world-shattering novelty there have been medium snakes in baskets, new, improved, smaller snakes in baskets, and even Jumbo snakes in baskets; and as the Indians have been keeping their snakes in baskets for hundreds of years, I feel I am being really original by producing a snake at last that is not in a basket. On the other hand, my snake produces a card as have so many of the others, so perhaps I'm not so brilliant after all.

This trick is no good for a stage, platform, or club show (that's what they call Negative Advertising!), but it's a lot of fun when you're doing a card trick for a couple of friends. It won't baffle magicians, but we'll bet they'd like one!

Somebody throws a pack of cards at you so you start doing tricks. Eventually you have someone take a card then allow him to shuffle it back all by himself. Suddenly you say: " Let me introduce you to Reggie, my Rattlesnake. Rattle for the Gentlemen, Reggie! "

Reggie duly rattles, then he suddenly pops out of your outside breast pocket with a small replica of the chosen card stuck between his teeth.

Doubtless some of the more mechanically-minded dealers could produce Reggie in a completely self-contained version, but for us simple types there is always a magician's thread or, in this case, thin fishing line. You will need a small tube of either glass or metal and a model snake that will fit in it. The size of the snake naturally depends on the dimensions of the tube, which will depend in turn upon the size of your left breast pocket. Big men definitely have the bulge here.

In the illustrated model there is a small lip on the rear side of the tube which stops the snake coming too far out. Attached to the snake, somewhere near its nether regions, is a widish ring which

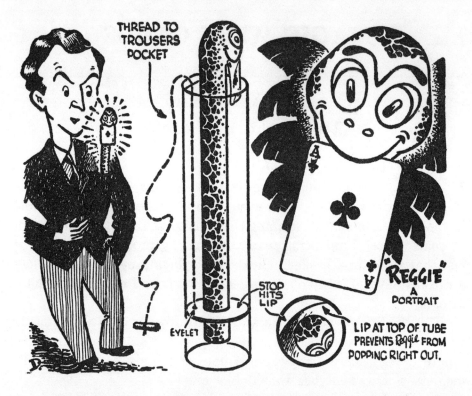

THREAD TO TROUSERS POCKET

STOP HITS LIP

EYELET

"REGGIE" A PORTRAIT

LIP AT TOP OF TUBE PREVENTS *Reggie* FROM POPPING RIGHT OUT.

hits against the lip and so stops catastrophe. Just by this ring there is an eyelet to which a length of thin fishing line is attached. This leads up out of the tube, through the lining of the pocket, and down into the left hand trouser pocket. If you'd rather, the movement may be controlled by the line coming down to the mouth of the left sleeve. However you do it, the end of the line should have a small bar or button attached to it so you don't have to fiddle about fiendishly for the end.

The card, as you surmised, is forced. A duplicate of the card you intend to force should be made, in miniature, and stuck into the snake's mouth with glue.

The "rattle" is caused by the right hand furiously turning the cog of a "Watch-Winder." This may or may not sound like a rattlesnake's rattle but we doubt if your audience will know the difference.

The snake is down in its tube and the end of the thread is in a position where it can be grasped easily. The card is forced from an ordinary pack and may be shuffled in by the chooser. The patter is gone through, the Watch-Winder wound; then the thread is pulled, and up comes Reggie. When the trick is over he may be pushed back down into the tube and you're all set for the next performance.

*   *   *   *

Ri-Ki-Ki Poker

NIGERIA is an amazingly cosmopolitan place. Recently I set in (rather like Rigor Mortis) on a Poker game in which one player was a naturalised Frenchman, one a Dutchman, and the third from the region of the Polish-Russian Frontier. Luckily we all spoke English . . .

At the end of the session (that is, when all the bottles were empty—and I refuse to divulge the results of the game !) the Frenchman told us a rather amusing yarn. It was new to us, although you've probably heard it before, but I thought at the time that if I could illustrate it with cards it would make a good trick and would demonstrate my ability to deal poker hands, without making that the only point, if you follow me.

First of all, here's the story. It appears that a gambler was playing poker with a comparative novice at the game. A hand was dealt to each, the novice discarded three and drew another three to take their place, and he found he'd got four Aces and the Joker which, in this game, was very, very wild. So he quite naturally started raising and, oddly enough, the gambler raised with him, all the way. Eventually the gambler " saw " him and the novice turned over with great pride his five Aces, whilst the gambler showed he'd got the Two of Clubs, the Four of Hearts, the Seven of Spades, the Eight of Diamonds, and the Queen of Clubs. In passing, Gentlemen, I would say that a hand like that is known out here as a Takoradi Straight and is worth exactly nothing at all.

The novice started to rake in the chips but was stopped by the gambler.

" Just a minute," he said, " That hand of yours doesn't beat mine. This is the Ri-Ki-Ki ! "

As there was about a £100 on the table the novice wanted to know what the ———— the Ri-Ki-Ki was, so the gambler told him that the Ri-Ki-Ki (pronounced, incidentally, Ree-Kee-Kee) Hand was the highest in the pack. The gambler duly won the day and the novice decided he'd better write that round off to experience. The cards were dealt a few more times until suddenly the same business happened the other way round, the gambler got the five Aces and the novice picked up the Ri-Ki-Ki. They raised each other as before. The gambler started to pull in the chips when the novice excitedly pointed out that he had the Ri-Ki-Ki which the gambler had told him only a few minutes before beat any hand there was.

" Oh, I'm terribly sorry," said the gambler sadly. " I quite forgot to tell you that Ri-Ki-Ki can only count once in an evening ! ! ! ! "

And with that he scooped the pool.

There are bound to be heaps and heaps of ways of bringing this about but the following has its points of interest, is exceptionally easy, and leaves you with an ordinary pack at the end. If you care to work out complicated sleight-of-hand methods for working it with an ordinary pack then by all means do so. Anything for the art, so to speak.

You will require a pack of cards containing the Joker, and duplicates of the following cards, AC, AD, AH, AS, Joker, 2C, 4H, 7S, 8D, QC, which have the same back-design as the pack.

The pack must then be set up in the following order, from back to face :—AC, 2C, AS, 4H, 10D, 7S, 8H, 8D, 2S, QC, AD, Joker, AH, 2C, AD, 4H, AS, 7S, Joker, 8D, JD, QC, 6S, AH, AC, the rest of the pack. Certain cards in the list are only indifferent and do not affect the trick ; in short, they could be anything.

The pack, set as above, is false shuffled and cut. Then two poker hands are dealt, the first to the " sucker," the second to yourself. This means that the man opposite you finds the AC, AS, 10D, 8H, and the 2S. In your hand will be the Ri-Ki-Ki. If the assistant knows Poker he will immediately discard three cards, the 10D, 8H, and 2S, and demand three more which you deal him from the top of the pack. Watch where he places his discards. He should now have four Aces and the Joker. Carry on with the story, then turn both hands over so that all can see them. Gather them up face-downwards on the table and add the three discards to their top. This packet is then placed on top of the rest of the pack in your left hand, but a break is held and, at a convenient moment, the packet is passed to the bottom. The top card in your pack should now once again be the 2C.

Continue with the story and then deal two more poker hands from the top of the pack, again starting with the helper. He will get the Ri-Ki-Ki and you will have AD, AS, Joker, JD, and the 6S. Discard the last two from the gambler's hand and deal the next two from the top, which gives it four Aces and the Joker.

Point out that there are five Aces in the gambler's hand as you turn it up ; then have the novice's hand turned over and tell the audience that it is the Ri-Ki-Ki. As they look at the cards and wonder at your astonishing skill, thumb-count ten cards from the bottom of the pack, palm off, and dispose of them into your pocket. Continue with the plot as outlined before, shoot the climax at them, then drop the rest of the pack on the table to give the sceptics a chance to get at it.

If you happen to be doing it for a bunch of magicians you may then stand back and watch them dive for the deck.

*   *   *   *

Silken Card Discovery

IN this we have attempted to improve on an old production box idea wherein the load is attached to the rear of one of the four walls, and the box is built up out of walls and base. Previously all sides of the walls could not be shown ; in this version they can see everything is innocent. The box consists of four walls decorated to resemble Giant Playing Cards. The base is merely a square piece of wood with four slits in it into which the " cards " may be stuck. The box assembled is shown in Figure 1, and the base in Figure 2. No further description of these is necessary as they are ordinary in every way.

The necessary "works" are in a stand which is used apparently merely for showing the cards. This stand is illustrated in Figures 3, 4, 5, 7 and Figure 3 is how it looks to the audience, Figure 4 is a side view, and Figure 5 is a view from behind. The two pieces marked X are runners into which slides a fake shown in Figure 6. This is made from a piece of thin metal painted black, and slightly narrower and shorter than one of the Jumbo Cards. Attached to this fake is the load chamber (marked in the drawing L.C.) and the size of this naturally depends on the size of the rest of the apparatus.

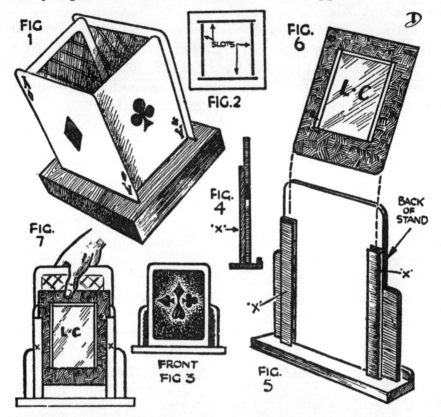

The fake is slipped down the runners at the back of the stand prior to performance, the load is in the chamber, and you're all ready to go.

The presentation is as follows. The box is exhibited to the audience already assembled. It is taken to pieces by removing the cards from the slits in the base one at a time, displaying them on both sides, then placing them on to the stand. They are then removed and returned one at a time to the slits in the base, the two sides and the back wall being placed in first. When the time comes to take the last card from the stand it is done as in Figure 7. The fingers are at the front of the card and the thumb at rear pulls up the fake also. As both are pulled clear of the stand the fake naturally slips into place at the back of the card and, as it's smaller both ways than the card, it is unlikely to slip to either side. The two together, card and fake, are then pushed down into the front slit. The box is now loaded.

Many plots will suggest themselves, but the following has been tested.

Fill the load chamber with all the picture silks you can lay your hands on, and the first silk to be put in should be a card silk, shall we say the Jack of Clubs, although a low sopt card is better in a big hall. This is the silk that will be produced last of all.

The box is taken apart and re-assembled then a plain white silk handkerchief is dropped into it. A card is chosen by a member of the audience who, needless to say, doesn't have the free choice he thinks he has ; in short, he takes the Jack of Clubs.

" Now," says the sorcerer, " I want you, Sir, to project your thoughts on to the white handkerchief in the box. Project them as hard as you can and if you succeed we shall find a picture of your card impressed on it."

The spectator duly does as he is told. The magician reaches into the box to find the result and withdraws a handkerchief with the picture of a beautiful girl on it (if you have that sort of silk in your kit !). He tries again and finds another handkerchief with Mickey Mouse rampant. And so on. At the bitter end he finds the handkerchief that tells him the name of the gentleman's card.

A different angle could be used at smokers. The three walls could be decorated to represent the local hostelry and the front would be a replica of the inn's sign-board. This time a glass of beer is produced. Instead of a load chamber attached to the fake you need only have a ring into which the glass fits upright. And, as the advertisers say : " No rubber covers used ! "

* * * *

The Travelling Phoenix

A MEMBER of the audience is asked to step forward, take charge of a sealed envelope, carry it to the back of the hall, and stay there until called upon. A pack of cards is shuffled and another spectator is given the choice of one card with, however, the provision that if he takes a court card he is to return it and take another until he has a spot card.

When he has finally located a spot card he is handed a pencil and asked to write his name on the face of the card, then to pass both pencil and card to three other people who also write their names. This business over, the card is returned to the sorcerer who, holding it high in the air, returns to his table.

A candle is lighted from a match magically produced and the card is burned to ashes but, to confound sceptics, whilst the card is consumed its face is towards the audience at all times.

The gentleman who, all this time, has been kicking his heels at the back of the hall is requested to open the envelope he has been holding. Inside is a card and he is asked to call out its name. It is realised that the card is the one just burned. The magician asks him if he sees anything peculiar about the card, and he replies that it has four signatures on it. The card itself is now taken to the man who drew it for verification of signature and, if necessary, the other three signatories may also check.

Required is a forcing pack consisting of 51 spot cards (we suggest something like the Two of Spades), and one court card with matching back. An envelope, and a pencil.

To prepare, remove from the pack two of the spot cards. On each of these scribble four signatures with the pencil. Obviously these signatures should appear as if written by four different people. One of these cards is sealed in the envelope and the other is placed face down on top of the pack. The single court card is placed in the pack in your favourite position for forcing.

To perform, present a member of the audience with the sealed envelope and request him to go to the back of the hall and stay there until called upon.

Force the court card on another spectator telling him, as mentioned above, to replace the card if it is a court card as there will not be sufficient space on it. He returns the court card and takes another. He may be allowed a free choice of all cards with the exception of the top one, the card with the four fake signatures on it. He takes a blank Two of Spades (or whatever your force deck consists of), and you give him the pencil so that he may write his name across the card's face. He is instructed to hand the pencil and card to three more people and, when they have written their names, the card is returned to you. You take it in the right hand between the forefinger and thumb, and the rest of the pack is held in the left hand face-downwards.

It is at this point that the first sleight takes place, the top change. This is a basic card sleight and should present no difficulty. The position is now that the card with four fake signatures on it is held in the right hand in full view and the genuinely signed card is resting safely face downwards on top of the pack.

On the return to the table the pack is placed down. A lighted match is pulled either from the pocket or beneath the lapel (from a match lighting fake) and the candle is lit. The card held in the right hand is now burned face towards the audience and, whilst this is going on, the pack is picked up with the left hand.

When nothing remains of the card but ashes the gentleman at the back of the hall is asked to open the envelope. He is asked to tell the audience what is inside. When he tells them there is a card he is further asked to name it. After it has been named as the Two of Spades the magician says :

" Is there anything strange or peculiar about the card ? I mean, is it different in any way to, say, any of the cards I have here ? " holding the balance of the pack up in the air with the left hand. He is told there are signatures on it. The volunteer comes to the stage and hands the card to the magician and, at this stage, the second sleight is used. This may be a top change as before or the bottom change. We prefer this as it is slightly more silent. What happens is that the card taken from the volunteer is changed with the card on the top of the pack.

The genuine card is handed to the spectator so that he may check his signature, and he may be allowed to pass it on to the other three people who signed their names.

One last point : The signatures you write on the cards should be comparatively indecipherable.

PUBLISHER'S NOTE. There was a great deal in Annemann's warning not to make an effect " too divine." We suggest that if the man at the back of the hall shows himself to possess the card which the performer has just burnt, although the magician has not approached him since the beginning of the effect, the audience's reaction must be that it is *not* the same card or that the performer is employing supernatural agencies. There can be no other explanation.

For this reason we recommend that the contents of the first assistant's envelope should not be disclosed until the envelope has been handled by the performer—however briefly and however cleanly.

The Snake Charmer

THE magician shows a piece of white rope a yard long, ties a knot in one end, then tosses it into a basket. He has three cards selected from a pack, they are returned, the pack is shuffled, and then that, too, is thrown into the basket.

The sorcerer dons turban and snake charmer's pipe then squats down by the basket and commences to play any mournful dirge he can think of. Slowly, up comes the rope, knotted end first, until it stands vertical about two feet high. And stuck to the knot is the first card that was chosen.

The card is removed, the rope pushed down, and the effect is repeated. The last time, however, there appears to be some difficulty and the rope is reluctant to rise. The magician plays louder. Then suddenly the rope shoots up until it is nine feet high, and the last card is attached to the top.

The performer whips out a pair of opera glasses and focusses them on the card.

" Was your card the —— of ——, Sir ? " he asks.

" It was ? . . . Well there it is ! " Curtain.

Once again, we're afraid there is nothing really new. But, as a stage card discovery with novelty this meets the bill as is proved by audience reaction.

Requirements are few and simple but an assistant is needed to pull the thread at the right time. You will need a basket of the flat variety, a piece of rope a yard long, another piece four yards long, some Scotch Tape, thread, a pair of opera glasses, a turban, a tin whistle, and a pack of cards.

The long piece of rope is knotted at one end and a piece of Scotch Tape is attached to the knot. A long thread is also attached, then this should be carried up over a stage batten and down into the wings. The assistant is now stuck to the end of the thread. The rope is next coiled up neatly and placed into the basket so that the knotted end is easily available.

To present, the performer shows the short piece of rope, ties a knot in it in the same way as he did in the larger piece, then tosses it into the basket well to one side so that it cannot foul the prepared piece. He then goes down into the audience with the pack of cards and has three selected and returned. These cards are brought to the top of the pack by your favourite method, then the pack is placed face-downwards in the basket near the taped end of the rope.

The magician dons a turban and picks up the whistle. He squats on the floor at the side of the basket and commences to play. Slowly up comes the rope. The magician pushes it back into the basket and, in doing so, presses the part with Scotch Tape on on to the top card. He plays again. The assistant pulls on the thread and the

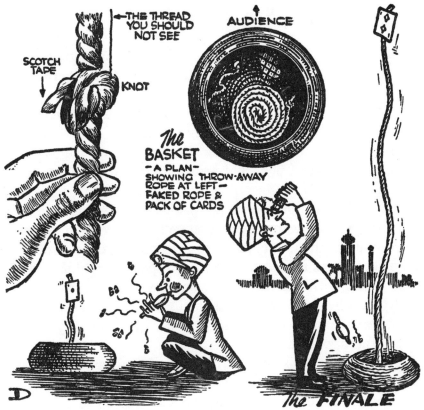

rope rises once more, this time with the first selected card attached to it. This is repeated for the second card because when the first card is detached the rope head is again pushed down so that tape comes in close contact with the top of the pack. The second card is removed from the knot and the rope pushed down on to the pack ; but this time the assistant does not pull on the rope immediately. The magus plays louder and, when he has almost reached the end of his endurance, the assistant pulls the rope right up quickly. The pipe is dropped, the sorcerer pulls opera glasses from his pocket to discover the name of the card and, when he receives confirmation of it, points dramatically to it.

MAGIC WITH THE MIND

Eve v Adam

A HUSBAND and wife are invited from the audience on to the stage. The husband is chained up with a length of chain and a padlock ; and each of six keys (the padlock key amongst them) is sealed in a separate envelope. The wife is invited to try to free her husband by discovering by her " intuitional faculties " the correct key to unlock the padlock. As there is usually a pretty strong sort of bond between husbands and wives, needless to say, she succeeds.

Required to work this effect is a padlock, preferably Yale, which comes with two duplicate keys. You will also need five other keys that are similar but not sufficiently so to unlock the padlock. One of the padlock keys is kept hidden in your pocket until later and the other is mixed with the five indifferent keys. A length of chain is necessary of a length to go round the average person's wrists twice and still leave enough to get the padlock into. Six pay envelopes complete the apparatus.

A married couple is invited on to the stage and you seat the lady on a chair on your right, and the gentleman on another chair to your left. The lock with the six keys is handed to the lady and special mention is made of the fact that only one key will open the lock. She may test this statement to her own satisfaction.

The keys are now sealed up in the envelopes and the lady may help in the process. Then the chain is wound tightly round her husband's wrists and the padlock is snapped closed over the ends. He, for the moment, is safely out of things.

You patter to the effect that there is always a bond of sympathy between all married couples, and the lady is then invited to try to pick out the envelope containing the key that will free her husband. Tell her to act immediately she feels the slightest impulse about any envelope she picks up.

Whilst this is being done the duplicate key is palmed out of the pocket by the left hand and concealed there by the fingers. When the lady stops at an envelope you take it and tear off one end. Actually it only looks like that to the audience. What you really do is tear off only *half* an end. If you refer to the illustration (Fig. II) you'll see what we mean. The envelope is then squeezed open and

apparently the contents deposited into the palm of the left hand (Fig. I). But as you hold the envelope with the open part of the end uppermost the key inside it doesn't fall out. The key is held up (that is, the key that was already in the left hand is held up) and the envelope with the other key still inside is screwed up and dropped into the pocket.

You take the key, walk over to the woman's husband, and unlock the padlock releasing the chain. You might try massaging his wrists " just to restore the circulation."

Prolific readers of magical literature will see in this yet another variation of " Seven Keys to Baldpate," and how right they are.

" Hail, O Swami "

AN effect for mentalists usable under pretty well any conditions, this is capable of giving the performer good publicity. A small card bearing a picture of a " Swami's head " and a crystal ball is examined and initialled by a member of the audience. It is then placed into an envelope just large enough to hold it. This is sealed, and the assistant's autograph is scribbled across the flap to obviate any dirty work.

Having shuffled a pack of cards, the performer hands it to the spectator, and asks him to deal off from the top of the pack face downwards as many cards as he has years in his life. He is then to look at the next card, replace it, and return the counted off portion of the pack back to where it came from.

The envelope is torn open and the card removed ; there in the white circle that represents the crystal ball is found the name of the card the assistant has just chosen. At each stage he may check his initials on the envelope flap and on the card itself. He may be allowed to keep the card (which could have your name, address, and telephone number printed in tasteful type on the reverse). And if you'd rather he didn't find the name of a card, but something else, that could also be easily arranged.

You'll be glad to know that the method isn't troublesome. The card is ordinary except for the fact that it should appear as illustrated, a Swami's head at the top, the white circle fondly pretending to be a crystal ball, and a couple of small triangles in which the spectator sticks his initials. The card should be completely black with the above items standing out in white. We suggest the back of the card also be black with your name and other details in white lettering, the idea being to give the impression of a *black* card. You'll see why shortly.

The guile in this particular instance is in the envelope. This has a hole in it which is slightly less in diameter than the diameter of the crystal ball, and in such a position that when the card is inside the envelope the ball on the card coincides with the hole. This hole should be on what is commonly known as the " address " side of the envelope, which should be of the type real workers collect their pay in. It should also be white in colour. We will now explain how cunning we are. The card, after it has been initialled, is slid into the

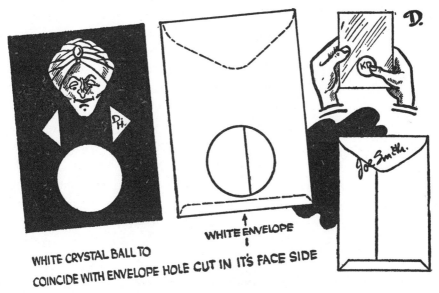

WHITE CRYSTAL BALL TO
COINCIDE WITH ENVELOPE HOLE CUT IN IT'S FACE SIDE

WHITE ENVELOPE

envelope in such a way that the ball and hole coincide. As the ball is white (and the customers feel it's a *black* card) and the envelope is white, if the audience should happen to get a flash of the faked side they'll think nothing of it because each side of the envelope is still completely white. And for that superb bit of subtlety we hereby award ourselves the Sorcerer's Star.

The envelope is sealed and initialled across the flap. Then the assistant is given a pack of cards and carries on as mentioned before. Whilst he's in the throes of working out his age the job is finished. This consists of scribbling the *initials* of the card (that is, the King of Hearts is written as KH) on the face of the crystal ball through the hole with a Nail-Writer stuck on the right thumb. At the moment of writing the card is held at a slight angle to the audience so they can't see what's going on.

The man finds his card, re-makes the pack, and is then asked to check his name on the flap of the envelope. The envelope is torn open, the card removed. He checks his initials on the card and is positively staggered to find the name of the card he's just looked at.

Now, of course, all you want to know is how the name of the card is discovered. No, there's no need for you to know the man's age before you start, all you require is a forcing pack, a pack containing fifty-one cards all alike, and an odd card on the bottom just to keep up appearances. It doesn't matter what his age is providing he's under fifty-two. If you'd rather use a stacked pack and a disc-locator by all means do so, but the Forcing Pack makes it all so easy!

Tangled Thoughts

IS it really necessary that all mental routines should be done with a serious, and often gloomy, face ? Or do you agree with us when we say let's have a little comedy and brighten things up? The mentalist introduces a slate, a paper bag, and a Jumbo card that stands back-outwards against a simple stand. These, he states, are Indications of the Future, in other words, predictions.

Three cloth bags are shown, each containing nine plastic counters, circles, tags, or Poker chips. In the first bag each counter has the name of a city upon it. In the second bag each has on it a number from 1 to 9. And in the last bag there are nine counters all of different colours.

The counters may be examined if necessary, then they are mixed up thoroughly in their respective bags. Three spectators in the expensive seats are asked to stand. The first is asked to reach into the bag containing counters marked with the names of cities, take hold of any counter he likes, then withdraw his hand. He should keep his fist clenched as he is not to know at this stage what he has drawn. The second spectator is given a choice in the same way from the second bag containing counters marked with numbers, and the last spectator chooses a counter from the bag containing coloured discs.

The magician (sorry ! " Mentalist ") returns to the Indications of the Future. He picks up the slate still, however, keeping its blank side toward the audience. Briefly he runs over what has happened, how the spectator has had a free choice and doesn't know himself yet what he's drawn. Ah ! But the Hidden Eye knows ! The slate is turned around and on it is written in large letters " CALCUTTA."

" Look at your counter, Sir," says the mentalist, " and you will find you have drawn the same city."

The spectator opens his fist and finds he's drawn a counter bearing the name " NEW YORK."

The slate is quickly reversed again so that the blank side faces the audience, and the mind-reader appears slightly deflated. " A slight error, Sir," he says, " but then, it's not easy to predict the future."

The Jumbo Card is removed from the stand and turned to face the audience ; it is seen to be the Four of Spades. The second spectator is requested to call out the number on the counter he has taken, and this number turns out to be a 2. The Jumbo card is quickly replaced on the stand whilst the audience stifle a yawn.

A green handkerchief is removed from the interior of the paper bag. The third spectator calls out the colour of the counter he chose; It is RED. The bag is dropped on to the table and the green hand-kerchief is dropped on top. The mentalist is in an extremely tem-peramental condition. Suddenly, inspiration!

" There are always two ways of looking at a thing," says our seer. " Let's try the second way."

The slate is turned around again and is seen to bear the name " NEW YORK." The Jumbo card is turned around and is found to be the Two of Spades. The green handkerchief is still in full view so appears to make things slightly more difficult. But no, the mentalist merely pulls it through his clenched fist and it changes visibly to the chosen colour, RED. Honour is regained.

Let us take the items required individually. The slate is the ordinary Flap Slate obtainable at most dealers. The green hand-kerchief is the old Colour Changing Hank. This is also a dealer's item and usually comes in red and green. That is, the handkerchief is either red, or green, and can be changed to the other by merely pulling it through the hand.

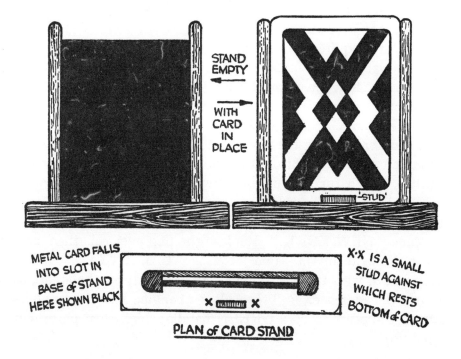

STAND EMPTY

WITH CARD IN PLACE

'STUD'

METAL CARD FALLS INTO SLOT IN BASE OF STAND HERE SHOWN BLACK

X·X IS A SMALL STUD AGAINST WHICH RESTS BOTTOM of CARD

PLAN of CARD STAND

The stand that displays, and changes, the Jumbo card is, we fondly think, our own origination. It consists, as shown in the diagrams, of two side pieces stuck into a substantial base and supporting a black back. It will be noted that the height of this back is less than the height of a Jumbo card, and it's that which makes the stand so deceptive. The base is made of wood an inch thick and, between the two uprights there is a slit a quarter of an inch wide, and as long as the distance between the uprights. This is shown in the drawing. There is also a small stud near the front against which the Jumbo card rests. With this stand a further fake is necessary. This consists of a piece of thin metal exactly the same size as a Jumbo card. It is painted on one side to represent the Four of Spades. The other side of the metal is painted matt black the same as the back of the stand. A genuine Two of Spades is also required. The Four of Spades fake is placed against the face-side of the Two of Spades and, both together, they are rested on the stand at an angle. The stud prevents them from sliding off.

The bags from which the counters are chosen are ordinary changing bags with the usual two compartments. We suggest that one compartment goes all the way down to the bottom of the bag and that the other has its bottom a little higher up. This ensures that when the spectator reaches in he will not feel the duplicate counters against his fingers through the cloth. Three bags exactly the same are needed.

Next are required three sets of counters. The ideal things are about one and a half inches in diameter and an eighth of an inch thick. In the first set you will need nine white counters each having a different city printed on them, and a further nine counters each having the name " NEW YORK." The second set consists of nine white counters bearing the figures 1 to 9, and a further nine counters all marked 2. And the third set is made up of nine differently coloured counters, and a further nine counters all coloured red. If plastic is beyond you, cardboard does almost as well.

Remove the flap from the slate and mark in chalk in bold letters the name " NEW YORK." Replace the flap over this then, on the flap itself, write in the same lettering " CALCUTTA." Have the Jumbo card, with its fake synchronised with it, on the stand, back towards the audience. Pull the Colour Changing Hank through itself so that it appears to be a GREEN handkerchief, then place it in a paper bag.

In the short side of one Changing Bag place all the RED counters, and in the opposite side place the nine counters of different colours. Prepare the other bags in similar fashion.

TO PERFORM

Introduce the slate, card stand and Jumbo card, and paper bag. Place these on one side but keep them well in view.

Pick up the Changing Bag containing names of cities. Reach into the long side and bring out the counters bearing nine different

names. Toss them back into the bag and, in having a spectator chosen, open the other side. Have him dip his hand in and remove a counter. Owing to the fact that every counter in the side he's feeling in bears the name " New York " we fail to see how he can get anything else. Have him remove his hand still closed and impress upon him the importance of not knowing at this stage what he has chosen.

This business is repeated with another spectator and the bag containing numbers, ending up with the number 2 being forced on him. And the third spectator finishes up with a counter from the third bag which is red, although he doesn't know it.

Proceed with the sucker dénouement. When you come to the Jumbo card, pick it up from the stand, keeping the fake pressed tightly against it ; it appears to be the Four of Spades. Immediately the chosen number is given as 2 replace both fake and card to stand but, in so doing, allow the fake to drop down the slit in the base whilst the card itself is retained between the fingers. Immediately the fake has entered the slit the Jumbo card is swivelled slightly outwards and allowed to rest against the stud as it did before. When it is turned around again it will show as the Two of Spades, and may be examined.

Pick up the paper bag and remove from it the green handkerchief. When red is called as the chosen colour drop the bag on the table and leave the green handkerchief in full view on top of it.

Go back to the slate. Before turning it round ask the first spectator what the name chosen was. He will tell you it was " New York." You take slate with you as you go to the footlights to reclaim his disc. Immediately he gives it to you turn the slate round to show the correct name. Deposit slate and disc on table. Remove Jumbo card from stand and ask second spectator what number he chose. He will say " 2." Take his disc back from him and turn the Jumbo card round. It is now the Two of Spades, so everybody's satisfied. Dispose of card and disc, then pick up the handkerchief. Ask third spectator what colour he chose. He tells you again that it was red. Take his disc back and then draw the green silk through your hand which changes it visibly to red. Retire exhausted whilst your audience stampedes to the bar.

And if you can't be bothered to make up the stand for the Jumbo card use an ordinary flap card box of the necessary size.

*　　*　　*　　*

The Devil's Key

A PADLOCK and key are given to a spectator for examination. Then he is asked to lock the padlock on to a handkerchief through the button-hole made in one corner of it. Another padlock of the same pattern is given to him to hold. The magician dangles the locked padlock into a borrowed hat without, however, allowing the end of the handkerchief to disappear from view, while the spectator locks the second padlock and still holds the key to the first.

The spectator is requested to unlock the padlock he holds, and when the magician withdraws the end of the handkerchief from the hat it is seen that the first padlock has unlocked itself in sympathy. Once again the lock may be examined.

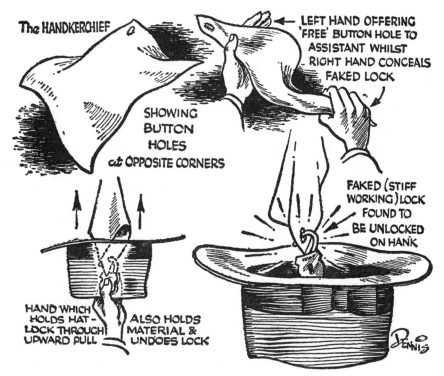

REQUIRED

You need two locks that are identical and that open with the *same key*. If you are able to obtain a third lock which opens with a different key then so much the better ; otherwise you will have to have another padlock which looks different. One of the duplicate locks is prepared only inasmuch as it will stay closed without being locked. This means that spring locks are definitely out. An ordinary padlock will usually do as it is, as the hinge on the arm is generally stiff. If the one you have isn't too stiff then you'll have to stiffen it a little. This can be done by hitting the part where it joins to the body of the lock with a hammer. But whatever you do to this lock has to be done to the duplicate, as they must be exactly alike.

The handkerchief is ordinary but has a button-hole in each of two opposite corners. The third padlock and key is as you buy it, without preparation of any sort.

The only preparation involved before the trick is to stick the duplicate lock which has the stiff hinge into one corner of the handkerchief. It is then closed so that it appears to be locked but actually isn't. This is placed on your table with the lock concealed under the corner on which it is closed. The other two locks, with their keys in them, are also on the table.

In performance, the lock which is the duplicate of the one already attached to the corner of the handkerchief is given to a spectator for examination. The handkerchief is picked up by the right hand which also conceals the lock already on it. The spectator is requested to push the lock through the hole in the opposite corner of the handkerchief and turn the key. The key remains in his possession.

Whilst a hat is being borrowed you slide the left hand down the handkerchief until it covers the lock just placed there by the spectator. The right hand approaches the left hand and reveals the lock it has been hiding all this time. The spectator's lock is concealed in the left hand and remains so for the rest of the effect. The second lock appears to be the same, as it is closed and a duplicate of the first.

This faked (?) lock is then dangled in the hat, which should be of the " soft " variety. The lock is allowed to touch bottom on the dent closest to you and is gripped through the hat's material by the right hand fingers and thumb. A slight upward pull by the left hand and the padlock is pulled open but it still remains in the hat and attached to the corner of the handkerchief.

Meanwhile the spectator has been given yet another lock and asked to lock it. It is pointed out that both locks are in the same condition. He is requested to unlock his padlock ; then the handkerchief is raised and the lock on its end found to have opened in sympathy.

N.B.—The " Majestic " Lock, of British manufacture, is ideal for this effect.

MAGIC WITH ANYTHING

No Knot

PERHAPS we'd better explain about this before you go getting a wrong idea. This is *not* a trick by itself, it is designed to be a part of a rope routine. We use a short routine before we cut our rope in which we try to tie a knot. Each time the knot is tied it just isn't there. Then, in disgust, we toss the rope round our neck and get on with another piece. Suddenly we stop and turn around as if we felt there might be someone immediately behind us. The rope is pulled from the neck and there is found to be a knot dead in the middle of it. " No Knot " is only one small part of the routine, it is also the only original part !

In effect, you tie a knot and, when the rope is pulled out, it isn't there.

If you glance at the illustrations you will see how easily this is accomplished. Figure 1 shows the rope held between the two hands. In Figure 2 the right hand has crossed over and pulled the rope

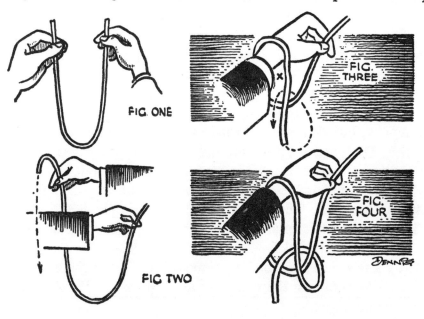

FIG. ONE

FIG. THREE

FIG TWO

FIG. FOUR

down over the left wrist then released its hold. This position is illustrated in Figure 3. The right hand next goes through the loop so formed (passing through at X and *not* at Y), picks up the loose end, then pulls it back through the loop as it withdraws. The movement of the rope is shown in Figure 4. Please note that the left hand doesn't release its grip on its end of the rope from start to finish.

Both hands are then pulled apart, allowing the loops to fall off the left wrist, and there is no knot where one ought to be.

* * * *

The Sympathetic Note Trick

AUDIENCES, we feel, are beginning to have a fair idea of what is coming when the conjurer asks to borrow a pound note. In an endeavour to fool them a little further we evolved the following plot to cover the usual Burned and Restored Bank Note.

The magician entices some unwilling member of the audience on to the stage, sits him down, and borrows his pound. So that there may be something on record the assistant is asked to write the number of the note on a slate with white chalk. The slate is propped up in view, written side away from the audience, the chalk is wrapped in a handkerchief, and the pound note is sealed in an envelope.

" Tonight," says the wizard, " I am going to show you an amazing example of Sympathy. I want you all to watch as carefully as the owner of the Bank Note is going to."

The envelope containing the pound note is burned to ashes. " Slates," continues the magician, " aren't usually in sympathy with money, but this one had the number of the note written on it. Look ! " The slate is turned around and the number has vanished.

" And chalk isn't usually in sympathy either—but that's gone, too." The handkerchief held by the assistant is pulled from his grasp, and no chalk falls out. Sympathy is complete.

The sorcerer bows for any applause that happens to come and then goes into his next trick.

After a few card fans the magician realises that perhaps, after all, it isn't quite as fair on the volunteer as it could be. He offers to see what can be done.

" This afternoon," he says, " I received a registered envelope from my Aunt Penelope ; that of course is only her Pen name. The shock was so great that I haven't opened it yet. But if you like I'll open it now in case it's anything valuable. I must warn you, however ; don't let it raise your hopes too much. The last time she sent me a registered envelope it turned out to be her Income Tax Form ! "

A large envelope that has been hanging in full view all the time is slit open. Inside it is another envelope slightly smaller, and inside that another, and another, and yet another which is similar to the usual pay envelope. And inside this is the very same borrowed one pound note.

You will require five envelopes, each larger than the last ; an ordinary letter envelope with the flap on the long side ; a thumb tip ; a piece of chalk ; a Devil's Handkerchief ; a flap slate ; and a cigarette lighter in the right hand trousers pocket. The five envelopes that are graduated in size should each be marked with a conspicuous blue cross. The Thumb Tip is inside the ordinary letter envelope.

Borrow the note and if you like have the owner autograph it. Write its number on the *flap side* of the flap slate. In propping the slate on the table, dispose of the flap. The chalk is disposed of by dropping it through the slit as you wrap it in the Devil's Handkerchief. The handkerchief is then handed to the assistant to hold " as security."

The note is folded up and deposited in the envelope, really into the thumb tip which is then withdrawn on the thumb. The envelope is sealed and may be burned without the magician losing his pound. In reaching for his cigarette lighter the magician disposes of the loaded thumb tip in his trousers pocket.

The note is burned in the envelope, the slate is shown to be blank, and the handkerchief is whipped away from the assistant showing the chalk to have vanished.

A bow, then a few card fans and flourishes. Eventually the nest of envelopes is taken from wherever it happens to be and each split open and the next in size removed. When you come to the last one the first thing to go inside it is your thumb, and on the thumb is the thumb tip which has again been stolen out of the pocket. The note is pulled out of the tip (the tip itself being left inside the envelope out of harm's way) and returned to its owner, who is probably swearing under his breath that he will never, never, never help another conjurer as long as he lives.

*   *   *   *

The Jeweller's Dream

IT has been said by experts that to have two effects in one is not by any means a good thing. This has just that. On the other hand, one effect without the other is rather weak, yet together they make a strong programme number.

The patter concerns a pearl necklace priced at £1,000 7s. 6d., a beautiful girl, and a slightly love-sick jeweller's assistant. Into the shop walks the girl and vamps the assistant into removing the 7/6d. from the price ticket, then each " O " in succession, until he finally sells the necklace to her at the price of £1. She places the pearls into her handbag and leaves. The owner of the shop comes in, races after the girl and brings her back, only to find her handbag empty. The necklace reappears on the stand, and even the price ticket is restored to its previous condition.

In short, it's " Fresh Fish " all over again with the story rather more illustrated.

Let us dispose of the price ticket first. It is only a length of paper, about 24 inches long by 4 inches wide, with " £1,000 7s. 6d. " printed on it black and clear. It helps if each tear is perforated by a watch-cog ; then the tearing becomes almost automatic. Stuck to the back of this strip is a duplicate strip folded up. It should be glued to the " sixpence " end as this is the piece that is torn off first. When it is torn off it is placed *behind* the first " 0," and so on, thus ensuring that when the tearing has all finished the duplicate folded strip is on the outside of the pieces at the back. If the pieces are now folded, the packet turned over, and the duplicate unfolded, the strip will have been apparently restored.

The stand may be any shape desired but a square area of black is necessary, as another piece of black material has to cover it to hide the duplicate necklace. Two long black pins hold the pearls in position. They should be curved upwards so that the fake may be drawn up off them. It will be understood that these two pins hold *both* necklaces in position. The stand is set up by placing the first necklace in position on the pins, then covering it with the fake; finally, the duplicate is hung on the same pins that stick through the fake. This fake, illustrated in Figure 4, has a small tab with a button attached to it extending from its top. This tab and button drop down over the back of the stand. This is shown in Figure 2.

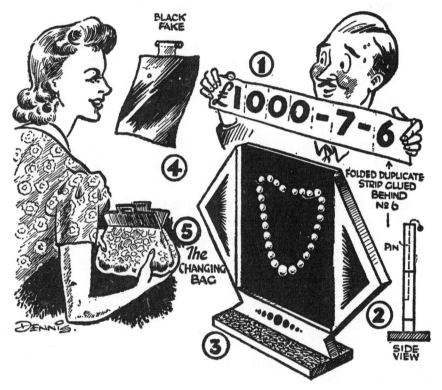

The handbag, one of those soft-cloth affairs, should have two compartments like the usual changing bag.

In performing, the stand is displayed along with the price ticket, and the story is told as the ticket is slowly torn up, nought by nought. The necklace is removed from the stand and dropped into one compartment of the handbag, and the stand is covered by a plain coloured silk.

The handbag is shown empty by opening the other compartment, the silk is removed from the stand—the fake being pulled away with it—showing the necklace has apparently come back, and finally the torn pieces are unfolded to show they've restored themselves in sympathy.

Which Witch ?

THE wizard introduces three cards of playing card size each with a picture of a witch on it, a small glass vial (or phial, just as you prefer), and a small model of a witch's broom, white, and of a size to enter the vial.

The miniature broom is sealed in the glass vial which is, in turn, wrapped in a handkerchief and given to a spectator to hold. The three cards, one depicting a green witch, one a yellow witch, and the last a black witch, are given to someone to shuffle, and then he is asked to lay them down face-downwards on the table in the form of a triangle. That represents, of course, the mystic, not the eternal, triangle !

Now comes no end of a jolly story until one is chosen freely and the magician is kept in ignorance of whether it's green, yellow, or black—perhaps.

The spectator holding the wrapped up vial is asked to wave the chosen card over it. The tube is unwrapped and the miniature broom is found to have changed from white to the colour of the chosen witch. No trap-doors are necessary, no wires, no threads, and the whole thing is done entirely without the aid of a net.

Required are three blank-faced cards of playing-card size with the usual backs. On each you'll have to draw the outline of what you think a witch looks like, leaving the hat and cloak in outline only, and making sure that not one of them possesses a broom between them. On one card the hat and cloak are filled in in black ; the second's hat and cloak are filled in with yellow ; and the third is touched up with Macbeth green. These three cards are suitably and secretly marked on their backs so you are able to tell one from the other.

Next required are four miniature broomsticks. These, naturally, should be authentic models ; if in doubt as to the appearance of a witch's broom slip round to your local fortune-teller, she may be able to help. They may be carved in wood or made of plastic but they must be of a nice size to just fit into one of the glass vials even when the cork is in. One broom should be white, one black, one yellow, and the last green. Four glass vials are also necessary and we suggest you take advantage of your local chemist and buy four tubes (20-Tablet size) of Veganin Tablets. If the drawing part of the trick gives you a headache then you are all prepared.

The last necessary piece of apparatus is a Devil's Handkerchief. This is the usual double affair with the slit in the middle of one side.

The three corked up tubes containing the coloured brooms are in your pockets in an order known to you. Show the empty vial, the white broom, and the three cards. Tell the audience about three witches who'd been doing a lot of flying and worn their broomsticks out. It seems they all went along to the ironmonger's (local

DEVIL'S HANK

Witches BROOM

...and PHIAL

name) to buy new ones but when they got there they found there'd been a rush on brooms that day and there was only one left in stock—a white one. This they bought, but they quarrelled so much on the way home as to who should have it that they had to leave the whole thing to the luck of the draw.

At this point the white broom is placed into the vial. The vial is corked and then placed in the centre of the handkerchief actually into the slit. This is given to someone to hold and you make certain he feels the vial is there.

Give the three cards to someone else to shuffle then have him lay them out face-downwards in a triangle. Suggest that as one has to be chosen he might try the following verse, starting at whichever card he likes :—

Three Little Witches,
Prisoned in a room,
Found they couldn't leave it
'Cos no one had a broom.

He recites the above, tapping a card for each word until he finally stops on one card. The colour of this witch is told from the back of the card and the tube containing the broom of that colour is palmed out of the pocket with the right hand.

The spectator waves the card over the covered vial to work the miracle, then you take the handkerchief, reach into its folds with the right hand and take out the tube with the coloured broom in it. Don't worry about the original vial; that's all taken care of in the double handkerchief.

* * * *

The Chinese Picture

A DELIGHTFUL piece of hocus-pocus that has been " under-done " of late is the " Handkerchief Frame." Here is a routine that is easy, colourful, and amusing. Further, the rather delaying part of pinning the handkerchief to the frame has been avoided.

You will need an ordinary Handkerchief Frame of the wooden variety; that is, the one in which one whole end slides down taking the handkerchief with it. Also required is a silk handkerchief with a Chinese Dragon painted on it (this was a dealer's item pre-war), and a piece of thin, soft material that gives the impression at a distance of being canvas. The silk should be of a size to just fit the frame, and the synthetic canvas should be cut to the same measurements then tacked to the silk. The frame itself should be painted with gold paint to resemble an old-fashioned picture frame. The picture is attached to the frame in the usual way, but the *bottom* of it should be tacked to the sliding end of the frame; this ensures that the picture will stay in position without being held up. The usual large, flat paper bag is needed (or a sheet of newspaper), a lighted cigar, a wand, a glass of water and an empty bowl, and a dagger that looks as wicked as possible.

The performer enters smoking the cigar and carrying the picture inside the paper bag.

"A little while ago," he says, "my Aunt Jemima died and left me a spot of the necessary. As the last present I gave my wife was her wedding ring I decided it was time I gave her something to show her I wasn't really as bad as she kept saying I was.

"I was walking down an old street in London when I stumbled on one of those Chinese antique shops. Knowing that my wife liked antiques—that is probably why she married me—I went inside. I was just going to ask the price of a wizened looking Chinese Buddha when it moved and turned out to be the proprietor, so I asked the price of this Chinese picture instead."

The picture is drawn out of the bag and shown back and front.

"The old man behind the counter said it was once the prized possession of a Chinese Mandarin who gave it up only because he was too dead to stop it being taken, but because he liked my face, he'd sell it to me for five bob and a packet of Players'. The addition of the cigarettes almost doubled the cost of the thing, but after all, my wife works very hard to keep me so I thought it was worth it. I bought it on the spot, cash down, and no coupons." The picture is returned to the bag. The bag is then turned upside down which allows the sliding end of the frame to slip down taking the picture with it.

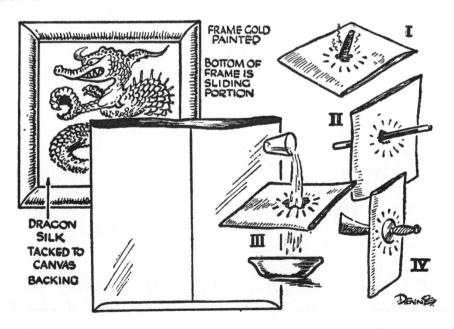

" I was on my way home holding the picture carefully . . . like this . . . " The bag is held in front of the body as if it were a tray, horizontally. " . . . when a bus went by and some silly person dropped a lighted cigar butt out of one of the upstairs windows. It didn't go on me but on to my picture. Naturally I was watching the traffic and didn't notice it until it had burned its way right through the picture."

The cigar is pushed against the centre of the bag until it burns its way through and falls to the floor. The cigar may then be discarded into an ash-tray on the table.

" I was very annoyed about that, but I blamed myself for holding it in such a ridiculous way, so I changed it to this . . . " The picture is now held edge-on to the audience, vertically. " . . . and the next thing I knew was that a lamplighter had stuck the sharp end of his pole through it." The wand is thrust through the centre of the bag and held there so that the audience can see that it sticks out from both sides. " I was very annoyed about that, too. I said some rather rude things to the lamplighter, but all he said was that it was lucky he hadn't stuck his wretched pole through *me*.

" I began to feel that, after all, the best way to carry the blessed picture was as I'd done in the first place, so I changed it back."

The picture is again held as if it were a tray.

" On mature consideration I thought a taxi home would probably be wise, and blow the expense, so I waited for one in the shelter of a block of luxury flats. But unfortunately a woman had decided it was time to water her flower pots and had forgotten they have holes in their bottoms. The water started to come down in a steady stream . . . not on to me . . . on to my picture."

The bowl is placed on the floor and the water from the glass is poured through the hole in the centre of the bag into the bowl. The glass is replaced on the table.

" I'd had about enough. I tucked the picture under my arm and joined a bus queue. And I was just about to get on a Number Nine when a man came tearing up waving a dagger at me. ' You've got the picture I've been after for years,' he shouted, ' but I'll see it's no good to you. Take that, and that, and that ! ' . . . and he stabbed my picture in its most tender part."

The dagger is picked up from the table and stabbed three times through the centre of the bag. The dagger is then returned to the table.

" I'm afraid I couldn't help it, I laughed full in his face. I told him that as far as I was concerned he could go the whole hog. I said that after having it burned, poked, and drowned I was darned sure that a silly little knife couldn't make the slightest difference. I told him all that had happened to my picture and when I'd finished he was almost in tears and genuinely apologetic. As a token of his regret he handed me the dagger, so I stabbed him dead and went home to my wife.

" I told her everything that had occurred and she said I must have been drunk, so I pulled out the picture to prove it."

The bag is turned the right way up which allows the slide to slip down to its original position. The picture now covers the entire frame. It is then removed from the bag. " And I guess I *must* have been drunk . . . but it taught me a lesson. Never again will I buy my wife a present ! ! "

*   *   *   *

The Fiddled Furniture

ON the very few times when we have entertained children we have discovered with amazement that while they're not one bit fooled by sleight-of-hand they just haven't a clue where a little mechanical apparatus is concerned. Whilst this effect is more or less intended for kiddies it still baffles those older and, although it is only " The Patriotic Billiard Balls " redressed, there is a story to play about with.

The apparatus consists of three brown cubes, three black cubes, and three green. There are also three houses decorated to match. The houses are only cut-outs of the front of a usual " detached " and the cubes are—just cubes ; there isn't a shell in the whole campaign.

The story is about three sisters, Lottie, Dottie, and Pottie (she was daft), who all encountered matrimonial bliss on the same day, one to Mr. Brown, one to Mr. Black, and the third, Pottie, to Mr. Green.

After the honeymoon (which, by the way, they all spent together) they commenced to put their houses in order. Now the girls' mother, christened Lottie and nicknamed Dottie and Pottie by the rest of the natives, had the wonderful idea that Mr. Black's house should be decorated with black furniture, Mr. Brown's with brown furniture, and Green's with green. The girls thought it was *such* a distinctive idea so they all pushed off to the local Jays to fix it up. They spent hours, and money, picking a wonderful selection of stuff. Then it was all crated up and addressed to the respective houses. Unfortunately Pottie had never learned to read so, to humour her, all the crates were painted according to their names, and as they all bought three crates full of the junk there were three black crates, three brown crates, and three green crates.

Oh yes! We forgot to tell you their pasts. The local village poacher, a nasty bit of work named Adolf, had proposed to each of the three girls in turn before their marriage without success, and he determined to have his revenge. He found he was short of money during the off-season for rabbits so turned to honest toil. He became one of the shifters in a firm of furniture removers and, oddly enough, they were the ones called in to move the Blacks', Browns', and Greens' furniture. Here, at last, was his revenge (dirty laugh from off!).

As the furniture van toiled on to the first house Adolf was thinking furiously. As this was an entirely new departure for him he was coming out in spots, but eventually he hit on a plan. Instead of delivering three crates of the same colour to each house he decided to throw a spanner in the works and drop one of each colour instead. Which meant that each house now had one crate that was black, one brown, and one green.

The three girls had all been spending the afternoon with their mother, gloating over their initial fight with their husbands, so it was a decided shock to them when they reached home to find what naughty Adolf had done. And what do you think was the first thing they did? Why, went back to mother, of course.

And mother, having been apprenticed to a witch decided that here was a case where she'd have to dust off the old broomstick and rout out the familiar. Which she duly did. And after the spells had been cast all the furniture was at its right house . . . and Adolf had a simply wicked attack of gout. And Lottie, Dottie, and Pottie lived happily ever after. Even if their husbands didn't.

No, Dear Reader, you don't have to palm an outsize block of wood, and the trick is entirely self contained. The blocks are of two

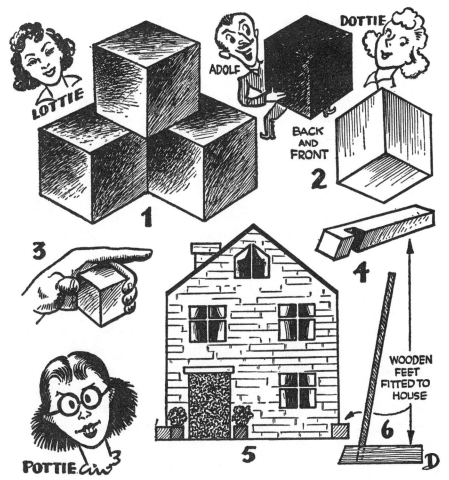

colours but this isn't noticed as the audience, try as it might, is only able to see three sides of a cube at the same time. Now please refer to illustration No. 2. This shows you one block from the front, and also from the back. The front three sides are painted brown and the rear three sides are black. As long as you have that in mind we can write out a list for the blocks, which will be as follows :—

(1)	Front	3	sides	BLACK.	Rear	3	sides	BLACK
(2)	„	„	„	BLACK.	„	„	„	BROWN.
(3)	„	„	„	BLACK.	„	„	„	GREEN.
(4)	„	„	„	BROWN.	„	„	„	BROWN.
(5)	„	„	„	BROWN.	„	„	„	BLACK.
(6)	„	„	„	BROWN.	„	„	„	GREEN.
(7)	„	„	„	GREEN.	„	„	„	GREEN.
(8)	„	„	„	GREEN.	„	„	„	BLACK.
(9)	„	„	„	GREEN.	„	„	„	BROWN.

Incidentally, when we talk of the " front three sides " we refer to the three sides visible when the cube is held as shown in Figure 3, that is, two sides and the top.

Now for the " houses." These are just cut-out fronts and may be made in cardboard or plywood decorated. One should be black, one brown, and the third, green. For ease in packing we suggest that each house should have two " feet " which hold it up and may be detached when necessary. Both house and feet are illustrated in Figures 4, 5, and 6.

The colour-change process is effected merely by turning the cubes over from front to back so that the front two sides and top become the rear two sides and bottom. It is very important that whenever the cubes are exhibited, either in the hand or on the table, they are always edge-on towards the audience as shown in the drawings. For a usual size hand we suggest cubes with two-inch sides.

The easiest way to perform the trick is to have all the blocks in a line on a very shallow tray. The " houses " should be one on each of three tables and during the course of the story they should be lifted up and shown on both sides. We suggest the black house be on your right, the brown house in the centre, and the green house to the left. In such a case the order of the cubes on your tray will be from right to left, three blacks, three browns, and three greens. If you refer to the table again you will see, by the numbers, what the cubes really are. From right to left—

Cube No. 1.   Black sides showing.
 „ „ 2. „ „ „
 „ „ 3. „ „ „
 „ „ 5. Brown „ „
 „ „ 4. „ „ „
 „ „ 6. „ „ „
 „ „ 8. Green „ „
 „ „ 9. „ „ „
 „ „ 7. „ „ „

If the blocks are on the tray in that order you will find there is no memory work involved in performance. All you need do is remove the first black block on the right, the first brown block on the right, and the first green block on the right and place them one at a time behind the black house. Then the second black, brown, and green from the right go behind the brown house. The remaining cubes, of course, are placed behind the green house. If you remember to turn *every* cube as it is placed down (under cover of the houses), then you can't go wrong. All the correct ones will be turned and the others are the same on both sides so it doesn't matter.

As three of the blocks are genuine it is a good plan to nonchalantly toss them into the air when you come to them. Don't, however, throw up the wrong ones or your audience may get an inkling of how this simply superb trick is worked.

* * * *

The Ju-Ju Man

SAYS the Magician : " Down in the forest something stirred. it was the Ju-Ju Man stirring up his black and murky spells." (Sound of tom-toms off.) " But there was one Ju-Ju expert I heard of who was having a pretty thin time raking in the shekels because a number of his spells were coming unstuck. It got so bad that when people came to him to ask him to kill their enemies or make their wives love them, they insisted on having results before parting with the cash. And that, as any Ju-Ju man will tell you, is fatal.

" However, he and I talked the whole thing over and, between us, managed to hit on rather a good thing. I'll show it to you . . . "

The magician proceeds to demonstrate just how the money was taken off the Unbelievers. A wand with a small skull and a few ribbons on one end is introduced as the witch-doctor's stick. A few large " African Pennies " with holes in their centres are shown, and the rest of the apparatus consists of two silken ropes and a bag which has a small hole in each side.

And here, Mr. Magician, we may as well confess that this is yet another presentation of that old classic " The Ropes, Silks, and Wand ! " On the other hand, it is a presentation that allows your histrionic abilities full play.

The magician obtains the help of two assistants from the audience. These are placed one each side of the stage. The ropes may be examined if necessary then they are tied round the centre of the wand. The giant " coins " are threaded, via the hole in the centre

of each, two on to each pair of ropes and then slid to the centre.
The bag is also threaded on the ropes so that the coins and the wand
come inside it. One rope from each side is dropped and a single knot
is tied binding the bag and everything in it to the ropes in a thorough
manner. Yet when the wand is pulled free of the ropes the coins fall
into the bag, and the bag itself comes clear and is held aloft by the
magician.

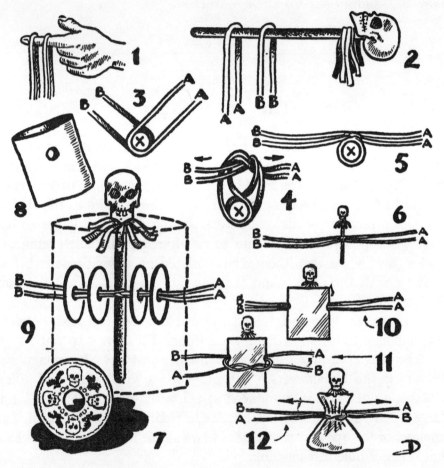

As diagrams are the simplest medium of instruction we have
prepared some that show all stages of the trick.

Fig. 1.　The two ropes are exhibited over the finger. They are then
handed to the two assistants.

Fig. 2.　When the ropes are returned they are placed over the wand.
This illustration gives some idea of the wand's appearance.

Fig. 3.　This shows how the ropes are separated. Notice that they
have now been designated A and B in order that the ends

may be followed easily. The circle marked X represents an end view of the wand.

Fig. 4. A single knot is tied by taking both ends of each rope in either hand, and considering both ends together to be just one rope.

Fig. 5. The single knot is pulled tight.

Fig. 6. This is merely a more distant view of Fig. 5. Ends B are held by one assistant, ends A by the other.

Fig. 7. A drawing of one of the " pennies." It should be cut from plywood and measure 6 inches in diameter. At its centre is a hole $1\frac{1}{2}$ inches in diameter. It should be painted silver.

Fig. 8. The bag. This may be any colour but a bright plaid shows up well ; witch-doctors have no colour sense anyway. It should measure 12 inches deep by 9 inches wide. The two holes (one on each side) should be $1\frac{1}{2}$ inches in diameter, and slightly more than halfway up from the bottom.

Fig. 9. Here are the " pennies " threaded on the ropes. The dotted lines indicate the position of the bag. In threading the bag both B ends are passed through the hole in one side from the *inside*. The bag is slid to the centre, the coins and wand deposited inside it, then ends A are passed through the opposite hole, again from the inside.

Fig. 10. This is how the finished threading should appear to the audience. The ends of the ropes are still being retained by the assistants.

Fig. 11. One rope is dropped by each assistant. These ends are tied in a *single* knot round the *outside* of the bag. In effect, each assistant now holds one end of each rope.

Fig. 12. The ropes are pulled tight. If the wand is now pulled from the ropes, the bag (with the " pennies " inside it) will be free, leaving the ropes stretched between the assistants.

PRESENTATION

" The Ju-Ju Man would tell his customers that it was hardly fair to make him work magic without actually showing him the money first and that, as they didn't seem to trust him, they could tie their money up on ropes in a bag so that it would be safe."

The ropes are examined and tied around the wand ; then the coins are threaded on. The bag is also threaded on and the ropes tied round it. Then the ends are held by the assistants.

It might be mentioned here that one's own assistants play this role rather better than volunteer assistants from the audience. The returning of spectators to their seats in the auditorium at the end of a trick nearly always, we feel, constitutes something of an anti-climax.

" The Witch-doctor would go into his trance, work the necessary spell that was required of him, then ask the natives for his fee. They would naturally laugh and tell him he'd have to wait until they'd seen some results. So he'd ask them to pull on the ropes while he removed his magic wand and, in front of their very eyes, he'd walk away with the money ! "

Whilst removing the wand the left hand holds the top of the bag. Immediately the wand is free of the ropes the bag comes clear and should be lifted up. The right hand dives into the bag and withdraws the coins, then both hands are lifted as a cue for applause.

* * * *

" Mud in Your Eye ! "

IF you don't mind slopping a spot of liquid about (and who does, in a good cause ?) then you may like this. In fact, as there's beer involved, *and* audience-participation, we don't see how you can possibly fail !

The sorcerer shows his audience a bottle of beer, a bottle of ink, three small whisky glasses, two glass tumblers, two empty tubes, two plates, and a glass jug of water. We doubt if he shows them all at once or there'll probably be no end of a smash.

To prove that the contents of the bottles are what they're labelled the magician proceeds to pour a little of each into a whisky glass, and a little water from the jug is also poured into a whisky glass to make it complete. A spectator is next invited up on to the stage to taste the beer and the water, and if he wants to taste the ink as well he'll just get a blue tongue.

That bit of misdirection over, the performer covers each large tumbler with a tube and rests a plate on each. The beer bottle is placed on one plate, and the ink bottle on the other. The magician tells the audience that he will show them a remarkable penetration.

He says he will cause the ink to leave the bottle, penetrate the plate, and land up in the tumbler underneath, and the same with the beer. But then, all of a sudden like, he has a brainwave. In order to make the feat more difficult (or perhaps you've heard that before !) he removes the plates from the tops of the tubes and pours water from the jug down into each tumbler.

" Not only shall the beer and ink filter down," he says, " but the water will also filter up. In short, they will change places." The plates and bottles are replaced on top of the tubes and everything's all set to go.

The magus further states that as a member of the audience was sufficiently kind to help out with the preliminary stage of the effect he will allow him (the member of the audience) to imbibe the contents of the glass immediately below the bottle of beer. That means there is now at least one spectator who is ardently hoping the trick will succeed !

The wand is waved, the fan is fanned, or the shot is shot. Then the beer bottle is removed from the plate and its contents poured into the empty glass jug. It is seen by those who happen to be watching that nothing leaves the bottle but clear cold water. The same thing occurs with the ink bottle, nothing but water is poured out, and that also goes into the jug.

" Well," says the necromancer, " the first part has worked so it follows that the second part must have, too." The obliging member of the audience is requested to remove the tumbler from the tube which supported the beer bottle whilst the magician staggers over to the tumbler which sulked beneath the bottle of ink.

" Here's mud in your eye ! " remarks the magician quaffing deeply of his ale, and the spectator has a slightly wild look as he discovers a glass of ink where it just hadn't oughta be. Not only have the liquids filtered, they've also transposed.

And, to close, the magician if he's any man at all, produces a glass of liquid hops from a gaudy foulard so that the repressed spectator doesn't wait at the stage door to bash him one later on !

The only requirements, apart from those mentioned in the beginning, are Beer Powder and Ink Powder. The beer bottle should be of a size that dishes out just one glass of beer, and of coloured glass. The ink bottle should be of a similar size and made of earthenware. Both labels should be nice and easy to read. The tubes are ordinary, a little wider than the diameter of the tumblers, and one inch higher. To further enhance the effect the tubes should be coloured to represent the contents of the bottles, brown if under the beer bottle, black under the bottle of ink. The plates may be borrowed or, if you carry your own (as you should), plastic jobs.

To prepare, half-fill one of the whisky glasses with beer and place it down on the table hidden by some other piece of apparatus, such as the brown tube. Into the second whisky glass place a small quantity of Ink Powder; the third whisky glass remains empty.

One tumbler has sufficient Beer Powder in it to make a full glass of beer by the addition of water, and the other tumbler has sufficient Ink Powder to make a full glass of ink. Both bottles contain water. The glass jug has sufficient water in it to fill two tumblers and one whisky glass. If possible, use two tables for the trick. On one table you have the ink bottle, the black tube, the tumbler containing Beer Powder, the plate, and the whisky glass with Ink Powder. On the other table you have the whisky glass half-filled with beer, the empty whisky glass, the glass jug of water, the beer bottle, plate, brown tube, and the tumbler containing Ink Powder.

Presentation is just as easy. Pick up the beer bottle and remove the top. Take the whisky glass with beer in it in the left hand making sure that it is almost entirely concealed by the fingers, and pour water from the beer bottle into it. This dilutes the beer a bit but it won't matter. The glass and bottle are replaced on the table then the jug is picked up and water poured out into the second whisky glass. The glass is placed down next-door to the glass with beer in it, then you cross to the other table and pour from the ink bottle into the third glass, again hiding the action with the fingers of the left hand. Result is a glass of ink. The contents of the three whisky glasses are offered to a spectator for tasting.

The spectator should now be stuck out of harm's way on a chair somewhere near the front of the stage whilst you get into the spirit of the thing. The tumbler with the Ink Powder in the bottom is shown empty (by hiding the powder in the bottom with your fingers in holding) then placed on the table and covered with the brown tube. A plate is placed on top and, on top of that, the beer bottle. A rapid journey is made to the other table and the same thing is done with the Beer-Powder tumbler, black tube, plate, and bottle of ink.

At this point you tell the audience that you're going to perform a penetration ; then, as an afterthought, tell them you'll make it even more mysterious. The plate covering each glass is removed and water is poured down from the jug into each tube. This will naturally have the effect of changing the empty (?) tumbler under the beer bottle into a glass of ink and under the ink bottle you have . . . well, vice versa.

The mechanics of the trick are over. You remove the beer bottle from its dizzy perch and pour the contents into the glass jug. Out comes water. The contents of the ink bottle are also poured into the jug, and they're water, too. You mention that the first part has worked alright so the second is bound to have done. Ask the spectator to remove his own glass of beer from inside the brown tube, whilst you remove the glass of beer from under the place where the ink bottle used to be. To get the full effect let the spectator remove his glass first, if you don't he gets an inkling (no pun) of what's coming.

It seems advisable to us for you to produce another glass of genuine beer from somewhere or other so that the spectator doesn't go away feeling too sorry for himself. Even a glass in your tail-pocket covered with a rubber cover would do, providing you get the cover off before it comes into view. Or you could use the method described in the " Silken Card Discovery " elsewhere.

*   *   *   *

Coins Rampant

WE present here a completely impromptu coin routine that can be done anywhere where the audience is in front of you. All that is required is a borrowed glass and four coins. Our choice is palming coins because they have usually a sharp milled edge which makes for easier palming.

Sleight-of-hand is hard to describe so we've prepared as many drawings as possible to illustrate the text. It is advisable to follow the moves with four coins in your hands.

Fig. 1.   Stand with your left side towards audience. Three coins are held in the left hand as shown in the drawing, and the fourth coin is back-palmed in the right which has its palm facing the audience. If you look at the figure again you will see a small arrow marked " audience," and this indicates the direction from which the audience is watching. It will be understood that the coins should be held in the left hand as naturally as possible so that their presence is unsuspected.

The right hand produces its coin, and the position is now that shown in the drawing.

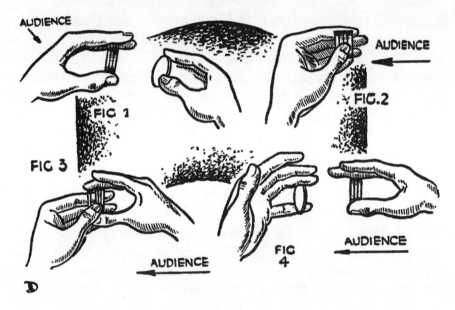

Fig. 2.   The left hand removes the coin from the right by adding its three coins to the face of the coin just produced. Now there is a complete swing to the left (so that the right side faces the audience) and all four coins are shown as one. This drawing (Figure 2) shows the magician's view from above, that is, looking down on his left hand. The audience's view is indicated by the arrow.

Fig. 3.   Still with right side to audience the right hand comes up and removes the coins from the left hand but, in this move, one important thing takes place. The three coins nearest the right hand are pulled away first, and then the last coin. This means that there is about a quarter of an inch gap between the single coin and the stack of three. It will be found simpler if the coins are removed with the second finger and thumb rather than with the first finger and thumb.

Fig. 4. The right hand now drops a little and deposits the separated coin between the third and fourth fingers of the left hand.

Fig. 5. As the right hand moves away the other three coins are finger-palmed.

Fig. 6. The right hand now reproduces its three coins as one from behind the right knee.

Fig. 7. These three coins are deposited again between the left-hand first finger and thumb, the right hand is shown empty, and the move described under " Figure 3 " is done again, only this time a break is made between the 2nd. and 3rd. coins. This separated coin is now deposited between the second and third fingers. This same move described in Figures 5 and 6 is repeated, the coin, after it is reproduced, being placed between the first and second fingers of the left hand.

The last coin is back-palmed and a swing made to the right. Then it is produced from the air. It is placed between the thumb and first finger of the left hand. On turning left again it appears as in Figure 7.

Fig. 8. The right hand comes over, removes the coins one at a time from the left fingers, and spreads them in a fan.

Fig. 9. Still with the right side facing the audience the right hand is turned (as in the drawing, which shows the audience's view) so that the palm more or less faces the audience.

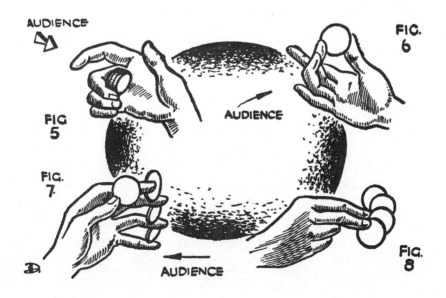

AUDIENCE

FIG. 6

FIG 5

AUDIENCE

FIG. 7

FIG. 8

AUDIENCE

Fig. 10. The left hand comes up and, hiding the coins, closes them up into a stack. The right hand now turns back towards the audience, and the middle finger comes up and joins the forefinger on the stack. As the left fingers close around the stack the middle finger and thumb carry the stack downwards, leaving the forefinger inside the left fist. This position is illustrated in :—

Fig. 11. Here you have an audience's view except that the coins are shown a little higher than they should be. The right hand should now be raised a little; the left hand moves away clenched as if containing the coins.

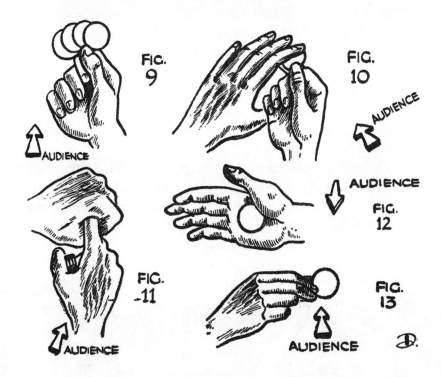

Fig. 12. As the right hand moves upwards to make a pass over the left hand the stack of coins is transferred to the palm proper. This is shown in the illustration. This view is, naturally, the performer's.

Fig. 13. The right hand drops to the side and the left hand squeezes the coins away. Immediately they are reproduced in a fan from behind the right knee. This time the coins are closed up in full view, held in the right hand. Then the "French Drop" is executed. The left hand again moves away as if containing the coins whilst the right hand transfers the stack from the fingers into the palm. The left hand squeezes the coins away and is opened to be shown empty.

Fig. 14. The right hand now produces one coin between the fore-finger and thumb, and it is placed between the thumb and forefinger of the left hand. Again a coin is reproduced by the right hand, and this is placed between the first and second fingers of the left hand. It is this stage which· is illustrated. The right hand produces the third coin and this is placed between the second and third fingers. The last coin in the right hand is transferred to the back-palm, a swing is made to the right, and the coin is produced. This is placed between the third and little fingers of the left hand. Once again the set of four is complete.

The coin is removed from between the third and little fingers of the left hand by the right forefinger and thumb. A swing is made to the left again (presenting the right

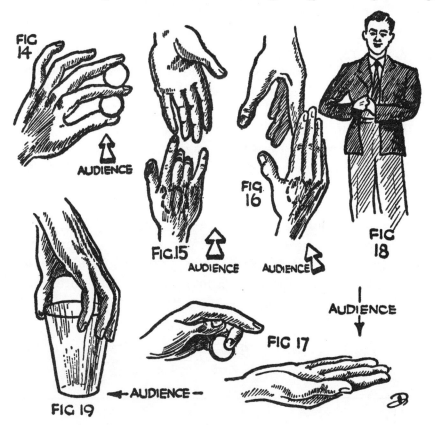

side to the audience), and the right hand apparently tosses the coin away. Actually it is palmed. This move is repeated three times more until all the coins have left the left hand and are palmed in the right.

Fig. 15. We now come to a very important move. The left hand is turned over so that its palm faces the audience and the right hand points to it as shown in the drawing. This gives the audience's view.

Fig. 16. The left hand half-turns its back towards the audience and descends towards the right hand. In this move the second and third fingers slip down one each side of the stack of coins and grip them. As this move takes place the body turns round to the right and the hands come together at waist-level. As the turn of the body continues the left hand will have its back to the audience and the palm of the right hand will also be visible to them.

Fig. 17. It is during this turn that the second and third fingers of the left hand (holding the coins) bend in towards the palm, and the forefinger extends so that it points to the empty right palm.

Fig. 18. The right hand draws back the jacket and the left hand enters. As soon as it is hidden from view the coins are brought to the fingertips and fanned, and then are brought to view.

Fig. 19. The left hand places all the coins into the right hand which, in turn, drops them one at a time into the glass. The last coin is not dropped in as are the other three but is apparently taken with the left hand (the French Drop). The right hand transfers the coin into the palm then grasps the glass by its lip as shown in the drawing. The left hand pretends to toss its coin up into the air and, after a suitable interval for it to travel over, the right hand releases its pressure and the coin drops into the glass with the rest.

The Cut and Restored Dope

IN the right hands this can become a hit trick. It is a " tongue-in-cheek " demonstration of hypnotism designed for the non-serious performer, and makes a change from the usual guillotine.

Let us give you the effect first. A lady from the audience is invited up on to the stage where she is given a chair on the left-hand side of the performer's (or should it be " operator's " !) table. On this table there is a box with a cut-away front which is shown to be empty. At one end of this box there is an elbow rest, and at the other a handgrip. The lady is requested to place her arm through the box (through two rubber star-straps provided at each end) so that her hand reaches the handgrip and her elbow rests on the elbow rest. Her arm can be plainly seen going through the box and remains in full view when it is in place.

The performer's ability as a hypnotist is now brought into play. The lady is apparently hypnotised and, to prove she is deeply under the spell, her left arm is raised from her side by the performer. As this is done there is a loud winding noise. This, it seems, proves she is suitably doped. She is blindfolded—so that the glare from the stage lights shall not waken her—and the effect proceeds.

The magician produces a bradawl and proceeds to bore a hole in the muscle of her right arm. A small funnel is placed in the hole and a jugful of green, anaesthetic liquid is poured in. Repeated hypnotic commands ensure that she feels no pain whatsoever at any stage of the operation.

A large rusty bread-knife is next introduced along with a loop of what the performer describes as stainless-steel cheese-cutting wire, and the audience is asked which they prefer. If the audience happens to be unduly bloodthirsty, the performer decides that he will use the cheese-cutting wire after all as it is more hygienic. The front slide of the box is pushed into place hiding the arm and interior of the box, then the cutting wire is placed round the wrist and apparently pulled right through. This same cut (?) is done at the elbow. Theoretically, at least, the centre part of the arm is now separated from wrist and elbow. Once again repeated assurances are made that no pain will be felt.

Suddenly the performer senses some doubt in the minds of the audience of his ability to restore the arm, so he searches for, and eventually finds, a recommendatory letter from a previous patient. This says how pleased the man was with everything that was done to him, and is signed by a Mr. Lefty Smith.

Now that everyone is certain of the complete success of the experiment the performer continues by reaching into the box and removing the portion of the arm that has been cut away. The front slide of the box is removed and the centre part of the arm is missing.

At this point the magician offers £1,000 to any charity the audience cares to name if he is unable to restore the arm to its normal condition . . . providing it is the charity the performer happens to be thinking of. Next comes a demonstration of a remarkable hypnotic fact. Our operator has found that he is able to stick pins

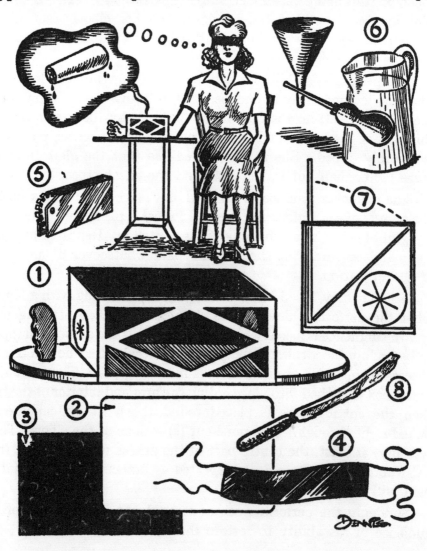

and swords into the detached part of the subject's arm whilst she is deeply under the hypnosis, and this is done. The pin (a long hat-pin) is jammed into the arm and, when asked, the lady says she feels nothing. The front slide is replaced in the box, then the forearm is wrapped up in a piece of newspaper (or grease-proof paper) and the subject is asked if she would like to take it away as it is, or whether she would rather have it replaced in its former position.

A red-hot soldering iron is produced and the lady's elbow and wrist treated with it. She is then de-hypnotised, and the blindfold is removed.

Suddenly the paper containing the arm is squashed flat and the arm has vanished. Simultaneously the front is removed from the box and there is the lady's arm as good as new and in its correct position. Applause. The lady removes her arm and is led to the side of the stage where the magician asks the audience to give her " a big hand " for the part she played for their entertainment. So you have two lots of applause in the same trick !

The basis of the effect is a cabinet built on the same lines as Stadelman's Live Stock Vanish combined with a large-size version of the Vanishing Wand. The rest of the build-up is supplied by gags and " bits of business " which may be altered, or left out, to suit the whims of each individual performer. The important thing is to remember that this represents an Hypnotic Demonstration; stress should be laid on that aspect, although it is burlesque.

The properties required for the presentation as described are as follows :—

The cabinet (as illustrated in Figure 1).

The front slide to the cabinet (Figure 2).

The black fake panel (Figure 3).

A blindfold (Figure 4).

A Comedy Watch Winder, obtainable from dealers (Figure 5).

A Magic Bradawl, small funnel, and Evaporated Milk Jug filled with milk coloured with green aniline dye (Figure 6).

A large " rusty " bread-knife (Figure 8).

A piece of steely-blue ribbon half an inch wide by sixty inches long. The two ends of this are stitched together so that an endless band is formed (Figure 9).

A dummy forearm made of paper with wood ends suitably decorated. This is shown in Figure 10.

A " soldering-iron." This is made of wood and the red tip should be coloured with red " silver " paper to simulate red heat (Figure 11).

A sheet of newspaper to wrap the forearm in.

A large hat pin.

THE CABINET

The cabinet is of a size to accommodate a lady's forearm, and is about eight inches high with a cut-out front as illustrated. The base continues out at both ends in a semi-circle, on one end is a carved hand-grip and the other remains flat and should be covered with a piece of felt. At the bottom, and to the rear of each side, is a rubber star-trap of a size to take a lady's hand comfortably.

The front of the cabinet slides in and out and is higher than the cabinet itself. This is so that the fake may be hidden behind it easily. The fake, shown in Figure 3, is black (to match the interior of the cabinet) on one side and the same colour as the front slide on its back.

A drawing of the action is shown in Figure 7. Front slide with fake behind it are slid down into the cabinet. The fake is pushed backwards until it reaches the rear wall of the cabinet so hiding the arm, the front slide remaining where it is. The position of the star trap is also clearly shown in this drawing. To reproduce the arm a reversal of these movements is made. It will be understood that the front slide can be withdrawn leaving the fake in position covering the arm.

THE DUMMY FOREARM—(Figure 9)

The best way we have found to make this is to have a semi-cone shaped piece of wood of the necessary size. The two wooden end plates are placed at each end of this then the tinted paper wrapped around and glued to one end plate (the narrow one). When dry, the block is slid out and the larger end plate glued in.

TABLE SET-UP

The title illustration gives some idea of how things should look. Immediately to the rear of the box is the dummy arm and, if you think the subject might be squeamish, it can be covered with the sheet of newspaper. Also on the table is the blindfold, the Magic Bradawl, the funnel, the Evaporated Milk Jug, the front of the cabinet with fake ready in position, the loop of ribbon, the dummy soldering iron, and the large hat-pin.

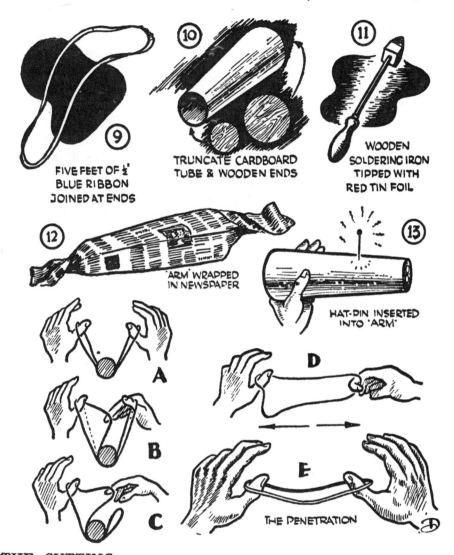

⑨ FIVE FEET OF ½'
BLUE RIBBON
JOINED AT ENDS

⑩ TRUNCATE CARDBOARD
TUBE & WOODEN ENDS

⑪ WOODEN
SOLDERING IRON
TIPPED WITH
RED TIN FOIL

⑫ 'ARM' WRAPPED
IN NEWSPAPER

⑬ HAT-PIN INSERTED
INTO 'ARM'

A

B

C

D

E

THE PENETRATION

THE CUTTING

Although this is exceedingly old there may be one or two who
do not know its mechanics so, for the sake of completeness, we
include it here. If you look at the illustrations marked A to E we
think you will understand it. The circle represents an end view of
the wrist. The loop goes under this then the looped ends are slipped
over the thumbs. The fingers of the right hand reach over and loop
into ribbon running over the left thumb. The ribbon from the right
thumb is dropped and the hands move apart quickly. The loop
stolen by the right fingers is transferred on to the right thumb and
you are left as you started except that the loop has apparently
penetrated the wrist.

PRESENTATION

If you've read the foregoing we don't think you'll find much difficulty in any of it. Once again we stress that the " Tongue-in-cheek " presentation is essential, remember, you're burlesquing a hypnotist and the more fun you can get out of it the better.

Little remains to be said, as most of the presentation may be gleaned from the description of the effect. When you apparently remove the portion of the arm from the box it is actually lifted up from behind.

The watch-winder is carried in the pocket for use when necessary.

THE CONTINUITY GAG

A LTHOUGH the dealers continue to flood the magical market with tricks of every description, very few Continuity Gags see the light of day. There are some however : the Continuous Cigar, Comedy Watch, and Abbott's Goofus Plant to mention just a few.

The ideal Continuity Gag, it appears to us, should be amusing without the necessity of a patter build-up, quick, mysterious, and with a surprise ending the last time it is performed.

The Gag in question can be of various types. The Vanishing Bird Cage invented by Jack Le Dair and performed so efficiently by Arthur Dowler is one, John Booth's Musical Gag is another.

We imagine there are few magicians who do not know what a Continuity Gag is, but for those few we will describe one. It is a gag of some sort that takes place immediately after your first trick. Usually you say you will perform something, try to perform it, fail, discard the apparatus, then go into your second trick. When that is over the apparatus is picked up again and a second attempt made. After the third trick a further effort is made to master it, and so it goes on until your last trick has been performed. This time, by the grace of the Gods of Magic, you succeed.

The Continuity Gag is a useful thing insofar as it helps to knit the act together. Most magicians' acts consist of isolated effects strung together. Apart from the fact that they have strong opening and closing numbers there is little cohesion. It is like having an evening's variety show without a compere. The compere knits an evening's show together and a good Continuity Gag helps to do the same to an individual act.

There are a large number of ordinary stock tricks which may be twisted to change them into Continuity Gags. This applies to some of the older ones, especially as, apart from helping the act as a whole, it often gives the tricks themselves a sufficiently new dressing to make the audience think they're new. We have compiled a few which may help you. We call the first :—

CHRONOLOGICAL

You will need a set of three nesting watches in the waistcoat pocket and a Giant Watch slung out of sight somewhere in the region of the " tails." After each trick a mention is made that as the show must run dead to time you must check to see that your're within schedule, so a watch is removed from the pocket, looked at, then placed on the table or into a hat. The last time you take out the Giant Watch and walk off.

MEDICAL

For children's shows, older children, we suggest you eat a piece of cotton-wool between each trick and, at the end, pull from your mouth a long paper streamer.

INTENTIONAL

A little while ago one could obtain quite cheaply an item called a " Flat Rabbit." It can be used effectively as a Continuity Gag by having it already loaded into a folded opera hat. After each trick you say: " I always like to produce a rabbit at least once each time I do a show—but before I do so I'll show you another trick." At the end you finally do spring open the hat and produce the rabbit, but you obviously kept him folded up too long.

The " Skilly Rabbit," a type of production rabbit that appears to be mostly skeleton, can be used in the same way, the tag-line being: " I should have produced him before—he's starved to death ! "

INFLATABLE

Another idea with a folded opera hat. Have loaded in the hat a model of a small pair of bellows, also four balloons faked with carbide in the usual manner so that they blow themselves up. Spring open hat between each trick and produce a fully inflated balloon. After the last trick produce the last balloon, then tell your audience that you like to show them how at least one trick is done—and produce the bellows.

(K)NOTABLE

Sometimes a trick that has been well-worn can be given a new lease of life. After your first trick a piece of rope is picked up and cut in the centre. The ends are knotted together and then the rope is wound around the hand. After a couple of magic words it is thrown out—but the knot is still there. After the second trick the same process is gone through with the same rope, and after the third effect, too. After the fourth trick you again pick up the rope, coil it, cut it, wind it round the hand then, give a heart-felt sigh of relief when it is thrown out and *all four* knots have vanished.

MEMORABLE

This, although not exactly a " gag," will be found to help the continuity of a Mental Act.

Once again we assume your programme consists of four effects. At the end of the first trick a member of the audience is asked up on to the stage and requested to write the figures 1 to 20 in a vertical line down the left hand side of a blackboard you have ready for him. The audience is then invited to call out the names of five objects, one at a time, and the assistant writes them down by the first five figures on the board. After the second trick the audience again call out five objects, and these are placed against figures 6 to 10. After the third mental masterpiece five more objects are written down, and the figures 16 to 20 are filled up after the fourth effect. You now go into the Mammoth Memory Trick.

INDESTRUCTIBLE

Quite a long time ago we had a Wrist-Chopper made for us but we never used it more than once. Although we used all the Guillotine Gags we could find we still had an anti-climax to overcome ; this was because the assistant had to withdraw her arm and walk back to her seat after the actual magic was finished. Now, although it may seem to some to be wasted, we use it this way.

The Chopper is the second trick on our programme. We demonstrate the sharpness of the blade in the usual way, in fact, we give the thing the biggest build-up we can. Then, instead of asking for an assistant from the audience, we bare our own arm and stick it through the hole. The blade is slowly brought down until it is just touching the skin, when we suddenly realise that perhaps the audience would prefer to see our next trick. We remove the arm, lower the sleeve, and do trick No. 2. This business is repeated before we start on Trick 3, and we invariably treat the guillotine as if we're not too sure about it. When the third trick is over we come back to it, but once again our nerve fails us and we go into the fourth effect. Then, and only then, are we able to screw our courage up to a sufficiently high pitch to push the blade down. Our arm is quickly withdrawn and shown unharmed and, with a rather hestiating smile, we say : " You see, there really *was* nothing to it ! "

COMBUSTIBLE

You will need a cigarette dropper on the right hand side under the coat, and a Lighter to Matchbox. This is a stock effect that is obtainable from the dealers.

After each trick a cigarette is produced from the air, via the dropper, and the Lighter (?) is picked up from the table and sparked furiously, without result. After a few moments of this the Lighter is returned to the table and the cigarette is lobbed away. This happens after each trick. After the last effect the same thing happens. When the Lighter has been unsuccessfully operated you turn to the audience and say you'd give fifty of these for one box of matches. The Lighter changes instantaneously into a match-box, a match is extracted, and off you go smoking furuiously to catch up on lost time.

HOROLOGICAL

A suggestion for a children's show. You will need one of the usual Crystal Clock Dials complete with hand. When the first trick is over you say : " That was Trick No. 1." We will now do Trick No. No. 2 and, so that you will all be able to know what number trick it is, I'll show you how my programme indicator works. Of course, in big theatres they use lights but my programme indicator works by magic."

So, after each trick, the hand is removed from the dial, altered, then returned and spun, and it should come to rest pointing to whatever number you like.

IMPERSONAL

If you are one of those lucky people who are adept at the almost forgotten art of Chapeaugraphy it might be a good idea to do one quick Chapeau impression between each of your ordinary tricks, the best one (of course) being kept till last.

The same thing would apply to a Lightning Cartoonist. He could have an easel and drawing board set up on one side of the stage. Between each trick he rushes over and sticks an odd line in here and there. After his last magical effect the drawing is finished off. It would be, preferably, one of those upside-down pictures. Both the above will give the audience the impression that you're a good deal cleverer than you really are !

INCREDIBLE

After each effect a fan of cards is produced from thin air, really from card clips beneath the coat, then discarded on to a tray. When the act is over the tray is covered for a moment with a handkerchief. The silk is raised and whipped away and there are all the cards built up in a Card Castle.

MEDAL

Some time ago there was an excellent effect published in *Abracadabra* entitled MEDALS by Jimmy Flowers. This makes an amazingly good continuity gag. The trick consisted of showing a neat stand empty then covering it with a silk Four coins were vanished one at a time over the stand and, when the silk was pulled away, there were the four coins each sewn to a ribbon in the form of a medal. All four were joined together so that they might be lifted off and pinned on the lapel.

Used in continuity it works this way. After you have performed your first trick a coin is picked up from a stand. The Medals stand is shown empty then covered with a silk and the coin is vanished, apparently being dropped into the stand.

After the next trick another coin is passed invisibly into the stand, and so on until you've performed your last effect. The silk is removed to show the medals. These are taken from the stand and pinned to the lapel; and you walk off!

UNCONVENTIONAL

Between each effect the magician walks to the front of the stage and offers some lucky spectator a free choice of one of five envelopes that rest on a thin tray. The magician takes the one that is left for him after the fourth trick, then all the spectators are asked to stand up and open their envelopes. As the tray was a " Just Chance " one the magician is the only one to find a pound note in his envelope, the rest each have two twopence-halfpenny stamps for their trouble.

GULLIBLE

To end this chapter here is a Continuity Gag we're rather proud of, although it needs careful rehearsal between yourself and a stooge. You will also need a set of Giant Find the Lady Cards on an easel. These should be on one side of the stage near the front, and the stooge should be sitting in the audience on the same side in the front row armed with some stage-money. After the first effect you ask if there is anyone in the audience who would care for a flutter. Up comes the stooge who lays down a quid. He loses. After the second trick he comes up again, and still loses. This goes on until after the last trick. Once again he comes up, and this time lays down four pounds. And, just for a change, he wins!

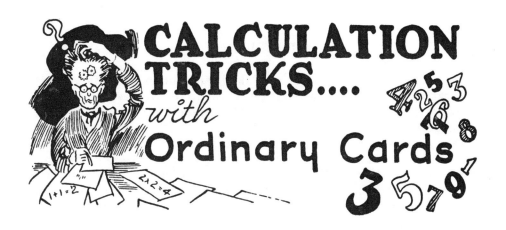

CALCULATION TRICKS....
with Ordinary Cards

EFFECT:—Any full deck is freely shuffled. Performer writes the name of a card on a slip of paper, folds it and hands it to a spectator who then calls a number. He counts down to that number and finds the card whose name is on the slip. This is repeated with a second person.

METHOD:—First check the pack to see there are 52 cards if there is a Joker, discard it. Hand pack out to be shuffled and in taking it back note the bottom card. Suppose it is the 8 of Spades. Write that on a slip of paper and hand it to a spectator to put in his pocket. Invite him to call any number between 30 and 40. Suppose he says 33. Mentally subtract 33 from 52, i.e. 19. Acting as though you had not heard you illustrate what he is to do. You say, "Suppose you choose 19, you would deal off cards like this . . . " Count off 19 into your right hand and keep your hands separated as you ask the spectator if he understands what he is to do. Then put the two packets together, but place the right packet under the left. Done casually and smoothly this will never be noticed. Hand the deck to the spectator, holding it with the right thumb underneath, fingers on top. Tilt the pack a little and note the bottom card, suppose it is the 3D. Write this on a second slip, fold it, and give to another person. Now ask first spectator what number he chose. He names it, deals off to it and turns the 8S. Ask him to take out his slip and read it . . . He finds the correct prediction.

Take the remainder of the deck and drop it on the cards dealt. You have the 3D the 19th card from the top. Ask second person to choose a number between 18 and 25. Put pack on table with the last few cards spread a little so that you can pick up the pack leaving a card or two on the table as if by accident. Suppose he calls 21. You have to add 2 cards to the top. In taking the pack leave two cards accidently on the table, put these on top, hand pack to spectator and have your prediction verified by him.

A PREDICTION

A spectator shuffles any pack. Take it and run over the faces of the cards, saying that you will take out two cards to be witness of your ability to foretell events. What you really do is to note the 19th card from the top, suppose it is the Queen of Hearts. From further down in the pack you take any Heart and any Queen, putting them face downwards on the table. Turn the pack face up and let a spectator remove any three spot cards from the lower portion, (the top 19 cards must not be disturbed). Tell him to lay them in a row face up, the highest card to the left; say they are 9, 6, 2. Hand him duplicates of these values to put in reverse order below, thus: 2, 6, 9. Ask him to subtract and call the figures, handing him cards of the corresponding values (6, 9, 3) as he calls them. Tell him to add these three figures (which total 18), then to take the deck and deal off that number of cards (18), and turn up the next card. He does this and finds the QH. You turn your prediction cards, a Queen of Hearts.

In selecting the cards for the subtraction sum, be careful to take the cards from below the 19th.

LONG DISTANCE MINDREADING

Mail to a friend a letter couched in the following terms:—"I am sending you by the next post an ordinary deck of cards. Read these instructions carefully and follow them implicity. Remove the cards from the case without disturbing their order. Fan them and examine them on both sides. Note that they are neither faked nor arranged in any way. With the cards face down cut as often as you please completing the cut each time. Then make a single ordinary dovetail shuffle. Cut again as much as you like, and finally cut the pack into two heaps as nearly equal as you can. Remove one card from about the middle of either heap, note it, and insert it anywhere in the other heap. Now select either heap, the one you drew the card from or the one now containing it, and shuffle that heap thoroughly. Mail it to me without saying which heap it is and by return mail I'll name the selected card."

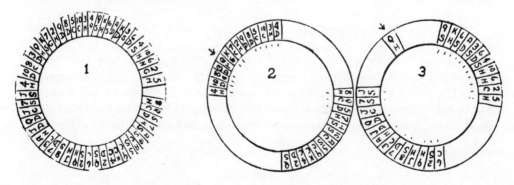

To do this you must shuffle the pack before sending it, but make a note of their order by jotting the names around a circle (Fig. 1). You probably know that complete cuts do not disarrange the sequence of the cards and that is true of a single dovetail shuffle; it merely distributes half the cards through the other half, but each half is still in the same order. The second cutting has no effect on the arrangement. When the deck is finally cut into two packets, the choice of a card from the middle ensures that it will not be an end card of one of the two strings that the original order has been divided into. The insertion of this card into the other packet, and the shuffling of that packet, seems to make its discovery impossible. But all you have to do on receipt of the cards is to mark them off, one by one, on the circle around which you had recorded the original order of the pack. When you have done this you will have either two separate runs of cards, with one card unchecked in one of them (Fig. 2) or, two separate complete runs with one, by itself, checked off somewhere else along the circle (Fig. 3). In the first case he has sent you the heap he drew his card from *and the unchecked one is it*. In the second case, he has sent you the half pack in which he inserted his card, and the isolated card you have checked off indicates his selection.

TWO CARD LOCATION

After a spectator has shuffled a pack of cards, have one freely selected, replace and bring it to the top.

Take about 8 cards from the top of the deck, spread them before a second spectator, face down, and ask him to indicate any one card and turn the index just enough to enable him to see what that card is. As he does this count the number of cards from the top card, (the first card chosen) to this second selected one; suppose it is five. Close the fan of cards, drop them on the pack and have the spectator cut the deck. Take it and rapidly deal the cards into four heaps, one card at a time. The two chosen cards must thus come together and you may allow the spectator to pick up the piles in any order he pleases. The cards are named, you order them to get together, the spectator goes through the pack and so finds them.

IMPROVED SUPER MEMORY

From any pack which has been freely shuffled allow 20 cards to be chosen and retained by different spectators. Collect them face down on top of the pack giving each person numbers from 20 down to 1. When card No. 10 is replaced on the others, secretly bend back the outer left corner with the thumb. When the last card, No. 1 has been taken back lift the top ten cards, the bent corner of the 10th card making this easy, and reverse the cards below. The pack is thus face up with the ten cards numbered from 1 to 10 face down on top of it; the other ten cards, numbers 11 to 20, on the bottom. Put the pack in your trousers pocket and have a blindfold placed over your eyes.

Announce that you will call various numbers, the drawers to name their cards as their numbers are called and you will at once find the cards. You call numbers in the following order:—

11, 2, 14; 1, 13, 5; 12, 4, 17; 3, 16, 8; 15, 7; 18, 9; 19, 10; 20, 6.
and you bring out the cards thus:—

Bottom card: second from top: third from bottom.
Top card: second from bottom; third from top.
Bottom card: second from top; third from bottom.
Top card: second from bottom; third from top.
Bottom card: second from top.
Bottom card: second from top.
Bottom card: second from top.
Bottom card.   Top card.

The patter goes that by intuition you get the thought waves of the persons who are thinking of their numbers and cards.
It's a case of 123; 123; 123; 123; 12; 12; 1; 1.

SPECTATOR'S CHOICE

From any freely shuffled pack deal 6 heaps of 5 cards each. A spectator chooses any two cards from the remainder of the pack, writes their names on a slip of paper, folds it and puts it on the table; he then puts his selected cards on top of any two heaps. Gather the heaps so that two of the five card heaps go on each of the six card heaps. Remark that you will also select two cards. Run through the packet, note the 6th and 22nd cards from the top and write their names on a slip, fold it and put it alongside the spectator's slip. Now deal the cards into two heaps beginning at the left and dealing one card at a time. The heap on your left contains the spectator's cards, that on your right has your cards.

Ask the spectator which pair, yours or his, he wishes to have finally left on the table, and which packet is to be "taken." If he chooses his cards and the left hand packet, discard the right hand packet and say you will discard the right hand pile throughout. If he chooses his cards and the right hand packet say you will "take" that away throughout. Use the same equivocal interpretation if he chooses your pair, to retain the right hand packet. Supposing he calls for his cards. Pick up the left hand pile and deal in two heaps as before. Discard the right hand pile and deal again. Continue until two cards only remain on your left. These two will be the cards whose names he wrote.

If he chooses your cards, deal in exactly the same way but discard the left hand heap throughout.

MENTALO

A spectator thinks of a number between 1 and 10. He shuffles the deck, which may be his own, counts down to the number thought of and notes the card, leaving it in the same position. This is done while your back is turned. When he is ready you turn around, take the pack, place it behind your back, rapidly count off 19 cards, reversing their order, and replacing them on the top. Do this as you say you will put the card at number 20.

Bring the pack forward and ask the spectator the number he thought of, say it was 6. Begin your count with that number, dealing the cards one at a time. When you reach 20 let him name his card and you turn it over.

KNOCK OUT COUNTING TRICK

A spectator shuffles his own deck and counts off any number of cards under 15. Suppose he chooses 6. He looks at the sixth card, remembers it and then replaces the cards in the same order. You turn away while this is being done. Take the pack, put it behind your back and count off 15 cards from the top and put them on the bottom, but do not reverse their order in counting them. Pretend to be trying to find the card without success; hand the pack to the spectator and tell him to transfer from the top to the bottom the same number of cards that he counted at first, but before doing that, to see that his card is not now anywhere near there.

This done, take the pack and again put it behind your back and transfer 15 cards from the bottom to the top. The bottom card will now be the card the spectator noted, and you can reveal it as you please. At first the result seems surprising, but a little thought will show that the two transfers of cards you make cancel out, so that when the spectator transfers the cards to the bottom he actually does the trick for you.

A CARD AND A NUMBER

Allow a spectator to shuffle any pack, select any card while the pack is in his own hands, note what it is and finally put it face down on the table. You have your back turned while this is done and keep it turned while he deals two even piles of cards of not more than, say 10 cards each. Then he is to put one pile in his pocket, place the other on his card, pick all these cards up and drop them on top of the pack. This done you turn around.

Pick up the pack and put it behind your back and as you expatiate on the impossibility of knowing the position of his card since you ask no questions, count off 15 cards from the top reversing their order and replace them on the top of the pack. Bring the pack forward and, as you say, to make the problem still harder for you, tell him to take the packet from his pocket and place it on top of the pack. His card will now be the 15th card from the top and you can reveal it as you please. You can reverse any number of cards on the top but such number must always be higher than the number contained in each of the heaps he deals.

PROJECTED THOUGHT

Some preparation is necessary. Write on 52 small cards "You will think of the   of   and it will be the 35th card in the deck." Fill in the name of a different card on each. Insert these in small envelopes and place the envelopes of each suit, in order from Ace to King, in four different pockets so that you can readily find the envelope which has the name of any particular card. Thus prepared and with any full deck of cards minus the Joker, you are ready.

Place a small sealed envelope in full view (this an extra one with a blank card in it). Hand the pack to a spectator asking him to shuffle it and merely think of any one card. Then tell him to deal, from the face down pack, four face up piles one card at a time. He is to place the pile containing his thought card face up on any two other piles and the remaining heap on those three. Again turning the pack face down he repeats the deal and picks up the piles in the same order as before. He deals a third time. You memorize the ninth card in each pile and watch which pile he puts on two others—the ninth card in that pile is the one for which you must find the corresponding envelope in one of your pockets. To gain time to do this tell the spectator to square the cards carefully, put them face down on the table and put both hands on top. Meantime you have secured the envelope and finger palmed it in the right hand. Pick up the original envelope off the table, fingers covering it with thumb underneath, and apparently transfer it to your left hand; really drawing it back with the right thumb and pulling out the other with the left thumb and fingers. Give this to a spectator on your left. Ask the first person to name the card he thought of, have the envelope opened and the slip read then have spectator deal 35 cards and this gives you your climax.

NE PLUS ULTRA

A key card is required, this may be a long card, a double card, any kind of key card that enables you to cut to it by feel. Have this face down on your table. Let a spectator take the deck, shuffle it freely, and take it to the others letting 5 cards be freely chosen. Take the pack, turn your back and ask the drawers to hold up their cards for all to see. Casually place the pack on the top of the long card. Ask your volunteer assistant to collect the cards face down on his left hand (note the order of the cards) bring them to the table, place them on top of the pack and then cut the pack several times. Finally you cut at the long card thus bringing the selected cards back to the top.

Next by way of giving them a thorough shuffle you lay the cards out a few at a time (really 4 cards exactly each time), the first 4 to A, the next 4 at B, then C and D. Continue dealing by fours in the same way until you have four cards left, deal one on A, the next on B, then on C, and the last card on D. Pick up the

C	B
D	A

packets by placing B on top of A, then C on B, and finally D on C. Take up the pack and deal into four piles, one card at a time as in bridge, and pick up the heaps in the same order as before. The spectators will naturally think the cards are lost in the pack, actually the top card is the second card selected, the third card stands at 14, the fourth at 27, the fifth at 40 and the first card at 5. These numbers are easy to remember, three of the cards being at intervals of 13 from the top card. You can then get the number 40 for the last card, deal face up and show that is right, mentally noting the 5th, 14th and 27th as you pass them, and then name them by mindreading. The remaining one, the top card reveal in as striking a manner as possible.

UNI-MENTALITY

EFFECT:—A spectator merely thinks of a card and the performer finds it and names it. Any deck may be used.

FIRST METHOD:—Spectator shuffles any deck and hands it to you. Tell him to think of any card and concentrate on that card. After a moment or two say that you have an impression of the color but not the suit, so in order to strengthen the spectator's mental picture of the card ask him to take a good look at it as you run the cards over with the faces towards him. Ask him to say "Stop" after the card has been passed so as to save time. When he calls "Stop," bend the inner ends of the cards in your left hand sharply by squeezing them between the thumb base and fingers. Drop the right hand cards on top and say that you now know the suit. This is a bluff but you have gained knowledge of the approximate position of the card under cover of a pretext.

Cut several times and finally cut at the bend in the inner end of the pack, thus you know that the card thought of is somewhere near the bottom.

Again spread the cards before him, fanning them very slowly and tell him to take out five cards, one of which is to be his card. Take your time so that he will have taken out four cards by the time you reach the middle of the pack. Naturally the card he takes from near the bottom must be the thought card. Note where he puts this card amongst the other four, and when you pick up the five cards get it in the middle with two cards above it and two cards below it. Spread the five in a wide fan and hold them up before the spectator asking him to make his mental picture of the card as perfect as possible. With the cards upright it is an easy matter to turn the lower index corner of the middle card with the left thumb and read it. Put the packet down and in your most impressive style read the card in the usual way, hesitatingly—color—suit—and finally its value.

When showing the faces of the cards to the spectator, insist it is done merely to strengthen his mental picture.

SECOND METHOD:—The procedure is the same but instead of bending the lower packet when the spectator calls "Stop," you push the top card of the deck, whose upper right hand corner you previously bent upwards a little, on the top of the packet in the left hand and close the deck. As before have five cards removed and simply watch the card that is removed just before you reach your key card, the one with the bent corner.

The pulling off of the top, bent corner card, to the top of the left hand packet is completely covered by the cards being held upright at the time.

(Note): A better plan than bending the corner of the top card is to put a light pencil dot on the back of the top card near the top left hand corner and another in the same place near the lower right hand corner. This can be done at any favorable opportunity before starting the trick. This card is then the one to be pulled over when "Stop" is called. When the cards are fanned the dot is easily found and the card taken out just before it is the one to watch.

In all three versions make a great point of the fact that you do not look at the faces of any cards.

For method with one-way cards see chapter 9.

EASY CARD DIVINATION

A spectator spreads a pack of cards, which he has shuffled, face down on a table. He removes a card from the upper part, notes what it is, and inserts it in the lower half of the deck. When the card is inserted make a mental estimate of about how many cards from the end of the row, i.e. the bottom of the pack, the card lies. Suppose you think it is about 14th. Gather the cards and place them behind your back. Count off to within four cards of the estimated position, in the supposed case this would be 10 cards and put them on top. Take off 4 cards from the top and one from the bottom and ask if the card is among the five. If not discard them and repeat the operation. When the card appears you know it is the one drawn from the bottom.

HOURGLASS CARDS

Any one shuffles his own deck and removes 6 cards. From these 6 he selects one and deals the remainder of the deck into two face down heaps, a card to each in rotation. He puts his chosen card on top of either half and the remaining 5 cards on the same heap, or the other, as best suits himself. Instruct spectator to place the half not containing his chosen card on the other half. The deck is laid aside and the time by the performer's watch is noted. Say it reads 3:26. Adding three to 26 gives 29, and the chosen card is found at that number in the pack.

The explanation is simple. The mechanical part ensures the placing of the cards at the 29th position from the top, and the trick is performed at certain times only, i.e. at 1:28, 2:27, 3:26, 4:25, 6:23, 7:22, 8:21, 9:20, 10:19, 11:18 or 12:17.

EASY CARD DISCOVERY

EFFECT:—Spectator shuffles his own deck and cuts it about the middle. Spread these two packets face up on the table, one below the other. While you back is turned the spectator takes a card from either row, inserts it in the other row, shuffles that portion, and puts the portion from which he took a card in his pocket. You take the shuffled portion and locate the card.

METHOD:—While you are spreading out the lower portion of the deck, mentally count the spots of the cards in the first row, subtracting 10 every time the total amounts to more than that and ignoring the face cards and the tens. If you finish with the number 7, there must be a final 3 for the second row as the two numbers will always amount to 10. When you turn back again ask which row the card was put into, if it was the top one, count the spots of the packet handed to you in the same way. Suppose you arrive at 9, deduct the previous number 7, and you know the card is a 2. If there are two such cards in the packet you must ask a leading question, such as "It was a red card, wasn't it?" to get information. If, however, the card was put into the lower heap you have the number 3, and you work in just the same way.

KEYSTONE CARD DISCOVERY

A borrowed deck having been freely shuffled and returned to you, fan the cards for selection of a card and secretly count 10 cards, holding an inconspicuous division at that point. See that the card is taken from further on. Divide the pack for the return of the card at the division, drop the ten cards on it deliberately and square the pack very openly. Riffle shuffle several times keeping the top eleven cards in top position. Explaining what is to be done, you count off eleven cards into a pile one at a time. Replace these on top of the pack and the selected card is now the top card.

Hand the pack to a spectator telling him to think of a number between 5 and 12 and "will" the card to go to that position. He deals face down the number he thought of and looks at the next card, it is wrong. Suppose, for example, he thought of 6, replace the packet of 6 cards on the top of the deck and hand the pack to a second person, telling him to do the same thing but to think of a card between 12 and 20. Suppose he thinks of 15 and deals to that number; he looks at the next card and again it is wrong. Replace the packet on the pack and hand the pack to a lady. Let the first two persons tell her their numbers; ask her to subtract the smaller from the larger and deal cards equal to the remainder, which in this case will be 9. She does so and turns up the next card, it is the right one.

Any numbers may be used so long as the second one is larger than the first.

ASSISTANCE CARD TRICK

From any deck take a packet of 16 cards. Run over the faces and put all the cards of·the suit of which there are most together. Rapidly add the values, counting J as 11; Q as 12; and ignoring the K. When the total goes above 13, or is 13, deduct 13 and start again with the remainder. Subtract the final total from 13 and remember the result. Ask spectator to take a card but to note the suit only. Spread the cards of the suit you picked so that he must take one of them.

Take the other packet of 36 cards and hand it to the spectator. From it he selects any card of the chosen suit he pleases and hand you the remainder. Run over the faces and add the values of the remaining cards of that suit in exactly the same manner as before. Subtract the final figure from the remainder you got from the 16 pile, the result will denote the value of his chosen card.

THE 52 CARD TRICK

A number is named and a party mentally selects a card. Pack is dealt into 4 face up piles, party indicating the pile containing the card. Pack picked up and again dealt in 4 piles, the pile with card again indicated. This is done twice more and the thought card is found at the number chosen .

The trick depends on the order in which the piles are picked up. All dealing is from the pack held face down, the cards being turned up as dealt. In picking up the piles put them face up on the left hand in the order indicated in the table, turn the pack face down and again deal into four piles.

Table to be memorized:—

1.	1. 1. 1.	5.	2. 2. 2.	8.	2. 2. 3.		
2.	2. 2. 1.	6.	3. 3. 2.	9.	3. 3. 3.		
3.	3. 3. 1.	7.	4. 4. 2.	10.	4. 4. 3.		
4.	4. 4. 1.						
11.	2. 2. 4.	12.	3. 3. 4.	13.	4. 4. 4.		

This indicates how to pick up the heap containing the chosen card after each of the first three deals when the number given is 1 to 13. After the fourth deal the heap is picked up first if the number is 13 or under. If the number is 14 to 26, subtract 13 from it, deal and pick up the first three times as the table indicates but, after the last deal, pick up the heap second. If from 27 to 39, subtract 26, follow the table, and pick up the pile third after the last deal. If over 39, subtract 39, follow table and pick the heap up fourth.

Examples:—Number given is 7. Pick up indicated heap 4. 4, 2. then first. Number is 22. 22 minus 9 equals 13. Pick up 3, 3. 3. then second. Number is 34. 34 minus 26 equals 8. Pick up 2. 2. 3. then third. Number is 49. 49 minus 39 equals 10. Pick up 4. 4. 3. then fourth.

THE MAGI'S DETECTION

EFFECT:—A spectator cuts a portion from his own shuffled deck You run through the cards once, then announce that you have memorized the cards. He secretly removes one card and hands you the remainder. You run through them once and name the missing card.

METHOD:—When you run over the faces of the cards add their values, counting a Jack as 11, a Queen as 12, and ignoring the Kings. Sub- 13 each time the total goes above that number. At the same time keep tally of the suits by counting Spades 1, Hearts 2, Clubs 3 and ignoring the Diamonds; subtract 6 when the suit total exceeds that number. The two numbers are noted mentally as you pass each card. Suppose the first five cards are QC, 5D, 3H, 9S and JC. you would count 12-3 plus 5-0...17-3; deduct 13 from 17 and go on with 4-3, add 3-2...7-5; add 9-1...16-6; deduct 13-6...3-0; add 11-3...14-3; deduct 13, and carry on 1-3. A few trials will show that the operation is easy since, there are no large totals, and as you are supposed to be memorizing the cards, a little hesitation is natural, however the quicker you do it, the more effective the trick.

When the packet is returned to you minus one card, simply repeat the operation and subtract the total from the former one, the remainder denotes the value and suit of the missing card. If the second value tally is greater than the first add 13 and then subtract. If they are the same, the card is a King. If the suit totals are the same it is a Diamond. Suppose the first total is 10-3 and the second 5-3, the remainder is 5-0 and therefore the card must be the 5D.

THE FLUSH TRICK

EFFECT:—The Aces, Kings, Queens, Jacks and Tens are removed from any deck and mixed. From the 20 cards placed under a handkerchief the performer brings out any Royal Flush called for.

METHOD:—Three simple tables have to be learned. Take the clubs face down in the right hand and the spades in the left, mix them by dealing in a single face down heap as follows:—

R.H. 1 card, L.H. 2 cards; R.H. 2 cards, L.H. 2; R.H. 2, L.H. 1; always one card at a time.

Take the Hearts in the R.H. and Diamonds in L.H. and deal thus— R.H. 1, L.H. 2; R.H. 1, L.H. 1; R.H. 1, L.H. 1; R.H. 2, L.H. 1.

Pick up the 10 black cards with the R.H. and the 10 red cards with the L.H. Deal again into a face down heap as follows:—

R.H. 1, L.H. 3; R.H. 1, L.H. 1; R.H. 1, L.H.1; R.H. 2, L.H. 3; R.H. 1. L.H. 1; R.H. 1, L.H. 1; R.H. 3.

Hand the packet to the spectator and have him deal them one at a time into 3 face down heaps, the 19th and 20th cards going on the first and last heaps. He is to pick them up by putting the third pile on the middle one and these two on the first. Fanning the cards will show the suits to be hopelessly mixed, but have him repeat the same deal exactly and cover the cards with a handkerchief. Impossible as it seems the packet is now arranged thus from the top downwards, 5 Clubs, 5 Diamonds, 5 Hearts, 5 Spades.

MODERNISM IN MENTALISM

Any pack may be used and it is a good idea to lead up to the trick by talking of telepathy and the scientific investigations now being carried on regarding it. Have a spectator shuffle the cards, take the pack and run them off one by one before his eyes, you carefully looking away, and ask him to merely think of one. Place the cards one in front of the other in the right hand as you show them so that they remain in the same order. When you have shown 9 cards ask if one has been mentally selected, if so replace the 9 cards on the top of the pack, but if not, put them on the bottom and continue in the same way with another set of 9 cards. If one is chosen mentally from these place them on top, if not, on the bottom, and continue until spectator says he has selected a card, and drop that packet of 9 on top and false shuffle the pack.

Say that you will use half the deck only and deal off 26 cards in three heaps and, since there is a Joker in the pack, you will take one more card to make the heaps even. Remarking that it is necessary for you to know if the card thought of is in that half of the pack, pick up the first pile of 9 and show the cards, if it is there pick up the three heaps with this one on top; if it is in the second put that on top, and if it is neither of the first two you know it must be in the third, so you say you will just take a chance. False shuffle and again deal three piles telling the spectator to watch for his card and try to send you the name mentally. Note the third card in each packet, one of them is the card thought of. With one or two leading questions you can ascertain the card and then name it in the hesitating way the mindreaders affect.

By having the row it is named, you know the card with certainty. In that case gather up the packets with the one containing the chosen card in the middle and it will be the 12th card down. Deal face up telling the spectator to think "Stop" when he sees his card. You stop at the 12th.

FOUR TO ONE DETECTION

Any one selects from his own shuffled deck any 16 cards. Take them and deal as follows, face down:

```
        1     2
     3  4  5  6  7
        8     9
    10 11 12 13 14
       15    16
```

Turn your back and tell the spectator to turn up any card, look at it, turn it face down again and leave it in the same place. This done you turn round and pick up all the cards in the same row as his, shuffle them and let the spectator shuffle them. Have the spectator put his cards on top of yours. Shuffle all the other cards and put them on the packet already made. Deal the cards as before face up.

Ask the spectator which row his card is in. It will lie at 7, 8, 9, 10, or 11. There are, therefore 4 chances of success to one of failure. The selected card falls at 11 if it is left on the face of his packet after the spectator shuffles; and if you have him shuffle with the cards face up he is not likely to leave it in that position.

A PSYCHIC CARD FEAT

Ask a spectator to take a coin from his pocket and write its date on a piece of paper. Then write the figures reversed and subtract the smaller number from the larger. Suppose the date to be 1935, this reversed would give 5391, and the remainder after the subtraction will be 3456. The spectator is then to take from the pack a card with the same number of spots as the first figure of the answer, and do the same with the other three figures. If there is a 0 he uses a king to represent it. The four cards must be of different suits. This done he is to lay them on the table face down and move them about so that even he cannot tell one card from another, then take any one and put it in his pocket without looking at it.

Pick up three remaining cards and as you add them to the top of the deck, slightly spread them so that you can see the indices. Note first what suit is missing, then mentally add the values and subtract the total from the nearest multiple of 9. In the case given above, suppose the three cards are the 3C, 4H, 6D. the missing suit is Spades, the total values 13, subtracting this from 18 leaves 5. Therefore the card in the spectator's pocket must be the 5S. The result is surprising since the spectator's himself cannot tell what card he picked up.

OUT ON LOCATION

Take any deck, after it has been well shuffled by a spectator, and run over the faces under pretense of taking out the Joker. In so doing note the bottom card, the fifth card further along, the fifth card from that and finally the fifth card from that one. Do not try to remember the suits of the cards, merely the values. Suppose the bottom card to be the 5D, the other cards at five card intervals being the 7C, 6H, and 3S—simply memorize the figures 5763 as you would a telephone number. This can be done easily as you run over the faces. Then turn the pack face down and undercut 7 or 8 cards from the bottom to the top and put the pack on the table. Invite a spectator to cut about the middle, complete the cut, look at the top card, bury it in the middle and square the cards carefully. Take the pack, run through the faces and find the original bottom card, the 5D. The figures 5763 will be recalled without effort. Count the cards between the 5 and the 7. If there are five only, count the cards between the 7 and the 6. Somewhere in these groups there will be five cards instead of four. One of these will be the selected card. Cut bringing these five to the top and glance at them again memorizing the values only. Place the pack behind your back and ask how many spots there were on the card. Bring that card forward and put it face down on the table. The suit is named and you turn the card over, it is the selected card.

In the unlikely event of there being two cards of the same value, put one on the bottom and the other on the top and bring the pack forward. In putting it on the spectator's outstretched hand sight the bottom card. Let him name the card and you turn the top card, or turn the deck over to show the card at the bottom as may be necessary.

COINCIDENCE EXTRAORDINARY

A full deck is required for this trick and it may be shuffled as much as the spectator wishes beforehand. Take the pack and deal the top card face up, then whatever its value deal single cards to make a total of 13. Suppose the first card is a nine, deal four cards on it. Deal the next card face up and form another heap in the same way. Suppose it is a 7 spot, deal 6 cards on it to make 13. The Jack is to be counted as 10, Queen 11 and King 13. Continue in like manner until you have too few cards left to make another packet. Turn the piles face down and ask a spectator to pick up and hand to you any piles he pleases, but he must leave three heaps on the table. The result of the operation so far is that the number of cards in your hands, less ten, equals the total number of spots on the top cards of the three heaps. That is to say, suppose the top cards to be an 8, a Jack and a 2, making a total of 21—then the cards in your hands will be 31 in number. Therefore, if you force a nine spot from amongst your cards and have it added to the three top cards the total will be 30; while the subtraction of that one card from your packet will leave you with just 30 cards, thus a "Marvelous Coincidence" is brought about.

To make the trick effective, the dealing should be. done haphazardly and great stress laid on the fact that the spectator has a free choice of the packets.

NECROMANTIC CALCULATION

From a shuffled deck of 52 cards a spectator is instructed to deal out, face up, a number of spot cards, say six or seven. Take the deck and deal cards on each of these to bring a total of 12. Suppose the first card is a 7 spot, deal 5 cards on it; the next a 3, deal 9 cards on it; and so on. This should be done casually without any appearance of having to count. Lay the pack down.

Turn your back and instruct your volunteer helper to turn face down any three heaps he wishes, to take the top cards of these three heaps and place them in his pocket; then to gather the three face down piles into one packet and put them aside. Finally he is to pick up the remaining face up packets, add them to the unused portion of the pack and hand them to you. Keeping your back turned tell the spectator to take the three cards from his pocket and add the spots. You seize this opportunity to count off 13 cards from the top of your packet and palm them in your right hand. When the spectator says he has the total, turn, put your cards on the table and with the right hand pick up the other packet which was made up of the three chosen heaps, thus getting rid of the palmed cards.

Now the number of spots on the three cards the spectator holds is the same as the total number of cards in the packet you have just laid down. Reveal this in the most surprising way you can devise.

CARD and MENTAL MAGIC
The Real Coincidence Trick

In the usual effect of this nature, the performer and another party each remove a card from different decks, replace the cards, take them out again, and all for no good reason. Here we have a coincidence trick that appears genuine in every way, and we claim that it is a PERFECT CLUB EFFECT.

In effect, you and the assisting spectator each genuinely shuffle a deck of cards. You place your deck in your inside coat pocket, and he does likewise. You each reach into the other's pocket and remove a card. Neither of you know the location of a single card— but YOU BOTH DRAW THE SAME CARD! Everything is simple and fair from the audience's viewpoint, and the method is simple and perfect in every way.

In your inside coat pocket is a one-way force deck of the same back design as the cards you are using. The duplicate of this force card is missing from your deck. Its duplicate in the spectator's deck is a short card.

The shuffle is real. You each place your deck in your coat pocket, however you really put yours in the upper vest pocket, and no one can tell the difference. You each reach into the other's pocket, and remove a card. You riffle to the short card in his deck and take that card—he will, of course, get its duplicate from the force deck in your pocket. The cards are held face down.

He holds up his card and names it—you hold up your card. THEY ARE THE SAME! Bring out a regular deck from your vest pocket, toss it on the table, and you are clean.

Telephone Telepathy

This is the book test that can be used where others cannot, because it is **absolutely impromptu**, and for that reason, I have used it a lot.

The telephone book and the pack of cards, which are the only articles used, are borrowed. A knife is inserted into the deck, and the card above it is removed without letting the performer see it. THIS IS A FREE CHOICE. A cipher is added to the denomination of the card selected, and this figure is used to indicate the page, thus spreading the choice throughout the book. The suit indicates the column, and the actual denomination indicates the word to be counted to. Then the performer, like the showman that he is or is not, slowly divines the selected name!

The reason that this is possible is that there are only ten possible selections, and you only have to memorize each of them in the proper order. The card is not forced, but it is glimpsed by tilting the inserted knife blade slightly to catch the reflection of the index. Use an ordinary table knife for this. Now the performer knows what card was selected, and he knows what each card, of the numbers from one to ten, will count to in, let us say, the second column.

Suppose the card selected was a Spade. After the spectator has found the page, the magician says, "If your card was a Club, take the first column; if it was a Spade, take the second column; if it was a Diamond, take the third; a Heart, the fourth." Do you get it? Whatever suit is selected, name that suit as indicating the second column.

Here's the idea: All court cards count ten. There are fifty-two cards, but you have, unknown to the spectators, limited the choice to ten possibilities, and you know the card selected as well, and also have memorized the ten possibilities. So that's all there is to it. It is impromptu because you can find a deck, a knife, and a phone book anywhere, and the books in the same town are all uniform.

In some towns the books have only two columns, so you call black cards column one, and red ones, column two, and vice versa. If using your own deck, have it set up and have the selection made from a spread. If you don't care to memorize the names or want to include the phone numbers as well, you can have them listed on a pad on which you write your divination (on another sheet, of course.) Or you may have this information written in pencil on a slate. Follow the first version though, and you will have something that you can use anywhere with good effect.

Telephone Telepathy Again

The force idea in this case is quite different. All court cards and tens are placed together in the center of the deck. It is now a simple matter to force one of these cards—there are sixteen of them—by the insertion of a knife blade into this part of the deck.

The glimpse a la knife blade is made, and the column forced as in method number one, thus absolutely forcing one name which may be predicted or revealed in any manner that the performer sees fit. This makes an excellent effect.

Alias Divination

This is an idea of Oscar Weigle, Jr., and is especially effective because of its impromptu nature (and good impromptu mental stunts are few and far between).

Several slips are handed out to a number of spectators. They all write THEIR OWN NAMES on the slips except one, who volunteers to write an "alias" or fictitious name. The slips are all folded in half and then in quarters. They are collected in a borrowed hat. The performer holds the hat and mixes the billets thoroughly. Then the hat is held up over the head while the other hand removes a slip. Almost immediately, or after a bit of concentration, the magician goes to one of the spectators and gives him the slip of paper, telling him not to open it just yet. Another slip is removed from the hat in the same manner, and again the performer dramatically hands the slip to another spectator. This is continued until every spectator who wrote a name, including the spectator who wrote a fictitious name, has a slip of paper in his hands. They are now all told to open their slips—and everyone has his original slip! Apparently the magician has correctly divined every slip.

But the real climax is yet to come. The spectators are requested to refold their slips and then to TEAR THE SLIPS IN PIECES THEMSELVES. The pieces are collected in a small dish. A match is lighted and the papers burned. The magician, gazing into the upcurling smoke, slowly calls out, or spells the "alias" name!

As many as nine slips may be passed out, but seven is about right. The slips apparently are passed out freely, but actually in a predetermined order—that is, according to some sort of numerical pattern so that you can mentally number each writer, No. 1, No. 2, etc. The slips are unmarked. However, in collecting them, they are marked in a subtle way. They are collected in the order which you are going to remember them and each slip nicked with the thumb nail according to a simple system.

You will see that when the slips have been folded, they will have four edges and each is distinguishable. There are a long folded edge and a short folded edge, a long open edge and a short open edge. Decide on a numerical order for these, and by nicking the proper edge you can mark 1, 2, 3, or 4. By nicking at the corner instead of on the edge, you can mark 5, 6, 7, or 8. No mark indicates 9.

You simply take the slip from each spectator between the thumb and forefinger and mark it on the proper edge as you drop it in the hat. That covers the first effect.

When the slips are dropped into the hat, the magician notes where the "alias" slip lies, and remembers its potition. When all the slips are in the hat, the performer mixes the slips about. He does this by placing his hand into the hat, taking hold of the "alias" slip in the right finger-palm position and mixing the OTHER slips around. Finally, he stops and leaves the "alias" slip in a corner of the hat, again remembering its position. If it is a felt hat, it may be placed in one section while the remaining billets lie at the other side. The hat is tilted slightly to show the slips as the hand comes out and is shown empty.

The hat is now lifted up above the performer's line of vision, or slightly over his head. The right hand goes into the hat, finds the "alias" slip, and OPENS IT IN THE HAT. It is opened so that the writing will be facing up. ANOTHER slip is removed as soon as posible and held up high.

When you see the mark on the slip, you can immediately associate it with its owner and subsequently hand it to him in as interesting a way as possible, pattering along the lines of knowing the slips by extra-sensory perception, or by getting a mental image of the owner, describing him before returning his billet.

Now, here's where the important part of the trick comes in. When you hand the spectator the billet, the hand holding the hat comes down, just naturally, right in front of your face. In this way you can actually see the "alias" name staring up at you! Even if the name is upside down, you can still decipher the name, as it's not hard. After glimpsing the "alias" name, the hat is immediately raised again. Because the spectators are seated and you are standing, they can not see the open paper in the hat. The right hand goes into the hat again, REFOLDS the open paper, and places it in its corner of the hat. Another billet is removed and by its mark you again divine the owner. Save the "alias" slip till about next-to-the-last. When you remove it, you need not even look at it. You simply place it to your forehead and "get" the correct owner. For the last slip you need not look at it either, for, by the process of elimination, you can easily see who its owner is.

When the slips have all been returned, the hat is shown empty. The spectators are requested to open their slips—and when they do, they find they have their original slips! This alone is very effective and leads the audience to believe that the trick is over, which is exactly what you want them to think.

You now remind them that one person wrote an alias—and that you will attempt an additional test with this name which its writer alone knows. Ask all the spectators to refold their slips and then to tear them in pieces. Meanwhile, you go around with a small dish and collect the pieces. A match is lighted and the pieces of paper ignited.

Now all that remains is to reveal the fictitious name as you see fit. A striking climax would be to have the name appear on the back of your hand after rubbing the ashes over it. This can be accomplished as follows: Place your hands behind your back as you stand watching the pieces burning. Now, stealing a piece of pointed soap or a grease eyebrow pencil from a clip under rear of coat, you will have ample time to print the name on the back of one hand. Bring hands forward keeping them above audience eye level and rub on the ashes to bring out name. If an eyebrow pencil is used, you had better have a Saturated Cleansing Pad (Woolworth's) handy to clean off the back of your hand. Another effective plan of revealing the name is to write it out, letter for letter, on a slate.

Instead of a fictitious name being written, the trick may be presented as a "Living and Dead" test. All the spectators but one write names of persons living and the one person writes a dead name. In the end, this name is divined. However, the "alias" presentation is a good presentation to try out, in view of the fact that "Living and Dead" has been somewhat overdone.

Magazine Miracle

If you were a genuine mentalist, would you use a lot of counters, cards, and what not in having the page of a book or a magazine selected? Not by a long shot, yet most effects of this sort require the use of these obvious forces. For a long time we have wanted to have a spectator turn to any page in a magazine, look at the first word, and have the performer write the word on a slate without any questions. Believe it or not, that is the effect of this trick.

Read this carefully; it is the exact effect from the audience's point of view: One of a number of magazines is selected and examined. A spectator places it behind his back. He opens it anywhere and looks at the first word ON EITHER PAGE at that place. The performer is standing at the other end of the room with his back turned and does not even see the spectator. As soon as the latter has made his selection, the magician writes something on a slate that he is holding and then places the slate, writing side down, on the table. Spectator now writes his word on another slate—shows it—magician shows his, and THE WORDS ARE THE SAME!

When you read the explanation you may have your doubts, but we have tried this and are now using it. It absolutely works and is entirely practical. The idea used to force the man to open at a certain place is this: A thin trade journal (of say 30 pages) is used, and all the pages are glued together at the edges except at this one place. When a magazine thus prepared is placed behind the back and one attempts to open it, it has to open at this place. As a trial will show, this feels perfectly natural, and no one will ever have reason to suspect anything to be wrong. We repeat that you must try it yourself to be convinced. It is suggested that you hurry the assisting spectator slightly when having him make the page selection.

If you think that they should look the magazine over before the test, the following ruse may be employed. A duplicate mazagine, unprepared, is used. The glued one is on top of the stack of about five journals. Force the unprepared one just as you would a card. All of the magazines are front cover side down. The spectator runs through the magazine he took, and pronounces it all right. Take it from him, and lay it back-up on the stack you are holding. Say, "Will you please mark the magazine?", and turn over both top magazines as one. He marks the front cover of the prepared magazine.

Turn the stack toward you, and remove this top marked journal and toss it on the table. Place the stack, front covers up, on the other side of the table. Hurry through this. Some may want to dispose of the examination and the switch and simply have a magazine selected by one of the well-known methods.

The slate used is a flap slate. On the slate is written the first word of one of the pages to which the magazine opens. This is covered with the flap, the under side of which is covered with part of a magazine cover.

Now to proceed with the effect: A spectator stands and is handed the "selected" magazine. The performer picks up slate and chalk, walks to the other side of the room, and gives instructions. "Hold the magazine behind your back, sir. Now open it to any place. Let's hurry. Now keep the place to which you have opened, and look at the first word of either page. Do you have it memorized? Now close the magazine, and put it aside. Take the slate and chalk lying on the table, and write your word on it. Please don't let anyone see what you are writing. I have already written on my slate." At this point you have finished writing the first word of the other page of the magazine on the flap surface of the slate, and you place the slate at once on the pile of magazines, flap side down, while the spectator finishes writing.

"Now, please show us what you have written." Spectator turns his slate around and you get the word. If it is the first word, you pick up the slate minus the flap; if the other word, pick up slate and flap together, finger holding the latter in place. In either case you at once pick up your slate and show that you have written the same word.

Strange Interlude

This is an ideal mental interlude for any act. It is a routine of two effects, both going on at the same time, and should appeal because of the directness of procedure and the strength of the climax. This paragraph may be too big a build up for what follows, but—well, try the following. You'll be surprised.

Here is what happens: The performer having given a bunch of number cards to a man to mix, goes on to someone else whom he requests to come up and help in the test. This man writes on a slip of paper the name of a dead friend and the year of that individual's death. The slip is pocketed by him. While he is doing this the magician goes to the first man and, forming his handkerchief into a little bag, has this gentleman drop the cards in to be mixed. The gentleman comes up front with the magician and draws a card, the rest of the pack being allowed to fall on the table. Magician gives the gentleman a magazine and himself takes a slate and turns his back while instructing the assistant spectator to open the magazine to the page indicated by his card and concentrate on the first three words on the first line of that page. Quickly, back still turned, the mentalist chalks something on the slates, and throws away the chalk. "Kindly read the words on which you are concentrating"—and holding up the slate, those words are seen to be chalked thereon.

Without an instant's hesitation, magician, back still turned and slate held high, asks the other man to remove his slip from his pocket and read the name he wrote. "When did this man die?" Immediately upon reply the performer wheels around and there on the slate is seen written the correct name and the year of the death!

Let us first explain how the magician gets the dead name. This is done by a carbon impression but in a most subtle manner. The magazine used in the routine is faked. It should be a house organ or trade journal about "Sphinx" size. On the inside of the back cover is glued a piece of carbon paper, carbon surface out, of course. On the page opposite the cover is lightly glued a piece of thin white paper —cheap typewriter paper is good. In the upper left hand corner of this page stick a piece of wax or diachylon, but do not press the cover on it. This magazine lies, back cover up, on the edge of table by which the spectator is to stand. But here is the subtle point. The table is covered with rather rough fabric and this makes it impossible for the man to write unless he places his paper on the magazine.

In operation, the man is invited up front to the table. Performer asks him to think of a dead name and hands him the slip, which should not be too small. Magician picks up pencil (which should be rather short and of hard lead) and places it on the magazine as an unspoken invitation to write thereon. If you will try this or think it over, you will see that without a word being spoken to that effect, the man quite naturally writes with the slip on the magazine. This has been carefully worked out and is quite perfect in both theory and practice.

As soon as the man starts to write, the magician turns his back, asking the man to fold and pocket the paper as soon as he is through, and proceeds with the other part of the effect.

Now all that we do in the magazine test is to force the page in the quickest manner possible. The best way I know is to have a set of all duplicate number cards in the double pocket of a Jap Bird Hank. This consists simply of two pocket handkerchiefs sewn together as shown in the sketch. This is placed in your pocket. A bunch of all different cards (make these by gluing numbers from a large calendar on cardboard—the cards should be about 2 inches square) has already been given a man to mix. You remove the handkerchief from pocket and without saying a word about it, simply bring the four corners together, forming an improvised bag. Take the cards from the man and drop them in and in mixing them open the pocket. It is into this pocket that the spectator reaches to remove one. At once, the ordinary numbers are dropped onto the table and the handkerchief is pocketed. A good point is to have the bunch of cards all different minus the force number.

You now pick up the magazine from the table, this being the first time that most of the spectators are aware of it. You illustrate that the man is to open it at the page indicated by the number and note the first three words, then close the magazine, keeping his finger in the place. As you explain this, you do just that—opening the magazine at the back page and a glance gets the name. Shut the journal, and in handing it to the man you squeeze the top outer corners and the wax now prevents acidental opening at the faked page. Here again the action has been simple and direct. It is what you would naturally do under the circumstances.

It is now time you knew that on the under side of the slate lying also on the table (but on the far side from the magazine and thus not interfering with the impression method) has been chalked the words on the forced page. While the gentleman is looking at the words on that page, you have picked up the slate, blank side out, and stand, back turned, chalk in hand. As soon as the man says he has the words, rapidly chalk the dead name on the slate and throw the chalk aside. Ask for the words to be read. At once hold up the slate—but you have turned it around, and they see the three words just read.

Let's go fast now. This is just the build up. Now the other man removes and reads his slip, you shouting your request quite dramatically, back still turned, slate held high. The climax comes when you wheel around and show the underside of the slate—with the dead name!

A Slate-Writing Method

The object here is to get a divined name onto a slate. Here is the routine:

Magician hands out a large window envelope to one man and a card to another. The latter is to write on his card the name of a dead person. In the meantime, the magician spreads a deck of cards on the floor before a man and one is freely taken. Let us admit right now that this is a force deck. As soon as the card has been taken the deck is dropped into the right coat pocket where a duplicate deck is standing vertically. The left hand removes a small drug envelope from the left coat pocket, and the man with the card slips card writing side down into the envelope and magician at once seals it and places it in view on the table, at the same time removing the duplicate deck and tossing it on the table for later inspection if need be. What they don't know about the envelope is that a window is cut in the face and magician thereby knows the secret of its contents.

Now the slate lying on the table has a flap, the under side of which is covered with the same material as the large window envelope. It covers the side of the slate on which has been written the name of the face card. The performer picks up this slate and turning his back asks the man to concentrate on his card. He writes on the slate, really writing the dead name on the slate surface. Then he turns the flap towards his body, and asks for the name of the card. At this moment the left fingers grasp the flap and hold it against the body while right hand quickly revolves the slate, and the flap goes in place again but over the just written name. Slate is now held up and it is seen that the magician has correctly divined the name of the card. This is just a quick trick for the nonce.

The slate is quickly erased on both sides, which are freely shown, and placed in the large window envelope which a spectator has been holding. This man initials the surface of the slate thru the window. It is, of course, the real slate surface which is toward the window. Magician asks the writer of the name to concentrate a moment while the spirits write with the chalk which has also been dropped into the bag. In a moment, the slate is removed minus the flap (which is invisible in the envelope) and the spirits have again scored.

The effect is further increased by two improvements for which we must thank Oscar Weigle, Jr., a New York magician with ideas. When he presented it, he faced the audience with the slate in front of him, flap side toward the audience (fingers holding flap in front securely), while he wrote the dead name on the real side of the slate. Then he turned his back for a moment, did the necessary maneuvering, and leaned the slate against some object, flap side to spectators, with the dead name covered. After the card was named, he merely picked up the slate and turned it around to reveal the name of the forced card. This is most natural and does not excite suspicion. It is, perhaps, more acceptable.

Another wrinkle that he used is this: Write the dead name with a chalk of a different color. Conceal a small piece (about an inch) of the colored chalk in the right hand, with the third, fourth and little fingers around it. Pick up the white chalk and hold it between thumb and first finger, in the natural position for writing. You show this casually, and you apparently write on the slate with this chalk. but under cover of the slate, the colored chalk is brought into position between the fingers, while the white chalk is finger-palmed. Write the dead name with the colored chalk, and just before executing the flap move, reverse the positions of the chalks so that the white chalk is again at the finger tips. You can let this be seen, in a casual manner of course, and then drop both chalks into the coat pocket. Later the spirits write their messages effectively in color. This is seen when the dead name is revealed on the slate. It is best to use yellow chalk, which shows up as well as does white.

It will be noted that when patter is given in this section it is in the form of short, stacatto sentences. It is a well-known psychological fact that short, direct, instructive phrases incite the assisting spectator to faster action, hence the reason for the patter being written as it is.

Slate Psychics

The ideas employed here may be used individually. Together they offer an unbeatable mental combination for any club show.

In the first effect, a prediction is written on a slate. The assisting spectator freely removes a card from a deck and holds it up for all to see. The prediction is read and it is correct. The effect is very direct. Now, for the follow-up, spectator is handed a slate on which he draws any geometric design and without showing it to anyone, holds it before his eyes and is instructed to concentrate on it while the magician draws on his own slate. When the slates are shown to the audience, it is seen that both have the same design drawn on them.

Required are two ordinary school slates, chalk, a sponge, and a gimmick similar to the well-known thumb tip pencil but containing a small piece of chalk. This has been used before to produce short messages on slates. In this case its use is very subtle and entirely unsuspected.

Invite a spectator up to the platform, and as he comes up inquire of him, "What is your favorite suit?" Upon his replying, hand him the deck and say, "Remove any card of your favorite suit —but first I am going to write a prediction." Pick up the slate and write— "The gentleman will choose the——— of (favorite suit)." Note that the blank is left on the right hand side of the slate. Place the slate with writing side down on the table.

Get the thumb tip gimmick on thumb from a convenient pocket while the gentleman is selecting his card. Have him hold it up, and as soon as you see what it is, pick up the slate, and misdirecting attention to the card, write the number or the initial in the blank place with the thumb tip pencil, this giving the denomination of the card. The slate is being held in the right hand, first finger and thumb on the inside, other fingers on the outside. At once, finger-palm the thumb tip, and hand the slate to another spectator to read aloud. The writing is the work of but a moment, and the effect is very clean and convincing.

Having disposed of the thumb tip, you are ready to proceed with the next effect. This is practically the same as the usual reflector method, but a wrinkle which we believe to be entirely new is introduced, which makes the working easier and requires no gimmick.

Hand the spectator another slate and piece of chalk, requesting him to draw some simple geometric design. While he is doing this, turn your back and wash off the slate upon which you have written in the preceeding effect. Now turn to him as you ask him to hold his slate directly before him and concentrate on the drawing. You hold your slate in your right hand, washed side away from the spectators, the man assisting at your left. He should be standing in good light and facing you. Step up directly in front of him.

Grasp his wrists lightly—"Up a little—hold it directly before your eyes"—and the surface of the newly washed slate held by the right hand now gives you a perfect reflection of his drawing. While the gentleman is staring fixedly at the figure, you walk some distance away and begin to draw quickly on your slate. Appear to have some difficulty and ask him to concentrate especially upon such and such a corner and you will get a laugh. Having finished your inspired sketch, you have the gentleman show what he has drawn. The big climax comes when you both show the slates and duplicate figures are seen.

There are many ways to use this last idea. Experiment for the most natural angle to get the reflection. Don't use too much water on the slate as you want it to dry as quickly as possible. Never show the washed side to the spectators when the slate is wet. You can rub it dry with a hank before drawing, but this is not necessary.

The Ultimate One Man Sealed Message Reading System

This system was designed to eliminate the obvious disadvantages of one ahead and transparancy methods.

In effect, the spectators themselves seal their cards in unprepared envelopes and write their initials across the flaps. The performer collects the envelopes and, holding the first one to his forehead, at once reveals its contents. The envelope is clipped open and the card removed and verified, and WITHOUT ANY SWITCH both card and envelope are returned to the writer. This is repeated with each envelope until all have been read. While the contents are being divined, the envelope is held at the finger tips and it is freely shown on both sides. The initials on the envelope are read and verified by the writer holding up his hand while his message is being read. No other one man non-apparatus method has such convincing features.

The system will be explained by parts so that each stage will be clear. I have gone into considerable detail to make every move and point of misdirection clear, but this does not mean that the method is involved or difficult. It is well known to magicians that if the extreme end of an envelope is cut off, the envelope will still pass as unprepared at even a little distance. This is the key to the system. At the beginning only one envelope is so prepared and this is the only preparation required. Any number of unprepared envelopes (drug envelopes that open on end—size No. 2) can be used—six is about right. In the right coat pocket is a pair of SHARP scissors.

Now let us proceed with the routine:

1. **Collecting the Envelopes**—The prepared envelope is on the bottom of the stack of envelopes and cards. All are passed out but this, which you retain as you give the last man a card to write on. As soon as he has finished, you ask the others to do as you illustrate. Holding the envelope flap side up and open, you ask the man to insert his card FACE DOWN. You seal the flap and, asking for the man's initials, write them across the flap, instructing the rest to do likewise. Now you collect the envelopes, flaps up, with the faked one on the bottom. You take each one in the right hand with thumb at one edge and fingers on the other, like a card, and tap the flap edge on the

envelopes in the left hand, before placing it flap up on top of them. This forces the cards to the flap end of the envelopes so they may easily be cut open at the bottom end. When you reach the front, turn the packet of envelopes face side up and place them in your right hand. Throughout the routine they are (unless otherwise noted) held in this hand, face side TOWARD you, and flap edges toward finger tips. This is important.

2. **Reading the Messages**—This is the easiest part of the entire routine and also the point on which the attention of the audience is the greatest. The message comes to view in the simple act of taking an envelope in the left hand and holding it to the forehead! This is because the right thumb nail has entered the open bottom of the first (faked) envelope, enabling the thumb tip to enter the envelope and press on the card therein. The left fingers grasp the envelope lightly at the flap edge making this easy. They then draw the envelope away leaving (because of friction) the card clipped by the right

RIGHT THUMB ENTERS ENVELOPE – RETAINS CARD – AND LEFT HAND DRAWS ENVELOPE AWAY.

thumb to the top of the packet of envelopes! The faked (now empty) envelope can be freely shown (as long as it is not held cut end on to the spectators), being held slightly convex between the thumb and fingers just as you hold two cards together after a double lift to show them as one. Holding the envelope to the forehead shields the eyes which read the message now reposing on the packet in the right hand.

3. **Returning the Card and Envelope**—As soon as the information has been revealed, the envelope is returned to the top of the packet (top of packet always faces performer), but it goes UNDER the card clipped there by the thumb. This offers no difficulty. Now pass the envelopes to left hand while right goes to pocket for scissors.

This results in the BOTTOM EDGES of the envelopes being toward the left finger tips. The top envelope is aparently clipped open at the bottom. Really, the ball of the left thumb presses on and pulls back the top envelope a fraction of an inch and it is the SECOND envelope which is clipped neatly open. This is perhaps the most important move to practice. Thumb at once pushes top envelope forward. The right forefinger reaches into the top (empty) envelope and the right thumb grasps the card, now clipped by the left thumb on the outside of the envelope, and it is apparently withdrawn from within and is at once read and verified and returned with its envelope to the owner. This completes the entire maneuver and leaves you in a position to show everything clean before continuing. Cards are returned to right hand.

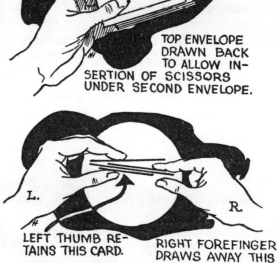

TOP ENVELOPE DRAWN BACK TO ALLOW INSERTION OF SCISSORS UNDER SECOND ENVELOPE.

L.   R.

LEFT THUMB RETAINS THIS CARD.

RIGHT FOREFINGER DRAWS AWAY THIS CARD ALONG WITH ENVELOPE.

This same routine is repeated with each envelope until the next to the last, so master it until you do not have to think which move comes next.

4. **Returning the Next to the Last Message**—When you replace this envelope on the last envelope, you place it ON TOP OF THE CARD instead of beneath it. The envelopes are transfered to the left hand as before, but as the right hand goes for scissors (which are naturally replaced in pocket each time), the left drops to side and turns the two over so flat sides are up, with the last envelope on top. The envelopes are now held horizontally so this is not noted. The card is between the two envelopes. Now you deliberately clip open the top envelope and actually remove the card therein, taking care to hold it writing side toward you. This is actually the last card. You apparently read this card but really read aloud what you have

already seen and revealed on the other card. Left hand has again dropped and reversed the envelopes so that, when the card is read, the right comes over and takes the top envelope. In doing this the card just read is naturally placed on top of envelope but it is slipped under left thumb, and right forefinger, in taking the envelope also clips the card which is under it (actual next to the last message) and brings it away with the envelope, leaving the other card behind the remaining envelope. Card and envelope are returned. This is the only time you have had to do a switch but it was an easy one and not looked for because of the previous open handling.

5. **Reading the Last Message**—All that reamins to be done is to hold the last envelope (card clipped behind) to forehead and reveal its contents. Envelope is clipped open and card apparently removed, but really from behind. You hand it to the owner for verification. You have done a perfect message reading act and there is nothing to be found at the end.

Notes:

In cuting open the envelopes, it is necessary that the card on top be clipped by the TIP of the left thumb so that part of the ball of the thumb be free to pull back the top envelope. (See illustration.)

When the spectators insert the cards as directed they invariably will be right side up when you get them. This depends upon the fact that people normally write with the right hand and will therefore hold the card in left hand and with this hand insert it (turning it face down, but not end for end) in the envelope. To make this more certain, it is well to avoid a stall between the time they finish writing and the insertion of the cards. This is exactly what is done when you illustrate what you want done about the writing, etc., on the cards and how you want the cards. They will all watch this, then immediately proceed with their own. However, when an occasional one comes upside down, there is nothing to worry about for you can read it by tilting the hand holding envelopes, so you read the line vertically instead of horizontally. In any case, getting the message is the easiest part of the trick.

Ask the spectators to write names, phone numbers, cities, etc.— any object upon which they can concentrate readily, rather than questions. In other words, we generally consider it better to present such things as a mindreading stunt than a question answering act. Of course you must use your own showmanship in revealing the information. And don't forget a supply of pencils for the writers. It will save lots of time.

This routine may be used to advantage with as few as three messages. In this case use a slate to write the divinations on. The third writer has been requested to draw a simple sketch. First you hold the envelope to forehead, then getting a flash of inspiration, replace on stack as usual and take same in left hand while right picks up slate and chalk. Slate is steadied by left hand and forearm with lower edge against body, while right hand chalks on the revelation, and then replaces slate, writing down on table. Envelope is opened and "contents" read—then slate is shown and it is right! Envelope and card are handed back to owner and any magician looking for a switch there will be fooled.

The second envelope is handled the same, but after "reading" card (see move 4), it is simply laid on top of envelope under left thumb and is not "returned" (switched) with envelope until the slate has been shown.

The last envelope contains the picture and as this would be hard for all to see and check, you fold the envelope and tear it up and pocket it, asking the man to come up and sketch it on another slate so all can see. You stand at the other end of room and duplicate it simultaneously on your slate for a strong climax. This routine, of course, is due to Annemann.

"PREDETERMINATION"

GENTLEMEN, BE SEATED

Before you read the following, let me have a word with you regarding predictions in general. How many of you realize that over three-fourths of the prediction effects in existence utilize the principle of forcing? An obvious fact? Certainly. But I doubt if one out of ten magicians realize it. This force may be accomplished in one of many ways—certainly there are enough methods available.

Then there is another alternative open to the magician. If he doesn't care to use a force, then his prediction must necessarily fall in the category depending upon discovering the name of the card freely selected and getting it in some way, either by the use of a "swami" pencil or by a switch, onto the slip of paper which supposedly carries the prediction.

Another of these facts so obvious that we are inclined to overlook them is put to use in this question. What is the difference between a card "discovery" and a card "prediction"?—and again we are forced to stop and think. And what indeed is the difference? And the answer—"The time element alone." But let us compare the two effects.

We review a "discovery". A deck of cards is handed to the spectator to remove one card, replace it, and remember the name of the card. Later, the performer reproduces the card in some way. He may deliberately remove it from the deck, having previously controlled it. He may cause it to appear reversed. He may do almost anything he is capable of doing, this depending upon his sleight-of-hand ability.

Again we review, but now, a "prediction" A deck of cards is handed to a spectator to remove one card, but this time he does not look at it, nor is it replaced in the pack. The card is kept and the pack is laid aside—there is apparently no card control. The performer has, by this time, written something on a slip of paper. Later, the paper is opened, and its contents divulged, and it is found that the card taken has been predicted—apparently the performer has controlled the spectator's actions in causing him to take the card predicted.

These are more-or-less obvious facts, and they are not given for the purpose of "padding"—instead, the author should like for the reader to put a little thought to the technical side of his work. Many magicians perform effect after effect (and perform them well, too) without realizing exactly what principle is involved. Not that this makes any appreciable difference in the effect, but it has always been the author's delight to study thoroughly his mode of presentation and the principles involved. In this way, many variations can be worked out, and thus a more flexible style of performance can be developed.

But enough discussion. The reader has asked for a prediction, so the stage is set and.......

THE CURTAINS PART

A prediction is written on a slip of paper, and the paper is sealed within an envelope which is, from that point on, used as a tray. A spectator shuffles the deck of cards freely, then spreads it out face down on a table and pushes one card out from the rest. This is a free selection, but as yet he does not look at the card. The remaining 51 cards are squared up and placed aside. At this point, the selected card is slid off the table onto the envelope, and a second spectator is given the card to hold.

After reviewing the conditions at hand, the performer opens the envelope and the prediction is read. The selected card is shown and it is found that it corresponds with the prediction!

AS SEEN FROM BACKSTAGE

A switch is responsible for the success of the experiment. but bold presentation and good showmanship make it appear miraculous. The switch in question is made with the card, and not with the slip of paper as some might imagine.

SETTING THE STAGE

In this section, I shall explain the preparation as I do it, then later on there will be given alternate methods. We will assume that the Nine of Diamonds is to be the card predicted, for simplicity of illustration.

The Nine of Diamonds is removed from the pack and is laid on the rear edge of the table with the face up, so that the end of it extends over the rear edge about an inch. Over this, the envelope is placed, flap side down, so that it too has its end over the edge of the table, and so effectively conceals the card. If you are using an envelope with a large flap (best results are obtained through the use of a short flap, as explained in the paragraph dealing with articles required), prepare the card and envelope as follows: Lift up the flap of the envelope and insert the card, face of card toward envelope, beneath the flap, as shown in Figure 1, and place the envelope flap side down on the table as explained before. The position of the envelope and card on the table is shown in Figure A.

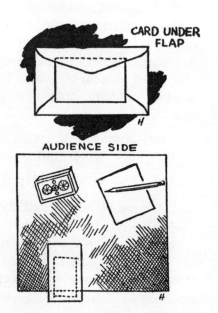

CARD UNDER FLAP

AUDIENCE SIDE

Place the remaining 51 cards on the table near the front, and also near this is the card on which the prediction is to be written, and a pencil This completes the preparation.

WE NEED

First—A full deck of 52 cards, unprepared.

Second—An envelope about 6″ x 4″, with a VERY SHORT STUBBY FLAP. This short flap makes the handling much easier than otherwise, as will be found when experimenting.

And Third—A pencil and a piece of stiff paper about 5″ x 7″, folded in half to be about 3½″ x 5″ when folded.

THE PLAY BEGINS

ACT I—Pick up the pack of cards and step forward to some spectator; hand him the pack, and request him to thoroughly shuffle it and cut it as many times as he might wish. Make no mention regarding the number of cards in the deck, or the possibility of any preparedness, as this experiment is intended to be, not a trick, but an exhibition of control by thought, and that ALONE. PRESENT IT AS SUCH.

ACT II—While the spectator is shuffling the cards, step up to the table, and write "You will choose the Nine of Diamonds" on the slip of paper. Fold the paper once, as required so that it will fit the envelope, and address the spectator, instructing him, while you carry out the instructions given in Act III. It is absolutely necessary for smooth performance to have this paper, on which the prediction is written, rather stiff and of such a size that it necessitates folding once to fit in the envelope. If such is the case, there will be no fumbling when inserting the paper in the envelope.

ACT III—After folding the paper, hold it in the right hand, and with the left hand pick up the envelope (and card beneath) in the following manner: Keep the back of the hand up, letting the four fingers go on the address side of the envelope, while the thumb reaches beneath the envelope, and presses the card against the flap side. This is a natural move, and easy to do. Bring the envelope up in front of the body, tilting the top of it slightly away from the body at an angle, as you would naturally do when inserting something in the envelope. It might help to stand with your right side to the audience. With the left forefinger, the other fingers holding the envelope and card, open the flap, keeping the card in place. Insert the slip of paper with the right hand, then bring the flap to the mouth, moisten it, and seal the envelope.

None of this is hard to do, every move being most natural, and should be preformed exactly as though it were an ordinary envelope, which it is. In fact, to the audience it appears to be just that—a container for the prediction just written.

ACT IV—During this time the spectator has, as instructed, pushed one card out from the rest and squared up the deck. Start toward him, and as you do so, hand the envelope into the right hand as follows: Take it with the palm of hand up, the fingers against the card beneath the envelope. If you hold the envelope at the level of your hips and hold it horizontally, there is absolutely no danger of this card's being seen. Just as you reach the spectator, take the envelope again in the left hand, but this time imitate the position of the right hand, i. e., the fingers of the left hand grasp the card and hold it in place.

ACT V—Still holding the envelope firmly in the left hand, lay the edge of it on the table, close to the selected card, and remark to the spectator that in order that he be sure no manipulation takes place, you will use the envelope as a tray and not handle the card with your hands. Using your right forefinger, slide the selected card onto the envelope—its face will be against the address side of the envelope, and your left thumb tip against it to hold it in place.

ACT VI—Have this spectator point out someone whom he wishes to act as a second assistant, and just as he does this (all eyes will be on the newly appointed personage), hand the envelope to the right hand and turn to the right slightly, this being done as follows: As was stated, when this second person is pointed out, it is only natural that all eyes should turn his way for an instant, and in this moment, you take advantage of the misdirection offered to accomplish the key move. Hand the envelope from your left hand to your right, first turning the envelope entirely over, this bringing the back of the left hand up, and of course, the flap side of the envelope and the Nine of Diamonds with it. With the right hand, palm up, take the envelope, letting the thumb go on top of the Nine of Diamonds (which the audience will believe is the selected card) and the four fingers against the previously selected card.

ACT VII—Carry the card on the envelope to this second person, who is requested to merely hold out his left hand. Slide the Nine of Diamonds from the envelope off onto his palm, and have him place his right hand over it, this action preventing him from looking at the card. His prematurely glancing at the card, and thus learning its identity, would not matter materially to the success of the experiment, but insofar as the selector of the card was not permitted to see it, this idea should be carried out completely, and no one allowed to learn the identity of the chosen card until the proper time.

ACT VIII—The envelope is now in the right hand, which is held palm up with the chosen card beneath the envelope and held by the right fingers. Now walk back to the first spectator who chose the card and take the deck from him, face up, with the left hand. Lay the envelope on the deck in the left hand, and address this spectator, reviewing the procedure as has taken place. When finished with the patter at this point, hand him the envelope to open, while you turn back to the table, taking with you the card previously beneath the envelope. The full deck, minus the card in the second spectator's possession, is dropped on the table.

ACT IX—Have the prediction read aloud, so that all may hear it. Then, turn to the second spectator and request him to hold the card up so that all may see it. IT IS THE CARD PREDICTED, and everything may be (but need not be) examined.

AUTHOR'S NOTE

This is, as it stands, a nice routine. Careful, snappy presentation is essential. Many effects have been spoiled by too much preliminary preparation before the actual effect takes place. The following are some notes that the author has made from time to time regarding the presentation:

Addenda

DISPOSAL OF THE EXTRA CARD

As an alternate method for the disposal of the selected card (see ACT VIII under "Presentation"), but one not quite so clean, you might proceed as follows: Begin at the point where you hold the envelope in the right hand, after having given the second spectator the Nine of Diamonds to hold. Hand the envelope into the left hand again which receives it with the thumb beneath (against the selected card) and the four fingers on the top-flap-side, keeping the back of this hand up. As you step back to review briefly what has happened, put the envelope (and card) into the left coat pocket, the card going next to the body—but be absolutely sure not to push the envelope more than half way into the pocket. IT MUST NOT APPEAR THAT YOU HAVE EXCHANGED ENVELOPES! This is most important.

ADDITION TO THE FORCED CARD

The method explained in the presentation is the one used most frequently by the author, and is in his opinion much the cleaner method; however, there are alternate methods, and these are given for the sake of completeness.

(1)—Lay the Nine of Diamonds on the back edge of the table, as previously described, and in front of it place a crumpled handkerchief. All other preparations are the same, except that the envelope lies near the front of the table with the pencil and paper.

After the prediction has been written, and is sealed in the envelope, the envelope is dropped onto the card, and the procedure is as before.

(2)—The Nine of Diamonds is, in this method, in the left pants pocket, with the back toward the body. When ready to add it, take the envelope with the right hand, and palm out the card in the left palm. Hand the envelope to the left hand which is back up, and turn the left hand over, this putting the Nine beneath the envelope as before—a most natural method, but not so clean as the first.

(3)—The following is a method I have used frequently at parties: On the table is a book which has a rather thin cover—one with a paper cover is excellent. To prepare, I insert the Nine of Diamonds, face up, between the cover and first page, so that it protrudes from the book about half an inch—just far enough that it may be grasped by the fingers. The envelope, paper and pencil lie on the book until needed. Insert the slip of paper in the envelope, and seal it, then lay it back over the book. Thus, in this method, the envelope can be handled more freely and with less danger of the card being seen. Before going to the assisting spectator, pick up the envelope, by using a sliding motion, toward you, at the same time, clipping the Nine of Diamonds against it and bringing it out beneath the envelope.

And A Routine

Because they cover the basic effects in the mental field, items from this section can be built nicely into an unusually strong club routine. We suggest:

1. Real Coincidence.
2. Alias Divination.
3. The Ultimate One Man Sealed Message Reading.
4. Slate Psychics (Two Effects).
5. Strange Interlude (Two Methods).

The result here being about a thirty minute routine, getting off to a good start with the coincidence trick, then the card prediction with the slate and the drawing effect. The Divination makes a nice interlude, and the Sealed Message reading can be worked as fast or slow as you want. The magazine test and dead name psychicism wind things up in a maze of baffling mentalism that will be remembered. How are you feeling?

There is little before-the-show preparation, other than setting the table for "Strange Interlude". The three slates are stacked with the one prepared for the last effect on the bottom. Be sure to have plenty of chalk and a damp cloth for the slate. The envelopes and cards and pencils for the Message Reading are stacked beside the slates, and scissors are in right coat pocket.

In "Strange Interlude" it is a point to dismiss the name writer as soon as he has finished and has pocketed the writing, and the magazine party as soon as you have held up the slate with the words. This leaves you clean at the end. Be sure to work fast as you near the climax.

Either "Magazine Miracle" or the "Slate Writing" may be substituted for the last effect and the Predetermination may be used instead of the Sealed Message Reading.

An Improved Four Ace Routine

This version of the Four Ace Trick is an elaboration of the familiar method employing double faced cards, but their use in this case is never suspected. It accomplishes about as genuine a vanish and reproduction of four aces as is possible under fairly close up conditions, and when accompanied with sparkling patter, is perfect.

There is but one move in the trick and it is scarcely a sleight, for it is done only under cover of the table top or body. It is simply the turning over of the deck while held in the left hand. This has been done in various ways in many tricks. The best plan in this case is to hold the deck well down in left palm, press thumb under upper index corner of deck, and, aided by the fingers on top of deck, lever the pack over. This is very easy to do and noiseless.

Four double faced cards are used. These are the AH, AD and AC, each backed with an indifferent card, and any other double faced card (different on both faces). Add these to the face up deck, first the indifferent double faced card, then the fake aces, ace faces down, and in known order. We are now ready for a most convincing routine.

A spectator is asked to assist. He is given the deck, face up, and asked to deal the cards one by one, face up on the table, and when he comes to an ace, to throw it to one side. The man thus goes through the entire deck, removing the genuine aces. The use of duplicates in the trick will seem out of the question (strong point No. 1).

Magician picks up the pack and places it face up in left hand. He places the aces back, face up, on the deck in the opposite order as the fakes were originally (order that they are now in) and the ace of spades on top. Magician is at right side of table, facing assistant who stands at opposite side. Therefore performer's right side is to audience.

Deal Ace of Spades on table, face up. Left hand drops to side and reverses deck while magician states that the ace of spades is the leader of the aces.

Left comes again and the three other aces (fakes) dealt off, face up, in a row by the ace of spades. The indifferent double facer still masks the fact that the deck is actually face down.

Left drops again and reverses deck twice, only the second time, the deck is not turned over, but the bottom card (double faced) simply pushed around and over onto the top (face) of the deck. The move is exactly the same as reversing the deck. Fingers and pressure against trouser's leg aid in doing this neatly and noiselessly. It takes no time at all and is done while magician explains, pointing to the four aces on the table, that he is going to deal three cards on each ace.

Deck is brought up (it is now actually face up but has the same card on the face as before) and the hand turned with deck face down in position for the glide, which is performed as the magician deals (face down from the bottom of the deck) three cards on the Ace of Spades (the three real aces), three cards on the next ace, etc. (They'll swear indifferent cards were dealt throughout—strong point No. 2).

Deck is given a quick overhand shuffle, faces out, shuffling the double facer to TOP, and deck returned to left hand which at once drops to side and reverses. Performer at this time picks up the Ace of Spades packet and places it aside or in a tumbler.

Now the three face up aces are transferred to the top of their respective packets. The deck is brought up (apparently face up) and the aces each deliberately buried face up into the deck. (Strong point No. 3).

The left hand is dropped and deck reversed twice (i. e. card transferred second time) while the three packets are collected. The deck is thrown face down on the table (double facer is on face) while both hands take the combined packets and count them. They are riffled and fase counted as twelve, indicating that the three indifferent cards in the tumbler have joined them. The cards are at once thrown face down on the face down deck which is handed at once, face up, to the assisting spectator to deal through (face up) for the aces. They are absolutely gone!

The man is asked to remove the cards from the tumbler. They are the four aces! Climax!

It is best to use this as a concluding card trick as it is a good effect and while the deck cannot be used afterwards, it is unprepared beforehand, the fake cards being palmed on immediately before the trick. It will be seen that the dropping of the hand with the deck is natural and not even observed when covered by suitable patter, for attention is on the aces, not the deck. Done as a table trick, the move is covered by the table top. Use of a card easel helps for a larger audience.

Selective Card In Pocket

Please visualize the effect, which is all that matters. A gentleman is given a card and pencil and asked to write in which pocket he would like a thought projected (right coat, left trouser, right hip, left upper vest, etc.). Another man selects a card from a deck which the magician spreads out on the floor before him. The card is at once returned and the man given a card and pencil to write the name of the card he thus freely selected. The deck is handed to a third man. Now the name of the card is read. The gentleman holding the deck runs through it but is unable to find the card. The first man reads what he has written and walking over to him, the magician allows him to reach into whatever pocket was named and remove therefrom the very card which number two has been thinking of!

The thing is a swindle from start to finish. A one kind force deck is used for the selection. One of the cards to be forced is in every pocket! In the left hand coat pocket is a card and pencil. In the right coat pocket is a straight deck minus the card to be forced. This deck is standing upright on end so as to be easily grasped when the force deck is dropped in the pocket. This is done immediately after gathering up the cards from floor, as both hands go to pockets for the card and pencil. The almost immediate search through the switched deck for the selected card throws them off completely as does also the writing of the first gentleman. The resulting effect is real magic in that the performer has divined both thoughts and somehow causes the selected card to find its way into the correct pocket.

An even more daring effect can be produced if it is convenient to work with an assistant in the crowd, placing the duplicate cards in his pockets. In this case, have whoever is sitting beside him write the selection of the pocket. At the end, ask him to give the card to the man sitting beside him (pointing) who is then asked to stand and read aloud what has been written. Then, showing hands empty, YOU reach into that pocket on his person and remove the vanished card!

This is one of those things which will appeal to the few who have the audacity (or are crazy enough) to present such a trick and maintain a straight face. It should be done exactly as described above as there are psychological points in every move. For example, it would kill the whole thing to have the spectator himself remove the card in the last version, while it builds the effect of the first presentation.

P. S.—If, in the first version, the right coat pocket be the one selected, the performer himself reaches into the pocket and removes the card from the force deck.

Si Stebbins Up The Sleeve

The magician holds the pack behind his back while a spectator selects a card and pockets it. Performer does not even bring the pack to front again, but simply faces the man and correctly names the card!

The title explains the method. A set up deck is used and this is cut at the place where the spectator removes the card. Magician faces front and, behind his back, slips the bottom card up his sleeve, between the right shirt sleeve and coat sleeve. He brings the right hand around front and up to forehead to aid concentration. With the hand shielding the eyes, he looks down the sleeve and spots the index which, by counting one ahead, gives him the selected card.

This little stunt has even fooled magicians who know the sleeve gag.

The Perfect Card Routine

The modest title is not without some occasion, for it would be hard to find a more effective and deceptive series of moves and effects than those which follow.

While the general effect was the idea of John Goodrum, credit for the sequence is due to Oscar Weigle, Jr., the cleverest originator of subtle ideas that we know. We have used this constantly since Weigle gave it to us.

The idea which makes the routine possible lies in a card vanish of Weigle's which is, briefly, as follows:

A double faced card is used—let us say it is the 8S-10H. Remove the "real" Eight of Spades and Ten of Hearts from the deck. One of these, say the Ten of Hearts, may be slipped into an unsuspecting spectator's pocket, into your own wallet (wrapping it securely with rubber bands around all sides), between sealed squares of cardboard, into a sealed envelope, or, for want of a more effective place, into your own pocket. The remaining card (8S) is secreted anywhere so it is out of the way—the hip pocket will do.

The double-faced card is already on the face of the deck proper, or it may be secretly added to that position. In this case, the 8S face of the card shows on the bottom. The deck is riffle-shuffled, backs up as usual, keeping the bottom card in place and being careful not to expose it. After the shuffle it is turned face up again and given to a spectator to place behind his back, with faces up. Ask him to cut the deck ANYWHERE, and then to place the cards cut off FACE DOWN on top of the half remaining—then bring the cards forward. You take the cards and spread them to the break, reminding the spectator that he cut anywhere. The first face up card is the Ten of Hearts (faked card). This face force is a variation of the familiar one with a double-backed card.

The cards in the left hand, with force card at the face, are held squared up, while the cards in the right hand remain in a slightly fanned condition. Have spectators take careful note of the 10H. With left thumb, it is pushed slightly to the right. The right hand comes over, and under its cover, the card is transferred to the bottom of that half—AT THE SAME TIME the left hand turns over clockwise onto the top of the deck, and the deck is squared.

This accomplishes a two-fold purpose. It creates the illusion that the Ten of Hearts is in the center of the deck and secondly, (and more important to the magician) the double-faced card is reversed so that now the 8S face is again at the face of the deck proper. The deck is immediately riffle-shuffled, again being careful not to expose the bottom card, and an overhand shuffle may be made without fear, always keeping the faked card at the bottom.

The sides of the deck are now riffled with a throwing motion to where the card should "go". If a pocketbook, the wallet should be in the hands of a spectator BEFORE the cards are even touched. The cards are handed to a spectator to deal ONE AT A TIME on the table and to look closely if he can see the 10H. As he deals the cards, you count out loud. There are only 51! Because, you having removed the real 8S, a duplicate never shows up which is a good point. The Ten of Hearts is absolutely gone, and if there's a cleaner way of vanishing a chosen card from a deck, we'd like to know it.

The cards when dealt onto the table one at a time by the spectator are, of course, held face up. The first card he deals off is the faked card, and this may be disposed of at your leisure.

Now the following routine puts to even more practical use the idea described above. Let us say the same double-faced card is used (10H-8S). The real 8S from the deck is placed in your coat pocket. The real 10H is placed in an envelope, sealed, and this is placed in the inside coat pocket. The double-faced card, with the 10H facing out, is placed in the right-hand trouser pocket. The deck is handed to someone to shuffle, and you're all ready.

When the spectator is satisfied, tell him to spread the cards face down on the table. While instructing him, stand casually by with the right hand in trouser's pocket, in an informal manner. Tell the spectator to pass his finger over the cards and when he gets the "impulse" to push forward any one card. He does this. With your left hand you sweep up the spread of cards, turn the deck slightly face up (in a vertical position) and ask the spectator to take a look at the card he selected. When he looks at the card, bring the right hand out of the pocket with the faked card palmed and add it to the bottom of the deck. Do not hesitate a second, but go right into a casual overhand shuffle keeping the bottom card in place. Even if someone is watching you, nothing is suspicious, as you apparently only brought out your right hand to shuffle the cards. The spectator is asked not to forget his card and meanwhile you cut the deck in the middle (backs up now). The spectator returns the card to the top of the lower heap and the top heap is placed on top. Just as the top heap covers the lower one, the left thumb pushes the selected card a bit to the right, and the left little finger goes UNDER this card, not over it as usual. The pass is not executed, but the cards are cut at the break, apparently at random. If there is a magician present, he will only think the selected card is at the top of the lower heap, but this is not so. The two halves are riffle-shuffled together—a few cards from the bottom half first, then the cards from the other heap. For the benefit of magicians, see to it that the top of the lower heap is riffled into the others, that is, let the cards in the right hand fall last. Push the cards together a bit, but not all the way, just to the point where the cards must be pushed together another inch or so to square the cards perfectly.

GLIMPSE

Pick up the deck with fingers at one side and thumb at the other, turn it face up, and IMMEDIATELY square the ends up. During that split instant, however, you catch a glimpse of the card selected, which shows as the first card at the top end over the bottom card. You must try it with cards in hand to get the idea of this glimpse, which is very simple indeed.

As soon as the glimpse is made and cards squared, the cards are handed to a n o t h e r spectator (whom we shall call No. 2) and he is asked to place the deck behind his back, face up. The same force as described before is done here, and he gets the 8S forced on him. You have said that you want everyone let in on the selection of the next card, hence the deck face up. To leave the selection to chance, the man cuts with the cards behind his back. This makes a very natural force. The cards in right hand are placed face up on the table and those in left hand placed over them. The "selected" card is in full view on the face of the deck.

The deck is handed to another spectator (No. 3) with similar instructions, and he, naturally, gets the 10H forced on him. The cards in right hand are placed FACE UP on top of this after the card is noted. The cards are now genuinely shuffled face up to apparently prove no control (and there is none). This also demonstrates, without so saying, that no card is reversed. The deck is turned face down and snapped. Spectator No. 2 (note) is asked to call "his" card, the 8S, to appear. The deck is spread out wide on the table and lo and behold, without a single false move, the 8S (faked card) is "reversed" in the deck. The 8S is REMOVED OPENLY, taking care not to reveal its other face, and laid aside. In this way we also get rid of the 10H. Marvelous, isn't it? (After the next part of the routine, we shall pick it up and drop it in our coat pocket, but if it would be dangerous to leave the fake card on the table, we drop it into our pocket here and now).

The deck is gathered up and spread FACE UP, with the request to spectator No. 3 to see if he can see his card. Again you accomplish a two-fold purpose, for what YOU do is look for the card you secretly glimpsed! This is spectator No. 1's card. You just look to see WHERE it is—nothing more. Meanwhile spectator No. 3 says he does not see his card.

Now at this point we have a choice of several plans, depending on how we wish to disclose the final card. If we wish to finish as quickly as possible, we ask spectator No. 3 to reach into our inside coat pocket and to remove the sealed envelope. He tears it open and finds the 10H! While he does that, we casually gather up the cards again, picking them up at the point where spectator No. 1's card is and scooping up the rest of the cards over it. When deck is turned face down, the glimpsed card will be on top. Execute the double lift, asking if that is the card. It is not. Place it face down again and take the real top card and put it in outside breast pocket, in full view. Again do the double lift, and of course that card is not the selected card either. It is placed face down and the name of the card requested. It is named and the spectator removes the card protruding from breast pocket—it IS the card.

THE VERSION USED BY ROBERT PARRISH IS AS FOLLOWS:

The trick is performed exactly as described, except that the deck is spread on the floor for the selection at the start and for the disclosures, rather than on the table. This is more effective under certain conditions.

When the deck is spread for the spectator No. 3 to see if he can see his card, the glimpsed card is spotted and this card cut to the second from the bottom in gathering the cards. The cards are handed to spectator No. 3, face up, with the suggestion that he deal through the cards until he comes to his (since he has not seen it when we spread the cards). He deals the cards face up into the magician's hand, and on the second card dealt (glimpsed card), performer starts mentally to spell this card, one letter for each card dealt (K-I-N-G-O-F-C-L-U-B-S, etc.) and on the last letter he suddenly stops the spectator (who is probably dealing rather fast). "Are you sure you haven't missed your card?" And so saying, magician throws the cards in his hand back onto those held by the man, and says, "Start over again and deal slowly, making sure that none of the cards stick together." The man goes clear through the deck and declares that his card is absolutely not there!

This is very convincing. It has the important added effect of (by reversing the cards the magician has replaced) getting the glimpsed card (about which no one is thinking at the moment) in EXACT POSITION FOR SPELLING FROM THE TOP OF THE DECK, when the deck is turned face down.

Now that we are sure the 10H has inexplicably vanished, we ask the man to reach into our inside coat pocket and remove the envelope there. He does so, examines it and finds it sealed. He tears it open and removes his card! It is most effective.

We take his card and the fake 8S which is lying on the table, and drop them into our coat pocket. We appear to have forgotten the card of spectator number 1. If he reminds us of it at this point, so much the better. In any case, we recall the matter and are a little worried about it. We ask if the man will name this card, the identity of which only he is aware. We pick up the deck, give it a false shuffle or false cut if we are able, and then very slowly spell it out, dramatically turning over the card on the final letter to reveal it as the chosen one.

Bringing out the two cards from coat pocket (we've switched the fake 8S for the real one in the pocket) we hold up the three cards that we have successfully located in a most amazing manner. We are now clean.

If you will go over all this again you will see how nicely it goes together and how we get ready for each climax before it is suspected, thus enabling us to get the maximum out of each effect. The routine is very easy to follow.

Mostly Manipulative with Glasses

Glass Of Liquid From Card Fan

In the lower right vest pocket is a whiskey glass half full of water. In a clip under coat on this side are a few cards, and a fan of cards is clipped under the coat on the opposite side.

You have been producing card fans. Finally the left hand goes under the coat. It grasps glass, holding it in the curved left fingers so that the top rim is held by the curve formed by the forefinger and thumb. The tip of the thumb and forefinger grasp the cards, and the hand comes out with them, as at the same time the right hand goes under the coat on the left side and comes out with a fan which is added to the few cards held in the left hand. The cards are squared together, masking the glass.

The left fingers, if held closely together, will hide the glass from the view of those who sit to the performer's left; therefore, the packet can be held almost edgewise with the back of performer's hand to his left front.

As the pack is held in left hand as described above, the empty right hand pulls up the left coat sleeve. The right hand now grasps the deck by lower right hand (not index) corner and makes a ONE

HAND fan; the left hand holds glass out of sight behind the fan. All four right fingers behind the fan clasp the glass thus: Little and forefingers between the glass and back of fan (the back of these fingers are against the glass), and the second and third fingers on the opposite side of the glass. The left hand, which is now free, pulls up the right coat sleeve slightly.

A turn is now made to the front, or rather to the right, under cover of which the left hand steals the glass from behind the fan and holds it in the same position as at the beginning when the glass was stolen. Having given the spectators a brief glimpse of the back of the fan, turn the hand over with fan and reach behind fan with the left hand which, under cover of fan brings glass to finger tips and emerges with it held thus. The effect is very pretty, especially if a colored liquid is used—dark colored is preferred.

The moves are easily learned, and they may be done very quickly, the production of the glass of liquid coming as a REAL surprise! The glass may be filled over half full with no danger of spilling.

Care must be taken when performing the change-overs not to let the spectators get a flash of the bottom of the glass—especially under a strong light.

Some Glassy Ideas

For those who would like to develop an act with glasses of liquid, we offer these suggestions—

The problem of having glasses readily get-atable for productions is neatly solved by arranging a little shelf under the front edge of the table. This is concealed by the table fringe.

This works well during a thimble routine. After several sleights, stand about eight inches in front of the table, and vanish the thimble. Produce it from behind the right knee. It is a simple matter now for the left hand to reach under the fringe and take one of the glasses from the hidden shelf.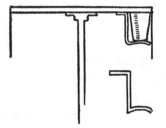

Vanish the thimble by throwing it into the air (thumb-palm) and produce the glass from the left knee. Right hand in the meantime has obtained three more thimbles, which it at once produces and drops into the glass.

Instead of a fringe, a regular table drape, cut with edges overlapping slightly in front of the shelf and weighted to insure its falling into place, may be used.

For the club performer who has to set up his tables in view of the spectators, here is a neat way of keeping the glass under the edge of table without danger of spilling. The under part of table top that the rim of glass presses against is covered with sheet rubber. The shelf, in this case, takes the shape of an angular piece of metal. This keeps the glass pressed tightly against the under side of the table, but it will be found that the glass may be easily removed from its position, and the table may be handled easily in moving without danger of spilling any of the liquid, as the sheet rubber makes it water tight.

In an emergency the left rear pocket may carry a large glass to be produced. You can carry a glass over half full of water (uncovered) in a tight fitting pocket without danger of spilling.

Glasses, Glasses, Everywhere!

Having brought your card manipulation routine to a close with the "Glass of Liquid from Card Fan", it is effective to follow up with the production of three more glasses.

A large tumbler of liquid is placed on the special shelf under the table, and directly in front of it are placed two whiskey glasses of the same size as in the previous production. They are half full of liquid.

As you turn to the left to place the deck on the table, left hand, screened by the body, gets the first little glass and holds it in the curved in fingers. See sketch. A swing is now made to the right, left forefinger pointing to the empty right palm; then left hand pulls up right sleeve a little more with free thumb and forefinger. Another turn is made to the left, under cover of which the glass is changed over into the right hand, which at once gives the left coat sleeve a pull in the same manner.

The hands are brushed together, the right hand reaches upward and produces the glass at the finger tips. Meanwhile the left hand has dropped and got the second glass. The left hand, with the glass palmed as before, meets the right hand, a turn to the right having been made, and takes the glass with thumb and forefinger while the right hand at the same time steals the glass palmed in the left hand and retains it in the partially closed fingers as the left places glass just produced on the table. In order to do this, the visible glass is held between the right second and first fingers so that the thumb and first finger can perform the steal. The move is covered by a turn to the left. The right hand immediately moves upward and plucks the second glass from the air. The right side is to the audience, and as the glass is produced and a little liquid slopped out, the left hand reaches under (or through) the table drape and takes the large glass from the shelf, holding it against the body as the right hand places its glass on the table. At once, the left hand with tumbler, travels down left leg as the performer reaches down with the right hand and grasps it, bringing it out from behind the leg.

None of this is overly difficult, but speed and smoothness are essential. All of the moves are covered by excellent misdirection. These glass productions are worthy of your attention if only because of their novelty and effectiveness.

It is recommended that the large glass be on a shelf under the front edge of the table, and the small glasses on a shelf at the side on which the performer is working. If a table with a circular top is used, this will present no problem.

If you are unable to use a special table, the following set-up will suffice: Rubber balls of slightly larger diameter than the glasses are plugged into the mouths of the glasses. Run a bolt through each ball (the bolt is about 1½″ long), and to this attach a short loop of cloth tape which is in turn attached to the belt loops on the left side. The glasses are hung on these plugs about two inches apart, the bottom of each glass being about two or three inches above the edge of the coat. Be very careful when hanging these so that you will get them the right distance from the edge of the coat, for it will be found that if the glasses are hung too low, when the left arm is raised, the bottom of the glasses can be seen because of the coat's being raised by the action of the arm. The larger glass is in the left hip pocket—the left hand rests naturally on the hip just before the steal. Credit for the rubber ball idea goes, of course, to Percy Abbott.

The Pause That Refreshes

In effect, four glasses of liquid materialize one by one under a silk. The working is easy, and the misdirection perfectly covers every move.

Small whiskey glasses are loaded in the vest as in Fig. 1. One glass is in upper right vest pocket. A stack of two nested glasses is vested beneath the vest flap on the right side, the bottom of the glass resting on the belt edge. In a similar position on the left side is a fourth glass. This glass should be farther to the side, whereas the stack of two should be close to the front. All of the glasses are uncovered, and they are half-filled with liquid. When filled to this depth, they can be tilted at about a 45 degree angle without danger of spilling.

A large silk (18″ square is a good size) is shown as follows: At first it is held as in Fig. 2. The performer faces left front and holds the silk with his left hand farthest from the body. The right hand rests with its thumb on the right coat lapel. The forefingers only

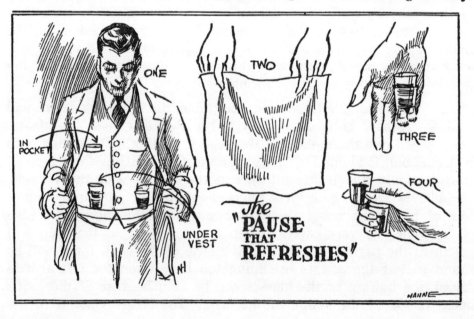

are on the audience's side of the silk. The hands are crossed now, the right hand being farthest from the body and the right arm in front of the left. This affords perfect cover for the glass steal.

The left thumb goes inside the glass in upper right vest pocket and removes it under cover of the coat. The hands are now returned to their former position (see Fig. 2), the glass being concealed by the left fingers and silk. The left hand, holding the glass, drops down behind the center of the silk, and the right hand, still holding a corner, drapes the silk over the left hand. The silk is now jerked away and the glass is seen to be resting on the left palm.

The performer turns to the left, and places the visible glass on the table, meanwhile the right hand has been busy. Nipping the silk between its forefinger and second finger it reaches under the vest with the third and little fingers, bringing the stack of two glasses out in the hand as in Fig. 3. At this time the performer is facing front, the silk being held in the two hands low in front of the body.

A swift turn to the left is made, the right hand releasing the silk, and the left snaps the silk out in "parachute fashion". The right hand is extended, the hank setting over the stack. Under cover of this the right forefinger and thumb disengage the topmost glass from the other and raise it so that the glasses are in the position illustrated by Fig. 4. The silk is removed and thrown over the right hand, while the left hand takes the visible glass from the right and sets it on the table. The silk is jerked off the right hand again, and there is a third glass.

The silk is, at this time, slipped between the first and second fingers of the left hand, and as the performer places the glass on the table with the right, the left hand steals the vested glass from the left side. A turn to the right is made, the right hand taking the silk from the left hand, and snapping it out to the right as before, the left hand, with glass palmed, is thrust beneath the silk as it settles, and then the silk is withdrawn. There, on the left palm is a fourth glass. Perhaps the production of this glass is an anti-climax. If you think so, use a lemon instead which appears in place of an expected glass of lemonade.

The vest should be very tight around the bottom for this routine. A strip of elastic around the bottom will help. There should be absolutely no lights behind the performer, unless the silk is very thick, and this is not desirable. Care must be taken that no light strikes the glasses, for the slightest reflection will be a give-away. Therefore, keep the fingers close together.

Drunkard's Dream

PREPARATION: On each side, under the edge of the coat, is sewn a paper clip. Mouth down, into each of these clips, is placed a small whiskey glass. If this causes the coat to hang poorly, secure the clips to the trousers. In the left coat pocket is a pocket flask. In the left breast pocket is a fairly large silk handkerchief.

Show the right hand empty, then swing to the left to show the left empty. At this time, using the right second and third fingers, steal the glass from under the right side of the coat. Fig. "A" demonstrates how the glass is held in the right hand. The hands are brought together, and the glass is produced. This glass is exhibited between the right forefinger and thumb while the left hand steals the second glass and holds it in the same manner. Now, facing front, the hands are brought together, and an important change-over move is executed. The left forefinger and thumb take the visible glass from the right hand, while under cover of the fingers, the left fingers extend and leave the glass palmed in the right hand, Fig. "B". The right

hand now reaches out and apparently extracts the palmed glass from the left elbow. These two glasses are placed between the fingers of the left hand as you would do billiard balls.

The performer removes the silk from his breast pocket and wipes the glasses, then places the silk over his bent left arm. This affords an excellent cover for the right hand to reach into left coat pocket and steal the flask there. Coming up under the hank, the right hand, holding flask, moves up in front of the face where the teeth grasp a corner of the silk and remove it.

The performer now proceeds to pour himself "two fingers", and tucks the silk back into the breast pocket.

A Glass Routine

A good routine with glasses should be a hit, so we offer the following: A large silk handkerchief is magically produced from which three small glasses of different colored liquids are produced, one by one (The Pause That Refreshes). As the third glass is shown, the glass vested on the left side is stolen by the left hand. Hank is placed in breast pocket and palmed glass is produced from the air, followed immediately by another glass and then a large tumbler, this being "Glasses, Glasses, Everywhere"! In effect so far the entire routine has been a fast and continuous production of glasses of liquid. As the glasses are produced they are placed on a tray on the table. Assistant transfers the tray to the side of stage, leaving the table free to work on. At this point, we suggest that you perform some such effect with the large tumbler as "Glass Thru Hat" or a "Milko" effect, or omit this and continue with the "Drunkard's Dream", producing the two empty glasses very quickly, followed by the surprising production of the bottle, which lends a comedy touch.

In conclusion the bottle suddenly changes to a bouquet of flowers. This is a U. F. Grant idea and is accomplished by quickly pulling a feather bouquet out of the sleeve in front of bottle, thus bringing a surprising finish to a surprising routine.

Those who are willing to spend the time and effort necessary to perfect these effects will have an act that is sure to create comment and will click because of its novelty and mystery. 'Nuf Said! Let's all have a drink.

THIMBLES

Duo Color Change

In this thimble novelty, two red thimbles are displayed on the forefinger and second finger of the right hand. The left hand is formed into a loose fist, and the thimbles are inserted. Upon the left hand's being opened, the thimbles are seen to be white.

Unknown to the audience, the two white thimbles repose on the right third and little fingers, which are curled back into the palm, out of sight. The performer's right side is to the audience. Now a turn to the right is made, and as the hands pass, the left hand masking the right, the right third and fourth fingers are extended into the left palm, where the left fingers curl around them, finger-palming them. Don't make a big sweep of the hands in this move—simply a natural gesture. After showing the right hand with its two red thimbles, displaying them on the  fingers, turn to the left and under cover of this move, thumb-palm the two red thimbles. They are not nested, but are placed in thumb-palm position and held in place by bending the thumb in and holding them side by side. The figure illustrates this. You'll not find this at all difficult. At any rate, you push the first and second fingers, which are now empty, into the left fist, where they pick up the two white thimbles and emerge to, let us hope, the profound amazement of the spectators.

This is good, and just to prove it we offer a complete routine based on the above move.

Continuous Color Changing Thimble Production

Sew a length of elastic tape to form pockets for six thimbles on the under side of the coat or vest on the right side. You may use any type of holder or arrangement that you like, as long as the right fingers can easily obtain the thimbles in pairs. The pairs consist of two white, two red, and two white thimbles, in that order. A red thimble is thumb-palmed in each hand. A complete mastery of the Duo Color Change is absolutely essential, as this is the key move of the entire routine.

Begin by producing the red thimble on the right forefinger. The hand is otherwise seen empty. The left hand reaches upward, and a red thimble appears on the left forefinger. Right hand has, in the meantime, obtained the two white thimbles on the third and little fingers, which are curled back out of sight. Left hand comes over and transfers its thimble to the right second finger, and under cover of this the right third and fourth fingers are extended into left palm where the white thimbles are at once finger-palmed, side by side, and the hand comes away, left forefinger pointing at the two red thimbles on the otherwise empty right hand. Now a turn to the left is made under cover of which the two red thimbles are thumb-palmed and the two right fingers inserted into the partially closed left hand. This is opened to show the two white thimbles now on the right fingers. All fingers of both hands are extended, backs of hands to spectators, and under a slight turn to the right the left first and second fingers are inserted into the red thimbles, which were thumb-palmed in the right hand, and at once curl back, the left forefinger thumb-palming its thimble and at once assuming a pointing position, directing all attention to the two white thimbles on the right hand, which is now turned palm to the audience. "But the red thimbles really didn't change," says the magician. They just went under my left knee." And left hand at once goes under knee and comes forth with the red thimbles on first and second fingers. During this action, the right hand has obtained a pair of red thimbles on its third and fourth fingers, which are, of course, curled in. Now as you turn to the right, do the change-over as in Duo Thimble Color Change. Right hand is palm to audience, and left is back to audience. Third and little fingers of both hands are curled in slightly. Now a little turn to the left, the thimbles on the right fingers are thumb palmed, and these fingers inserted into the two red thimbles in left fist, which is opened to show the change.

You do almost exactly what you did before, but this time left third and fourth fingers steal the two white thimbles from the right thumb-palm, under cover of a turn to the right. Again both hands are being held with third and fourth fingers curled in, right palm to audience. "Of cours you know what happened—the thimbles went under my knee," and left hand goes under left knee to appear with the two white thimbles, making a complete display of four thimbles—two red, two white, on that hand.

By this time the right third and fourth fingers have stolen two white thimbles. You will be relieved to know that there is no change-over this time. With a downward, striking gesture, you apparently insert right first and second fingers with their red thimbles into the left, which closes over them. The thimbles, needless to say, are thumb-palmed. Pull the left fist away, seemingly taking the thimbles with it. Slowly open left hand—turn it over—the two thimbles have vanished. "But the thimbles really didn't vanish; they just went behind my—no, not my knee this time—my elbow" —and you go behind left elbow and come out with the four thimbles on right hand, these matching those already on left hand.

Lost And Found

Have you a sure-fire method for vanishing a thimble? By this, I mean some method that rids you entirely of the thimble—something such as the "Jim Dandy Vanisher" or a cork thimble vanisher. If you have, try this: During the course of your routine, place the thimble into the left fist (into vanisher) and "let-'er-go", but do not show the hands empty as yet. Perform several passes, then open the hand, showing the thimble gone. Reach out with the forefinger of right hand and pantomine surprise when the thimble does not appear on its tip. Try again, this time with the left hand, then with both hands at the same time.

Now begin a diligent search between the fingers, lift up a hair on your hand, and appear to look under it; look up the sleeves, and finally under your fingernails, all in your effort to find the missing thimble. At this time, pretend to notice dirt under a finger nail, so reach in your vest pocket, remove a nail file, clean the nail, and return the file to the pocket. This is sure-fire comedy, especially when presented in pantomine.

It has the added advantage in that the replacement of the file offers a splendid opportunity for stealing out thimbles for subsequent productions.

The Passing Thimbles Again

In effect, 5 thimbles pass from one hand to the other, but in accord with the originator's aim, there is no moving of thimbles from one finger to another, this feature making the effect faster and cleaner.

Six thimbles are used, their placement being as follows: One is on each of the right fingers, and two, nested, are on the right thumb.

The left hand is empty. The little finger's thimble is large enough to nest over the one on the forefinger, and the third finger's thimble fits over the one on the second finger.

Show the hands by first showing the back of both, then turn both hands palm to the audience. As the right hand turns, back palm the outer of the two thimbles nested on the right thumb, and rest it in the crotch of the second and third fingers of the left hand. See Figure. Turn the left hand over and get the thimble onto the little finger. You can easily do this by placing the left second finger tip on the thimble rim and rolling the thimble down to a position in which the little finger can be inserted.

Swiftly back-palm the right thumb's thimble, and at the same time, straighten out the left fingers showing the thimble on the little finger.

Lay the right hand over the left, as in illustration, letting the palmed thimble's tip go into the crotch of left first and second fingers. Get this thimble on left third finger as you turn the hand over.

Turn the right hand back out, and remove the little finger's thimble with right thumb and second finger, place it on the thimble on the first finger, nesting the two. Thus the right little finger's thimble apparently melts away under cover of a tossing movement. It appears on the left third finger.

Both hands are turned back out. As this happens, thumb-palm the outer thimble of the two on right forefinger, and steal it with the left thumb. Bend the thumb into left hand, finger-palming the thimble; then roll it onto left second finger.

Now, the thimble on right third finger is removed with the thumb and little finger and is placed on the second finger OVER the thimble already there. As this thimble apparently vanishes, the left second finger is straightened and the missing thimble shown thereon.

To make the next thimble travel, thumb-palm right second finger's thimble and show it on the left forefinger.

The thumb-palmed thimble is got onto left thumb, which is held bent in. The thimble from the right forefinger is caused to pass onto the left thumb. The remaining thimble can be dropped into a pocket unobserved, or it may be nested over one of the thimbles on left hand.

The Super Thimble Vanish

As seen by the audience, at any time during the act a thimble disappears. The hands are shown to be absolutely empty, fingers wide apart and hands separated. There is no place in the hands for concealment, yet the thimble is under absolute control at all times. This is really a perfect thimble vanish. The idea was taken bodily from "AT YOUR FINGER TIPS" by Shannon and Leroy; however I have applied the principle in a much different way.

To the second vest button attach a hair 15″ in length or longer, and on the end of this put a pellet of wax.

At any time get this hair attached to the inside of the mouth of the thimble, placing the thimble on extended right forefinger. Push this thimble into closed left fist, and when the thimble is in, turn right hand palm out, remove forefinger from the thimble, and move right hand up and away from left fist. As you do this, let the hair go between the right second and third fingers, this action bringing the thimble against the back of the right hand and pulling it out of the left fist. Move the left hand by the side of the right and open it, turning this hand also palm to the audience. Thus, both hands are shown empty at the same time—a feature never before embodied in a thimble vanish, to our knowledge.

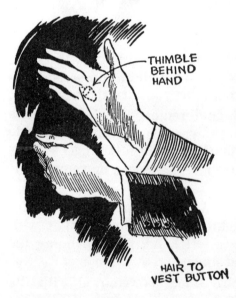

THIMBLE BEHIND HAND

HAIR TO VEST BUTTON

Turn the left hand back out now, and move the right hand down; let right fingernails brush against the back of left hand. This allows the hair to go between the left second and third fingers—the thimble is in left palm. Now, you are at liberty to show the right hand on both sides.

Form the left hand into a fist around the thimble, and reproduce it on the right forefinger from the fist.

Although there are a number of change-overs possible with this device, they will be left to the ingenuity of the reader.

A Nu-Idea Thimble Holder

You will use this holder for a stack of thimbles. The drawing speaks for itself. The plate A is concave, being designed to hold the tip of the outermost thimble. Part B is a piece of spring wire curved to fit in the mouth of the innermost thimble. Part C is a safety pin with which the holder is attached on the under side of the coat.

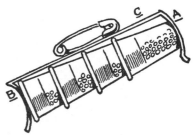

A slight pull is sufficient to release the stack from the holder.

A Contrast Screen

The idea of using a contrast screen for use in manipulation is far from new. Whether it has ever been applied to use with thimbles, we know not, but it certainly adds beauty to a thimble routine. This screen is of modernistic design with a black velvet drop to act as a contrast for the hands and thimbles.

Only the principle and some ideas for the use of this clever piece of apparatus will be given. The construction, should the reader wish to make his own screen, will be left to the purchaser.

The performer's monogram in the upper left corner is more than a decoration, for it conceals a cleverly-arranged black art well, into which may be dropped any article you may desire to be rid of. Later on, in the routine, moves are given for the use of this.

Thus, the vanishing angle is taken care of. Production is taken care of just as easily, by the use of small black pockets or flaps, which hide the thimble to be produced. The screen's being black makes it perfect for using the black-art principle and carrying it to the extreme.

This is the idea "in a nutshell". We suggest the use of a very modernistic design, and also the use of a modernistic side table placed in front and slightly to the left of the screen. On this table rests a bowl of clear, shallow glass, which acts as a receptacle into which are dropped the thimbles as produced.

A Routine

This routine is fast and full of surprises and makes use of the contrast screen, the bowl for holding the thimbles produced, and several of the moves described.

Though there are several different colored thimbles used, it is suggested that the tip of each be painted the same color, because of the use of the paper shell which has no tip at all.

REQUIREMENTS AND PREPARATION

1. On the table is an orange thimble and a paper cone about 3" high. In the upper left vest pocket is a nail file, and in a clip on this pocket is an orange thimble nested in a green one. 3. A thread or hair arranged for the "Super Thimble Vanish." 4. In a paper clip under the coat on left side is a white thimble covered with a green paper tube, so that it gives the appearance of being a green thimble. This is secured to the thimble with a LIGHT dab of diachylon. 5. In a "Nu-Idea Thimble Holder" on the left side is a stack of 4 white thimbles. The innermost will go on the third finger, the next on the second finger, next on forefinger, and the next is really two nested together for the thumb. These conform to the size for "The Passing Thimbles Again."

THE ROUTINE

1. Use a series of vanishes and productions with the single orange thimble picked up from table. Four moves are sufficient.

2. "Lost and Found." In this, you get rid of the orange thimble by means of a vanisher. As you replace the nail file, steal out, on the right second finger, the orange thimble nested in green, but do not show them as yet.

3. Load green thimble in left fist as the hands pass, then produce the orange one from the right ear. By any method you may care to use, change the color from orange to green, leaving the orange thimble in left fist. As both hands are back out in front of the well on the screen, it is a simple matter to toss the orange thimble into it.

4. "The Super Thimble Vanish." Vanish green thimble, do a couple of change-over moves; then reproduce the thimble.

5. Start to place thimble on table, then change your mind apparently, and replace the thimble on forefinger. As you lean over, steal the white thimble covered with green paper shell from under coat on left side. Hold this concealed in left hand. Face front and work the concealed thimble onto left forefinger. Lower both hands to the sides at the knees and apparently pass thimble from right hand to left. This is done by thumb-palming with right hand and extending left forefinger with thimble.

6. Face left again and hold left hand palm out about shoulder high, rather close to the body. With right forefinger, point to left hand, at the same time dropping real green thimble into left sleeve. Show right hand empty, but make no remark about it. Remove left hand's apparently green thimble and place on right forefinger, letting left hand drop to side. This shoots green thimble into left hand, which can easily drop it into coat pocket on that side.

7. Pick up paper cone from table, place it over the forefinger and thimble. Lift it, taking the shell with it, and show that the thimble is now white. Crush the cone in left hand, and drop the white thimble into the bowl on the table.

8. Close left fist around the crushed paper, and hold hand in front of the well. Pull up left sleeve, then with right hand, hit the back of left hand smartly, opening it at the same time. This propels the paper into the well.

9. Show left hand empty first, then turn and show right, first back and then front. At the same time, steal out the stack of nested white thimbles from the holder. Produce the thimbles as you face front, bringing them out one by one on the proper fingers for—

10. "The Passing Thimbles" as described in this text.

A Coin, A Match, And A Thimble

A cute trick. The performer removes from his pocket a half dollar and a match box. Taking a match from the box, he breaks off the head, which he places on the center of the coin, and hands the rest of the match to someone to hold in his fist. To complete the arrangement, a thimble is placed on the coin to cover the match head.

But when the spectator opens his hand, he holds a complete match with head restored, and when the thimble is lifted from the coin, the head is of course gone.

On say, the heads side of a half dollar, place a dab of diachylon wax. Another match head is neatly glued to the end of a match, which is returned to the box.

Now show half dollar and spin it on the table. Show thimble and place beside the coin. Open match box and remove faked match, keeping real head concealed by fingers. Do not call attention to the match—everyone can see it.

Appear to break off the head (fake) of the match with left fingers and place this head on coin. Place stick in spectator's hand and close his fingers over it.

Place coin (with match head thereon) on open left palm near the heel of the hand. Over this apparently place the thimble, mouth down. As the right hand, holding the thimble, comes over the left palm, and thus hides the coin momentarily from view, drop the left hand slightly, and it is this movement which flips the coin over so that it is now tails side up. The thimble is placed mouth down over this empty side of the coin.

Performed as a table trick (and it should be), with spectators looking down on the coin, the coin with thimble may now be passed once from hand to hand, so fingers may be freely shown empty. (The match head is stuck to bottom of coin.) When back in left hand, grasp half dollar and thimble together with right fingers and place them on the table, at the same time retaining the head in the left fingers.

Everything is now ready for the spectators to investigate at the climax.

MISCELLANEOUS MAGIC

The Flying Light Bulb

In this flashy and surprising illusion, a bulb is removed from a lamp, vanished with a bang, and it instantly appears in the lamp—lighted.

We are assuming in the following explanation that you are using an assistant. For convenience in operating, a small lamp and bulb are used. The base is of the type shown in the figure. The shade should be a square one and it has a clip (or a strip of elastic) on the outside to which a duplicate bulb is fastened as shown. The other bulb is in the socket, lighted.

The shade is removed and shown to the audience, as illustrated, the right hand and arm concealing the bulb. The shade is replaced, and in so doing, the bulb is stolen off the shade by the right hand, which goes within the shade now and, with the help of the left hand, apparently unscrews the lighted bulb. In reality, the assistant turns off the light from offstage, and the magician pretends to unscrew the bulb and comes out with the duplicate bulb.

Picking up a paper sack, the magi places the bulb therein, but again there is a deception. The bag rests on the table in front of a black art well. The right hand, with the bulb, goes into the bag, apparently—really going behind the bag and dropping the bulb into the well. Keeping the right hand concealed behind the bag, the left hand lifts the sack and here is the point at which the bulb is apparently dropped into the sack. The bag is held between the thumb and forefinger of the left hand, and as the right hand makes the motion of dropping the bulb into the bag, the left second finger thumps the bag, creating a "thud", while the left hand drops a couple

of inches. This creates the illusion perfectly that the bag has absorb-
ed the shock of the bulb's being dropped within.

The sack is then inflated, screwed up at the top, and burst. The
assistant at once turns on the light from offstage, and when the
shade is removed from the lamp, the missing bulb is seen.

A VARIATION

Have a real light bulb screwed in the socket of the lamp, and, on
the INSIDE of the lamp shade—in a clip provided—have a duplicate
faked light bulb as used in the floating light effect. At the start, the
real lamp is burning, and the shade is lifted off and replaced, there
being no real need for showing the inside of the shade. Reach in and
apparently unscrew the burning bulb, but really turn on the fake
bulb (at the same time, the assistant turns of the real bulb) and remove it from the shade. It appears that you have unscrewed a lighted bulb which remains lighted. Now, just before dropping this
bulb in the sack for the vanish, blow it out as follows: Hold the bulb
in the right hand. Now blow up the left sleeve and at the same time,
with the right fingers, turn the light off. This is a good gag. Drop
this unlighted bulb in the sack, vanish it as described, and it apparently re-appears back in the lamp as it was in the beginning.

The Ideal Hank Box

This is a brand new way of presenting the classic "Jap Hank
Box." Let us state at the beginning that the box is absolutely unprepared. Everything is clean-cut and natural in operation.

Suggested dimensions for the box are given in the sketch. The
bottom is loose. The fakes are shown in Figs. 2 and 3. The first
is a wire hook, the large loop of which holds the load, while the small
loop fits over the edge of the box. This hook, holding a load of ten
or more silks rolled into a compact bundle hangs inside the box.
The hook is, of course, painted to match the box. Another load is
in the right coat pocket hanging on a hook, as shown in Fig. 3. The
hook extends over the edge of the pocket. Two 36 inch rainbow or
emblem silks, folded so that they form a flat bundle about 4 inches
square, are secured by a thread which is run thru a loop in the hook.

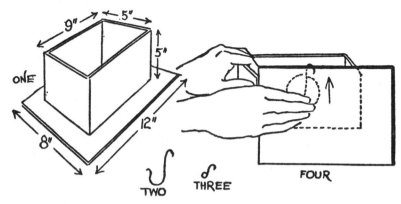

Pick up the box, and place it on the left palm. Grasp the bottom in the right hand and the box in the left, and move the bottom upward in front of the box, hooking the load on the upward journey. See Fig. 4. Let the box slide over the left arm to complete the upward gesture. Lower the arm and show the box proper all around, then reverse the above move, replacing the load back in the box in its original position. Replace the box on the bottom, and produce the load of silks. During this production, steal out the hook.

Pick up the box, dismantle it, and hand it out for examination. The bottom goes to a person on the right, the box going to someone on the left. Take back the bottom first, and hold it bookwise in the right hand. As you receive the box in the left hand, swing to the left, and bring the right hand, with the bottom, up, getting the load in right coat pocket hooked on its top edge. This last move is performed as you step back to the stage or platform, so the covering is perfect. DO NOT HURRY this move, as you have ample time, and to do so would excite suspicion. Load the box naturally.

The production follows. This second production really puts the trick over, for no one expects the trick to be carried further after the examination of the box. An additional production, such as "The Stack of Bowls" production, from the silks could follow to close a flashy and mystifying routine.

SPELLO

A magazine is freely chosen from a stack, and its cover is torn off. This is folded into a cornucopia and a ribbon dropped in, its ends protruding. A number of cards, each bearing a letter of the alphabet, are dropped in also. The performer states that if he had not known which magazine was selected he could easily have solved the mystery by removing the ribbon. He does so, and there, strung on it, are a number of the cards spelling the name of the selected magazine.

First is the preparation of the cards: A set of them is threaded along the middle of a ribbon, which is about four feet in length. Now, the cards are folded into a compact stack, and each end of the ribbon is pleated and the whole put together as in the figure at the right. There are six sets of these to correspond to six magazines. Those used should of necessity have short titles as "Life", "Look", "Time", etc. Let us suppose that they are deposited as follows: "Life" set in the upper left vest pocket; "Time" set lower left vest pocket; another in upper right vest pocket, and so on, one set in each pocket, where they can be conveniently reachd.

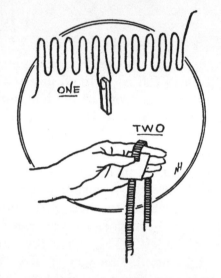

Suppose that "Life" is chosen, and its cover folded into a cone. Reach into the upper left vest pocket, and remove the set, holding the stack of cards concealed in the fingers as in Fig. 2. Let the ends of the ribbons unfold. Now drop the cards (unseen) into the folded magazine cover, and push the ribbon in, letting the ends protrude. Drop the mixed set of letter cards in.

When ready for the climax, pull the ribbon out, showing the cards strung on it. Dump the letter cards on the table, and no one will suspect anything, as the number of these cards was not noted before they were deposited in the cover. Everything may now be examined.

A Sleight of Hand Rope Method

This is a good method to use as an encore after your regular rope trick.

The trick lies in the way the rope is coiled. First make about three or four loops (until about half of the rope is coiled) then start to make another loop. As the right hand comes over grasp loop A, which is the first loop that was formed, and pull it thru the other loops, as in Fig. 2. Make one more loop very deliberately so all can see it is the actual center of the rope, and place it with loop A. Turn to the left slightly and pick up the scissors. At this moment let the last formed loop drop. Now, openly cut loop A.

This move has actually cut a piece off the END of the rope. This piece, about 8 inches long, runs thru the first three or four loops formed. Grasp the MIDDLE of this small piece and the third loop (the loop next to loop A in Fig. 2) and let the ends of the rope drop—the appearance is now as in Fig. 3. Bring the ends up together in the hand, and clipping one end of false piece to one of the real ends with the fingers, let the other real end drop, and another rope has been cut and restored.

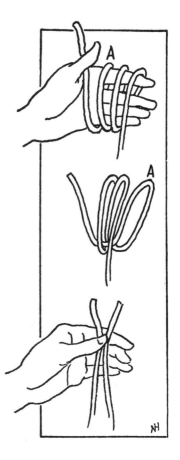

P. and G. Cut and Restored Ribbon

In this effect, a marked ribbon is cut in two pieces, which are separated, and then restored. The marked ribbon may at once be handed for a most careful examination. There is only one ribbon used, and when it is cut the two halves are actually separated.

Two ribbons? No. Merely a ribbon one and a half times the length visible to the spectators. Use a fine silk ribbon not more than one yard long and one half inch wide. One foot of this length is folded in accordion pleats near one end of the ribbon and secured with a thin loop of thread. Thus you have what appears to be a two foot length of ribbon. The only piece of apparatus used is a large size thumb tip. This is placed in the right coat pocket along with a small pair of scissors. If your coat is made "that way", you might place the thumb tip in the small match and coin pocket at the mouth of the pocket.

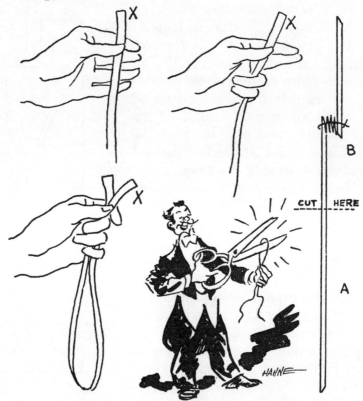

Follow this presentation carefully: Hold the ribbon in the left hand (Fig. 1) with the folded section under the thumb. Display it freely, and if you wish to heighten the effect (and who doesn't?) you may allow someone to mark the X-end for later identification. The folded section is effectively concealed by the left fingers.

Reach into the right coat pocket and get the scissors—at the same time get the thumb tip on the right thumb. Now take the lower end of the ribbon and bring it up by the other end, holding it under the thumb as in Fig. 2. As you place this end in the fist, load the thumb-tip into the fist also, it being finger palmed by the curled left fingers. Cut the ribbon as shown.

Hold the hands apart, displaying two separate pieces. In the left hand is held the B part (the 2 ft. piece), and the right hand holds part A. These pieces are held as shown in Fig. 3. Place both pieces in the left hand and push them into the fist, the A part going into the thumb-tip. The scissors are held in the right hand all the while by the curled third and little fingers.

Tap the left fist with the scissors, and get the thumb-tip (with part A of ribbon in it) on the right thumb. Show the right hand empty in a casual manner, but DO NOT CALL DIRECT ATTENTION TO IT. Place the scissors back into the coat pocket, and leave the thumb-tip there. Slowly pull the ribbon from the fist, and hand it out for examination.

We believe this to be the most practical and clean-cut "Cut and Restored Ribbon" effect ever conceived. The handling of the ribbon is clean and deliberate, and the marking of the end makes the restoration appear to be a miracle. There are no awkward moves, no exchanges.

A Magical "Flash" Routine

This routine has been put together only theoretically, but the practicability of the individual effects should insure success. The act should run from three to five minutes.

1. The Flying Light Bulb.

2. The Cut and Restored Rope.

3. The Ideal Hank Box with Stack of Bowls Production.

The opening effect is done very quickly and is a good attention-getter—an ideal opener.

Of the rope trick there are many good versions, but if something quick and spectacular is required, the following is something to which some serious thought should be given.

Up the right sleeve is a pull. We prefer a simple pull running around to the left wrist. A hank is slipped thru the catgut loop and is allowed to go up the right sleeve. When the pull is required, openly reach up right sleeve and pull out the hank, bringing the pull along and getting the loop over the right thumb. This is the oldest way and the best.

The rope must be soft and about 4½ feet long. One and one half feet are folded as in the "P. and G. Cut and Restored Ribbon" and secured with white thread. This prepared end of the rope hangs over the back of a chair. Magus picks up the rope with both hands, left covering folded rope and right slipping gut loop over unprepared end. The right hand moves down to about 9 inches from its end, and both hands are extended out in front of the body, holding the rope horizontally for the assistant to cut in the apparent middle. One piece in each hand, the magus shows the rope—cleanly cut in half. A slight turn to the left is made, and as this is done the hands come together, the right hand releasing its piece which is whisked up the right sleeve. The right hand grasps the loose end in left hand and the hands separate, left hand retaining its end—this action stretches the rope out to full size. This is but one gesture—once tried, there is nothing to worry about.

And here, dear magnus, for the first time in the history of magic a rope has been genuinely cut and VISIBLY restored into one unprepared length without the tying of so much as a false knot.

After the rope has been tossed out, the hank box, loaded with three or four 36 inch rainbows (depending on the silks and size of the box) is shown. The silks are produced slowly and the box is again dissected, showing first the bottom and the sides. These are put together and the second load, consisting of a 48 inch butterfly silk, is quickly produced. This is thrown with the other silks over the decorative screen which stands in back center stage, while the box is quickly shown and thrown aside. Picking up the silks, they are draped over a small, low taboret and raised to reveal the stack of bowls which may then, if desired, be emptied one by one into a pail. Now you might vanish the water or produce a duck from the pail. The duck is then vanished and ————— perhaps we'd better stop here!

The mysteries of a prearranged ORDINARY pack of cards

PRESENTATION

When a trick depends on a prearranged pack it is not enough to merely show the deck and proceed at once with the effect. Either a convincing false shuffle and series of false cuts must be made, or the deck, which has already been used for several tricks and has been handled freely and shuffled by the spectators themselves, must be exchanged, "switched" to use the accepted term, for the arranged deck.

False shuffling, like all sleights, requires practice but a very easy and convincing method is given in the last section of this book which treats the indispensable sleights for the proper presentation of tricks with cards. A method of false cutting is also included. Once these are mastered, a matter of very slight application, it is hoped that the reader will be sufficiently interested to go more deeply into the subject by studying Erdnase's "Expert at the Card Table," the "Card Manipulations" series by Jean Hugard and other text books.

Several easy methods for switching the deck follow.

SWITCHING THE DECK

1. Place the set up pack in your inside coat pocket on its side; take any three cards, memorizing them, from the pack to be used for the preliminary tricks (the back must be the same, of course) and put them in the same pocket but on their ends. When you are ready to introduce the arranged pack, have the pack in use thoroughly shuffled by a spectator, take it back and, standing with your right side to the front, pretend to put it in your inside coat pocket. Really put it in your lower right vest pocket and as you do this with the thumb and first finger, insert the other fingers in the pocket so that the spectators see the pocket bulge out as the pack apparently goes into it. Now give an example of the sensitive nature of your finger tips by bringing out the three memorized cards from behind the arranged pack, naming each one first. Pretend to replace them in the pocket, really sliding them into the vest pocket with the same finger subtlety as when the pack was put there. Let a spectator remove the

pack from the pocket and you are then ready to begin your pre-arranged tricks.

2. In this case the set up deck is placed beforehand in the upper left vest pocket and its three top cards are memorized. The same three cards are forced from the pack, replaced, and the pack shuffled by a spectator. The pack is really placed in the inside coat pocket, but the duplicates of the three forced cards are taken from the deck in the vest pocket and this pack is finally removed as if it came from the coat pocket. Three cards are put on top in their proper order and you are ready for the set up trick.

3. **Al. Baker's Method.** No. 1. The duplicate deck is carried in the lower left vest pocket. With the pack to be exchanged in the left hand turn towards the table, drop the pack into the outside left coat pocket at the same time take the pack from the vest pocket with the right hand and put it in the left.

4. Al Baker's method No. 2. Place the prearranged deck in the right hand outside coat pocket, lying on its side. Sight the two bottom cards of the pack beforehand. Force the duplicates of these two cards from the deck in use and have the pack shuffled by a spectator after the two cards have been replaced in it. Take the deck and put it in the pocket with the prearranged pack, but on end. Have the selected cards named and bring out the corresponding cards from the bottom of the set up pack. Then bring out the rest of that pack and the exchange is made.

A MOVING REVELATION

This is one of the best non-sleight of hand tricks extant. The effect is that the performer appears to be able to divine the exact number of cards secretly moved from one end of a row to the other, and is able to continue doing the trick ad lib. without rearranging the cards.

To prepare you place 11 cards in sequence from 10 to Ace with a Jack following the A, regardless of suits, on top of the pack. The J is to represent 0. Deal these cards face down on the table from left to right thus:

10. 9. 8. 7. 6. 5. 4. 3. 2. A. J.

Explain that you will turn your back and any spectator may move as many cards as he pleases, one by one, from the right end of the row to the left but not more than 10. To illustrate this you move six cards from right to left. The cards will then lie thus:

5. 4. 3. 2. A. J. 10. 9. 8. 7. 6.

The J has been brought to the sixth position from the right so that 6 will be your key number for the next move. Turn away and the spectator moves, say 2 cards from right to left making the lay-out——

7.　6.　5.　4.　3.　2.　A.　J.　10.　9.　8.

Turning around you gaze intently at the spectator, announce that you have read his mind and to prove it you will turn up a card with the same number of spots on it as the number of cards he moved. Turn the 6th card, the two spot. For the next key card simply add 2 to 6 which gives 8, the present position of the J, therefore no matter what the number of cards moved the 8th card will give it by its number of spots. This may be continued indefinitely, whenever the number amounts to more than 11, subtract 11 and continue with the remainder as the key number. If the J turns up then no cards have been moved.

After divining the number two or three times announce that you will give an illustration of the dominant power of your thought. Pick another spectator and tell him to think of any number between 1 and 10. Tell him that you have selected a number mentally and that you will force him to choose the same one. To prove your assertion you take a slip of paper and write, "Turn over the .... card," filling the blank space with the key card calculated for the next move. Put the paper down folded and lay the pencil on it. "There is my number," you say, "Now please move the cards to the number you thought of". He does so, reads the slip and turns the card showing that number of spots. Gather up the cards, mixing them up, replace them on the pack and shuffle.

The trick is very effective as it is but with the ability to make a false shuffle and false cuts it may be made into a little miracle. With the pack set up execute several false shuffles and cuts, then deal out five or six of the set cards. Make another false shuffle and several cuts, then deal the rest to complete the row. Any suspicion that you may know the faces of the cards cannot then enter into the minds of your audience and the feat is thereby made very much more effective.

DIVINING DECK

Prearrange the top ten cards of a pack so that they run from the 10 down to the Ace. These cards may be of any suits. In offering the cards to a spectator for him to pick one, count the first 10 and hold an imperceptible break at that point, making sure that he takes a card from those further on. Close up the pack and when the spectator has noted his card, cut the cards at the break, lifting the 10 cards, and have his card replaced there. Drop the 10 cards on top of it and square the deck very openly.

Spread the top ten cards and have the spectator touch any one of them; turn the card face up where it lies, the spots on it will denote how many cards further on the chosen card lies.

THE TRANSPOSED CARDS

Beforehand place 13 cards of mixed suits running from the King in order of decreasing value down to the Ace. Begin the trick by false shuffling the pack, leaving these cards on the top. Put the pack down and have a spectator cut it into two parts. Force the selection of the lower heap by the "your right or my left" equivoque and have him count off any small number of cards, less than ten, while your back is turned, and put them on the other heap. This part is then put on top of the cards remaining in his hands. The 14th card from the top will now denote the number of cards counted.

Take the pack, false shuffle if you can, then deal about 20 cards face down, throwing them carelessly but allowing the 14th card to be a trifle more exposed than the others. Have a second person choose one of these: if he takes the 14th, simply ask how many cards were counted off and have the card turned up. If not have two more cards taken, if these do not include the 14th draw it out yourself, put these four in a row and force the right one by having first two cards then one touched by a third spectator, making the eliminations to suit your purpose.

THE CIRCLE OF CARDS

Beforehand arrange ten cards on the top of the deck, of any suits, but with the values running from 10 down to the Ace. False shuffle and cut as freely as you can and finaly have a spectator cut about the middle. Let him choose a heap: if he selects the top half say that you will have him deal some cards on that heap from the other one: if he chooses the lower one let him take it: in either case he gets the lower heap. Turn your back and instruct him to count off any small number of cards, less than ten, look at the bottom card of the packet, remember it and place the packet on top of the other pile. This done, you turn around, take the remaining cards from him and put them under the other packet.

To discover the noted card and the number the spectator counted off, deal 10 cards in a circle, and then four cards in the center; all face down. After much mental exertion and much uncertain hovering over the cards turn up the lowest card of the packet of four, the 11th card dealt, the spots on it will denote the number of cards counted by the spectator and also the position in the circle of the card he noted. You secretly take note of its location, mix the cards up, apparently in a haphazard way, but keeping track of it. Finally draw it aside, have the card named and turn it over.

A TRICK WITHOUT A CLUE

With any deck secretly arrange ten cards of mixed suits, running from 10 to Ace, the 10 being the top card; false shuffle leaving these 10 cards in position. Bend up a corner of the bottom card. Place deck down and have a spectator cut it about the middle; from the lower part instruct him to cut off a few cards after you have turned your back, count them, shuffle them, then note and remember the bottom card of this packet, place it on top of the other part of the deck and finally put the lower half of the pack on the top of both. He is then to cut the deck several times with complete cuts. Turn and take the pack, cut several times, finally cutting to send the bent corner card to the bottom. You now have the pack in the same order as it was before the spectator cut. Deal ten cards rapidly on the table, lift the next one, sight it, then as if you had suddenly changed your mind, drop the card back on the pack, pick up the cards dealt and replace them on the pack. The number of spots on the 11th card that you secretly looked at, denotes the number of cards taken by the spectator, and the same number subtracted from 11 will give you the position from the top of the pack, for instance if the 11th card is a 4, then four cards were cut and the card noted will be 7 from the top.

To reveal this knowledge in a striking way, have the spectator cut the pack in half, and each half again, making four packets; keep track of the original top portion. Call the piles A, B, C, D, and suppose D to be the original top portion, to get the 7th and 11th cards on top of two packets simply have spectator move 6 cards from D to A, then 1 card from D to B; next 3 cards from D to C. This will leave the required cards on B and D. Place one of these on top of each of the other two. Let the spectator take the two top cards and put them face down on the table. He names the number of cards he took and the card he noted. Turn the two cards for the climax.

EYES ALL ROUND

EFFECT:—A spectator thinks of a number between 1 and 10, counts that number of cards from a pack handed to him, shuffle the packet and puts it in his pocket while the performer's back is turned. Without turning around performer has him remove cards from the top of the deck until he calls "Stop." Taking the card stopped at performer touches the spectator's pocket with it and has the number of cards put there called, suppose it is 8. He turns the card in his hand, it is an 8 spot. The trick is repeated several times with the same results.

METHOD:—To arrange the deck put 4 sequences of cards regardless of suits, running from A up to 10 on the top, the court card in any order going below them. When the first person thinks of a number show him what to do. Suppose the number is three, count off three cards, one by one, mix them and put them in your pocket. Take them out, put them on the bottom of the pack which you hand to the spectator. Turn your back. Since the trick works in tens, deduct 3 from 10 and remember 7 as your key card. Turn away.

The spectator counts off the cards to the number thought of, shuffles them and puts them in his pocket. Keeping your back turned tell him to take the packet again and remove a card, then another and another and so on until 6 cards have been removed. Tell him to place the rest of the pack on top of those counted off. Turn around and have him hand you the next card from the top. Touch the card to the pocket and ask how many cards he has there. He replies "Eight." Turn the card, it is an 8 spot.

Put the cards from the spectator's pocket, also the 8 spot on the bottom of the pack. Mentally deduct 8 from 10 and remember 2 as your next key card. Repeat the experiment once only since after that you might get into the court cards. The spectator's shuffling is merely to destroy the arrangement which might be noticed otherwise.

COUNT YOUR CARDS

A card is taken, noted, replaced and the pack shuffled and cut. The deck is handed to the spectator with the request that he find his own card and save the performer worry and trouble.

Ask him to start dealing the cards face down, to stop at any number he may think of between 1 and 10 so that the trick may not become boresome. He deals and turns up a card. You ask if that is his card and the answer is a negative one. Suppose this card happens to be a six. Tell him to deal another pile and turn up the sixth card. "Is that your card?" you ask and the answer is "No." Suppose this time the card turned up is a 10. Continue, "Three times and out. You may have one more chance and if you fail this time I'll have to find the card myself. Count one more pile and turn over the tenth card."

He deals nine cards and you stop him. Ask him to name his card. He does so, turns the next card and it is his.

METHOD:—Beforehand you arranged the first 11 cards, regardless of suits, to run in sequence from 10 to Ace, followed by another 10. After a false shuffle you have a card selected from below these 11 cards and in so doing secretly count 15 cards and hold a break at that point. While the spectator is noting his card count another five cards beyond the 15 and slip the tip of your little finger under the 20 cards. For the return of the chosen card cut off these 20 cards and drop them on top, making the selected card 21st from the top. False shuffle and false cut, if you can.

Hand the deck to the spectator and the effect works itself as described above. Regardless of what the first number is the second card must always be a 10 and the chosen card is tenth beyond that.

PYTHAGORAS

Take 11 cards of the following values but any suits and arrange them in this order: A, J, Q, K, 5, 6, 7, 8, 9, 10, Joker the A being the top card of the packet and the Joker the bottom card. Place the packet face down on the table and invite a spectator to take off any number of cards from the top, not altering their order, (not dealing them) and place them on the bottom while your back is turned. Illustrate by taking off three cards and putting them to the bottom. Mentally you subtract 3 from 11 and remember 8 which becomes your key number. Turn away and the spectator does as directed. Turn back and put your left hand on the pack saying that the cards affect your heart beats so that you can tell the number transferred; also that you will not only discover the number but that you will turn up a card denoting the number by its value. Explain that a J counts 2, Q counts 3, King counts 4 and the Joker—0, the other cards according to their spots.

You have merely to turn up the 8th card which will give you the number of cards transferred. To repeat glimpse the bottom card of the packet and subtract from 11, this will give you the key card for the next transfer. If no cards are moved you turn up the Joker, value 0. The trick can be repeated indefinitely.

KNOCK 'EM DEAD

Take out the Hearts from Ace to 10, place an indifferent card between each and an indifferent card on the top. Prepare a small wooden plug with ten holes bored in it, in each of these holes place a slip of paper rolled into a pellet, each slip bearing the name of one of the ten Heart cards. Put this plug in your right hand outside coat pocket, the slips arranged in order so that you can instantly find any one required.

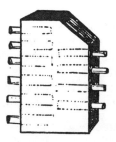

Provided with the prepared pack, the plug with the pellets, a slip of paper and pencil and having a hat on the table, begin by writing something on a slip of paper pretending to drop it into the hat and have a spectator call any number between 1 and 20. If the number called is even, hand him the deck and tell him to count down to that number and note the card, if the number called is odd he is to count down to that number and look at the next card. In the meantime you have simply to halve the number to obtain the value of the card, remove the corresponding pellet from the plug and drop it into the hat secretly as you bring it forward to have your prophecy verified.

SELF WORKING MYSTERY

With a deck of strippers arrange the first ten cards to run from a 10 down to an ace using mixed suits, and reverse them. Begin by shuffling the cards thus—strip off the top ten cards and make a riffle shuffle. Apparently cut the pack, really strip the ten cards out and drop them on top. Invite a spectator to freely choose a card from anywhere but the ten top cards. For its replacement cut off the ten cards, their reversal making this easy, have the card put back, drop the ten cards on it and square the deck. The chosen card is now the eleventh card and you false shuffle, keeping it in that position.

Again cut the top ten cards and put the remainder of the pack on the table. Fan the ten with both hands and let spectator remove one card. Separate the cards at the point from which this card is taken, with the left hand drop all the cards that were below it on top of the pack, then pick up the pack and put it on top of the cards remaining in the right hand. The spots on the card taken from the ten will indicate the position of the chosen card from the top of the pack. The counting must, of course, be done faces down.

STOP AND THINK

Separate the cards of any full deck into their suits, then separate each suit into odd and even cards, J and K being odd and Q even. You thus have 8 packets. Put the two red odd with the two black even cards and shuffle them thoroughly; do the same with the two red even and the two black odd cards. From these two packets take one card alternately in one pile until the cards have all been taken. The cards will appear to be well mixed.

With the pack so arranged begin by having it cut several times with complete cuts. Deal the cards into 4 heaps, one card at a time. Suppose the letters A B C D represent the heaps it will be seen that if A and C are put together and also B and D we have the two original packets, red odd and black even, and red even and black odd. Ask the spectator which he will have, the odd packets or the even. Whichever he takes let him put them together and shuffle the cards. You do the same with the remaining packets.

The spectator takes any card from his and pushes it into yours which you give to him to shuffle. Taking it back you have only to find the one card that does not match up with the odd and even cards that you hold. It may be an odd black, all the rest of the blacks being even and so on.

NOVEL CARD DISCOVERY

To set up the deck first separate the odd cards from the even, the J and K being taken as odd cards and the Q as even. Put 13 odd cards face up on the table, on them put 13 even cards, then the rest of the odd cards and finally the remainder of the even cards. Turn the pack face down. Now if it is cut at the middle the odd cards will be on the top of each portion and the even cards at the bottom, therefore if the two packets are riffled together the top part will consist of odd cards and the bottom of the pack will have the even cards when the riffle shuffle is completed. There will be a few mixed cards in the center but that will not interfere with the effect.

After the arranged pack has been riffle shuffled, have it cut into two packets as near equal as possible. Invite a spectator to take a card from the middle of either heap and push it into the middle of the other packet. The cards being dealt the one even card amongst the odd cards or vice versa, must be the chosen card.

IMPROVED MARVELOUS PREDICTION

In this trick you actually set up a borrowed deck into the odd-even arrangement. Deal the cards into four heaps by putting in the first two only odd Spades, and Hearts, and even Clubs and Diamonds. Into the 2nd two heaps deal only even Spades and Hearts and odd Clubs and Diamonds. Put first two heaps together and have a spectator shuffle them while you shuffle the other two. Cut the spectator's packet into two portions putting them side by side. Cut your packet placing the halves on top of the other two packets. Top of each now contains even Spades, Hearts odd Clubs, Diamonds, bottom portions of each are Spades, Hearts even Clubs, Diamonds.

Have a spectator riffle these two packets together. There will be only a few cards of both kinds mixed in the center, the cards at the top and bottom of the pack remain as set up. Have the pack cut into three nearly even piles, discard the center one and have two spectators each take one of the others. Each selects a card from the other's packet and shuffles it into his own. Have the packets put together, the original top heap going on top.

The cards are now called one by one from the top of the deck. The first odd Spade or Heart, even Club or Diamond is one of the chosen cards. After a card or two more has been called, have the packet turned over and have the cards called from the face of the deck. This time listen for an even Spade or Heart, odd Club or Diamond. This will be the other card. Reveal the cards as you please.

READY RECKONER

To prepare for this trick sort out the odd and even cards of each suit and reassemble the pack by putting the odd Spades and Hearts with the even Clubs and Diamonds in one packet, and the even Spades and Hearts with the odd Clubs and Diamonds in another. Put the packets together making a bridge between.

Thus prepared, take the deck and hold a break at the bridge with the deck face down in the left hand. Let half the cards below the break drop on the table, then drop the rest of the cards below the break besides the first lot. On each packet drop half the remaining, now dovetail the two packets together and as the lower half of each packet consists of one kind of cards and the upper half of another when the shuffle is completed the pack will be in two kinds of cards, with a few mixed in the middle.

Instruct a spectator to cut the deck into three heaps, pocketing the top packet and handing you the middle one. By merely glancing at the cards you tell him how many cards he cut. The only kind of cards he can have in his pocket are odd Spades and Hearts and even Clubs and Diamonds. A glance at the cards handed you will show how many of such cards are in it, subtract the number from 28 and you get the number of cards cut.

Follow this with "The Pair Detection."

THE PAIR DETECTION

This trick is designed to follow the "Ready Reckoner."

While the spectator verifies your total, secretly add the spots of the only odd Spades and even Clubs in the packet which you still hold, subtracting 13 each time your number exceeds that, and you know the number of points in his packet when all the 13's in it have been cancelled. Tell him to shuffle his packet and to remove any pair from it, pocketing it.

The only pairs in his packet must consist of a card of each color, either a Spade and a Heart, or a Club and a Diamond. Place the packet you hold face down on the table and put the other packet, which has not been touched, on top of it. Taking his packet, you merely add the spots of the black cards in it, subtracting 13's. Subtract this total from what the total should be and you have the denomination of the pair. If it is odd they are Spades and Hearts, if even, Clubs and Diamonds.

Follow with "Dead Easy Location."

DEAD EASY LOCATION

Continuing after "The Pair Detection," have the spectator replace the pair and put his packet on top of the deck after he has thoroughly shuffled it. Tell him to cut the pack at about the middle, note the card on top of the lower portion, put it on top, reassembling the deck and make several complete cuts.

Then tell him to deal the deck into several rows, turning the cards face up. You can now locate the card. Owing to the way in which the two lower portions were placed, cutting the deck at the middle forced the spectator to choose a card from among the even Spades and Hearts, odd Clubs and Diamonds, and this is placed on the original top of the deck, his whole packet of cards being of the other variety. In glancing over the cards dealt, locate the long string that must have been his packet and the card dealt next before the first of this string must be the selected one.

ODD OR EVEN

The trick requires a special arrangement. First sort out the suits and arrange each to read from back to face,

6, 4, 10, A, Q, 2, J, 7, 8, 5, 3, K, 9.

cut each of these packets so that a card of different value is at the bottom of each. Riffle shuffle the Spades and Hearts together once only and do the same with the Clubs and Diamonds. Put the two packets together with a bridge at the division.

To present, cut at the bridge and riffle shuffle once only, then cut the pack. Fan the deck from left to right, the faces outwards and have a spectator choose a heap. Pass the cards from left hand to right and as spectator tells you that a card is of a suit chosen, place it face down on the table. When complete the cards are in the set up order except for being cut. On a small card, which you can palm on to the back of the rest of the deck, you have the following table.

OOOO-8	EOEE-6	OEOO-2	EEOO-3	OEEO-10
EEOE-4	OOEO-J	EEEO-K	OOEE-A	
OOOE-7	OEEE-9	EOOE-Q	EOOO-5	

A spectator cuts the packet with complete cuts and you turn your back. He puts the top card in his pocket without looking at it or letting anyone else see is He deals the 12 remaining cards into four face down heaps, a card to a heap in rotation. He then turns the top card of each heap face up and calls Odd or Even for each, J is odd, K Q even. Consulting your table you at once name the card in the spectator's pocket the face of which no one else has seen.

If desired you can repeat with any one of the other suits.

THE WONDER FORCE

A. This can be used as a prediction trick or as a method of forcing a card for any other trick.

Suppose you wish to force the QH. First divide the pack into its red and black cards. Place 6 red cards face down, on them 12 black cards, then 6 more reds and on them the QH, and on it any black card. Arrange the rest of the pack in another pile, first a black card, on it 7 reds, then 12 blacks, and lastly the rest of the reds. Put the second packet on top of the first making a bridge between them.

If you are simply making a prediction write "Queen of Hearts" on a slip of paper, fold it and give it to a spectator to hold. Cut the pack at the bridge and riffle shuffle them together. The center portion of the pack will consist of black cards. Ask a spectator to give the pack another riffle shuffle and as he must cut amongst the black cards no red card can fall above the force card, the QH. Tell him to take out the first red card he comes to Your prediction is read and the card shown.

Two or more cards of the same color can be forced in the same way.

B. Second Method. Place a duplicate of the force card next above the bottom card of the original upper half of the deck. When shuffling let these two cards fall first. This time there is a force card the first red card from either end. Spectator riffle shuffles and then cuts the pack into two portions. He chooses one, if the top half, he takes the first red card from the top, if the lower heap, the first red card from the face. Again you may use two different red cards and have from 20 to 30 cards dealt into a heap, reversing their order so that the first red cards taken from each heap will be the force cards.

PSYCHIC PREDICTION

Here is an arrangement which will force the number 27. It may be used simply as a prediction effect, the number being written beforehand on a slip which is placed in an envelope, sealed and held by a spectator, or in any effect requiring the forcing of a number. Other numbers can be arranged for on the same lines. For 27 arrange cards as follows:—

2S, 3H, AS, KH, 9S, 10H, 5S, JH, QS, 4H, 8S, 6H, KS, 3H; AS;
2H, 9S, 10H, 5S, QH, JS, 4H, 8S, 6H, 7C, KD, 2C, 10D, 4C;
AD, 3C, 8D, 9C, QD, QC, 4D, 7C, 2D, JC, 10D, 4C, AD, 3C; 8D;
9C, JD, KC, 4D.

Bridge the cards so that you can cut at the 6H.

With cards thus arranged, first write the prediction, then cut at the bridge, riffle shuffle once only and call attention to the genuineness of the shuffle. Show the faces of the cards rapidly, the duplicates will not be noticed and the cards appear to be perfectly ordinary. Hand the cards to a spectator telling him to think of a suit. Cutting the deck wherever he pleases he picks off a card at a time from the top, noting each. Those not of his suit he places face up. No matter where the pack is cut or what suit he selects the total for six cards thus taken will be 27.

PROPHESIED SPOT TOTAL

Remove the 3's, 9's, K's, 6's, A's, 4's, 7's, 10's, J's, and 5's, and paying no attention to suits, arrange them in four sequences, so that all four sets of 10 are in the same order. Place these sets together and on top of them put the remaining 12 cards of the pack.

With the pack thus prepared, begin by writing a prediction, 69, on a slip of paper, fold it and give it to someone to hold.

Take the pack, deal off 10 cards and openly add their spots, spectator checking. Replace them on top, then put half a dozen to the bottom and again deal off 10 cards, the values of these are added and checked, giving a different total. Invite a spectator to cut the pack, deal off 10 cards and add up their values. He does so and gets a total of 69. Your prediction is opened and read aloud. It is the same.

The arrangement does it all, any 10 cards of the 40 taken in sequence add up to 69. It is advisable to have the spectator cut about the middle.

CAGLIOSTRO'S VISION

The deck used for this trick must be a complete one of 52 cards. Arrange the following cards in this order at the bottom of the pack: 2H, AC, 2C, 3C, 4C, 5C, 6C, 7C, the 2H being the bottom card.

To begin, make a riffle shuffle, leaving these cards in position at the bottom. Put the pack on the table and turn away. Instruct the spectator to remove two cards from the middle of the deck, putting one at the top and one at the bottom so that you cannot possibly know the cards occupying these positions. Tell him to fix on any number between 1 and 10, deal a face down row of cards from left to right to that number, look at and remember the last card of the row. Next he is to go back to the first card of the row and deal one card on each one in the row, continuing as long as there are enough cards to complete a deal on the whole row. When there are not enough to do that he is to lay them aside. Tell him to assemble the heaps by placing the last heap on top of the next one to the left, these two on the next and so on, finally cutting the complete pile several times completing the cut each time.

Turn around, note the number of cards left over; if there are none his card will be the next behind the 2H the pack being face up. If there are two cards left over, his card will be next behind the 2C, if three over, next behind 3C and so on.

QUADRUPLE DECK MYSTERY

Take the AC from each of three red backed packs and discard one of them entirely. Place two of the A's at the rear edge of your table, the ends projecting over it slightly and conceal them by laying a blue deck in its case over them. Have the three red decks thoroughly shuffled, placing them together as one huge deck. Pick up the blue deck with the two hidden aces below it and taking back the triple stack rest the blue case on it for a moment leaving the Aces on top. Lay the triple deck down and hand the blue deck, taking it out of its case, to a spectator. Turn your back or leave the room.

Instruct the spectator to take any card from the blue deck and put the rest of the pack in his pocket. Ask a second person to deal a row of cards face down from the triple deck on the table, the second person to stop him at any time and put his blue backed card face down at the right hand end of the row as the last card. A small identical number of cards is then dealt in turn on the back of each card in the row and the heaps are to be assembled by picking up the one first dealt at the left end, putting it on top of the second, these two on the third and so on. A third person now takes the deck so assembled, cuts some and, holding it face up, deals the cards one by one, calling their names as he does so. When he calls the first AC you start counting the cards to and including the next AC, the number will be the number originally in each heap and the chosen blue backed card will lie exactly that number of cards from the second AC.

You call "Stop" and turn around. The second spectator names his card, it is the one the third spectator has in his hand. He turns it over, it has a blue back.

MEPHISTOPHELES' TOUCH

Take out all the 2's, 3's, 4's, 5's and 6's from a complete deck and arrange the remaining cards in four sequences of 8 cards, thus:—

9S, 7H, KC, 8D, QS, JH, AC, 10D.
9H, 7C, KD, 8S, QH, JC, AD, 10S.
9C, 7D, KS, 8H, QC, JD, AS, 10H.
9D, 7S, KH, 8C, QD, JS, AH, 10C.

It follows from this arrangement that no matter what card is taken the 8th card down from it will be of the same value and the next suit in the order of S, H, C, D. Place the 20 low cards on the top of the arranged packet bridging them.

Begin by showing the deck, cut at the bridge and riffle shuffle the low cards into the others. Have a spectator cut. Take the pack face up and throw out all the low cards as you come to them. The arrangement of the remainder is unaltered though no spectator would believe this even if you told him.

Turn away, ask a spectator to make a complete cut and note the top card, putting it face down on the table. Tell him to deal 8 cards on top of it, lay the pack aside and shuffle the 9 cards. Turn and spread the packet face up. There will be one pair of cards amongst them and his card is the one that comes first in the suit order. For instance KH-KC being the pair, the spectator's card will be the King of Hearts.

FAIR AND SQUARE

With any deck arrange the cards according to suits only. Rotate the suits throughout the deck, paying no attention to the values. For instance, you may have the suits C, H, S, D, C, H, S, D, and so on all through the deck.

Cut the deck several times with complete cuts. Fan the deck for the free selection of any card. While the spectator is looking at his card run off four cards from the point at which he removed his card and have it returned there. Square up the cards and have the spectator make several complete cuts.

To find the chosen card you have simply to run through the faces of the cards and note when you come to the two cards of the same suit together. The selected card will always be the one of these two which is nearest the face of the deck.

YOUR CARD

In doing this feat lay great stress on the fact that you never see the face of any card. You hold the deck behind your back and allow a spectator to freely remove one card. Still holding the deck behind your back, bring forward two cards and lay them face down on the table. State that these two will reveal the chosen card, one telling the suit, the other the value. And they do.

You have the deck stacked by the Si Stebbins system in which the suits and values rotate regularly. When the spectator cuts the pack behind your back for the selection of a card, have him take the top card of the lower portion, take the cut from him and place it below the lower packet. In short the deck is cut at the point from which the card was taken.

Now because of the system the fourth card from the top of the deck will be of the same suit as the selected card and the 13th card down will be of the same value. So that all you have to do is to bring out these two cards to reveal the suit and value of the chosen card.

NOTE:—When removing the 13th card behind your back slip the tip of your left little finger in marking the spot. You can later on easily put it back in its proper place. The card taken from the fourth place can be replaced in position and you have your set up ready again.

ONE IN FOURTEEN

The deck is arranged in the "Eight Kings," the Si Stebbins, or any other system in which the sequence runs in four cycles of 13 values; such system as Nikola's is not suitable for this feat.

False shuffle the deck and allow a spectator to make several complete cuts. When he is satisfied that the cards are well mixed invite him to take the top card, look at it; put it face down on the table and deal 13 cards on top of it. The remainder of the deck is put aside. Tell him to pick up the 14 cards, shuffle them thoroughly and then hand the packet to you.

To find his card you have simply to look over the faces and find a pair of cards of the same value. There will be one pair only in the 14 cards and one of the pair will be his card. Suppose the pair to be the King of Clubs and King of Hearts, and the arrangement of the suits in the stacked deck to be C, H, S, D.—the spectator's card will be the one that occurs first in the suit order, thus in this case it will be the King of Clubs.

Having found the card so simply, reveal it in as magical a manner as you can devise.

NOTE: In running through the packet to find the selected card re-arrange the cards in the same order. Take out the selected card and drop the cards on top of the pack. Replace the chosen card on top and you have the pack in order for any other trick depending on the arrangement.

THE FIFTEENTH CARD

From any pack take out all the black cards and arrange them in the order following:

A, K, 2, Q, 3, J, 4, 10, 5, 9, 6, 8, 7, 7, 8, 6, 9, 5, 10, 4, J, 3, Q, 2, K.

There will be one Ace left over, place it on the top of the pack. It will be noted that the arranged cards make two sequences, one ascending value, the other descending, and that any two adjacent cards will total 14 or 15 in value, the J, Q, K, being reckoned as 11, 12, 13. Put the black cards, thus arranged, on top of the red, note the red card that is 15th from the bottom and put the deck in its case.

To show the feat, begin by writing the name of the 15th card on a slip of paper, fold it and give it to a spectator to put in his pocket. Take the pack from its case, split it at the lowest black card and mix the cards calling attention to the genuineness of the procedure. Hand the pack to the spectator and have him deal the cards one by one into two piles, the red cards in one heap, the black in the other. The cards will be in the same order but reversed, the noted card being now 15th from the top of its packet.

Ask the spectator to choose one of the packets. If he takes the blacks go right ahead with the effect. If he chooses the reds tell him to put those cards in his pocket and to remember he chose the packet freely. Have him thrust the blade of a knife into the black cards and let him take the two cards below, the two cards above, or the single card above and the single card below the blade. Any of these pairs will total 14 or 15. If 14 tell him to deal 14 cards and lay the next face down on the table, if 15 to put out the 15th card, then to take the slip from his pocket, read your prediction and turn the card he arrived at.

The precedure is so apparently genuine that it will puzzle any one not acquainted with the secret.

SENSATIONAL CARD MYSTERY

The secret is that cards are generally arranged in a certain order when they come from the makers, usually H, C, D, S with values from the Ace to the King.

Introduce a new pack and hand it to a spectator to open. He takes the pack out of its case and puts the cards face down on your left hand. Invite five or six spectators each to cut a small packet of cards from the top, look at the face card of the cut and then hold the packets against their chests so that neither you nor anybody else can get a glimpse of the face cards. Retain a few cards on your left hand and in returning to your table sight the top card of this packet. This will indicate the face card of the last spectator's cut. Suppose your sighted card is a 9S, you know the spectator cut an 8S. Take his packet, drop it on top of the cards in your left hand, sight its top card and so get knowledge of the next cut card.

Proceed in exactly the same way for the rest of the spectator's cards.

NOTE:—The reader is advised to test the various makes and brands of cards before relying on this "secret."

NEW X-RAY TRICK

Use the "Eight Kings, etc." arrangement and introduce the trick after switching the arranged deck for one that has been freely handled and shuffled by the audience.

Have a spectator freely select a card and pass all the cards below it to the top. Sight the bottom card and so memorize the chosen card. Go to a second spectator, have him cut off a packet, shuffle it, retaining one card and passing the rest to a third person to do the same. This person hands the cards to a fourth who also picks out a card. Have these cards replaced in different places in the arranged pack retained by you.

Drop the cards into a goblet and throw a handkerchief over them. Talk about the progress being made in telepathy, now a proven scientific fact and so on. Ask each person to concentrate on his card and after much stress name the first card. Take the cards out of the goblet, run through them to remove the card just named and note another card out of the regular order. Put the cards back in the goblet, cover them and proceed to get the name of the card you just noted. Continue with the rest in the same way. Shuffle the cards after you note the last card and you can let anyone remove the cards from the goblet after you name it. There will be nothing for anyone to find as a clue to the trick.

SHARK FOOD

Pack is in any arrangement you prefer to use. If you cannot make a satisfactory false shuffle, the deck in use which has been freely handled and shuffled by the spectators should be secretly exchanged for the arranged deck. Hand this to a spectator and have him make several complete cuts. Turn your back and tell him to deal cards face down on the table, stopping whenever he pleases, then he is to take the next card, look at it, insert it in the cards he holds and shuffle them. This done, turn around, take the cards from him, open the packet for the return of the cards dealt on the table. Slip the tip of your left little finger under the top card of this packet, lift off all the cards below it and shuffle them on the top. This leaves the last card dealt by the spectator at the bottom of the pack. Sight it and you know by the set up what his card is and you can reveal it as you wish.

THOUGHT FORETOLD

EFFECT:—Performer writes a prediction, seals it in an envelope and hands it to a spectator. This person chooses a color, red or black and from a shuffled pack draws one card. This he puts in an envelope and burns it. He segregates the cards of the color he chose. One card is missing and its name is found to have been predicted by the performer as proved by the slip in the sealed envelope.

METHOD:—Separate the red and black cards of any deck and take out one red and one black card, remembering their names. Cut the two piles in half and put the black halves on the red halves. Bridge the two packets and put them together.

Thus prepared ask a spectator to chose between red and black. Whichever he names, write the name of the card of that color on a slip of paper, seal it in an envelope and give it out to be held. Divide the pack at the bridge and give it a careful riffle shuffle calling attention to its genuineness. The shuffle will put all the black cards together at the top and all the reds at the bottom of the pack, with perhaps a few mixed in the middle. Whichever color was named, fan the half of the deck of the opposite color for the selection of a card. This card is not looked at but placed in an envelope and burned. This ensures that when the spectator picks out the cards of the color he chose there will be one card only missing. Naturally this is taken to be the one burned since the card named in your prediction is missing.

MYSTERIOUS DETECTIVE

EFFECT:—Spectator cuts a pack and takes the top card of the lower heap, and two other people do the same. The performer takes a card from the deck touches each man's pocketed card and names them correctly.

METHOD:—Arrange the red cards from face to back—AH, 2D, 3H, 4D, etc., to QD, KH, AD, 2H, etc., the suits alternating and the values in sequence. Do the same with the two black suits. Cut the reds bringing 8H to the face, and the blacks with the 2C in same position. Put the two packets together, bridging them.

To present, cut at the bridge and riffle shuffle. Show the faces rather rapidly, deck looks well mixed. Allow first spectator to lift off a packet, laying it aside, then take the top card and pocket it. A second spectator lifts off another packet in the same way and pockets card, third spectator follows suit. Assemble the pack by replacing the packets to bring pack to its original order except for the three cards removed. Note the bottom card and name a card a few points lower in value which will be near the top of the pack, saying that card is your detective card. Run through the pack face up and note first two cards of the same suit near together without a card of the same color but different suit between them.

Suppose you see the 8C and 10C and no Spade between them, you know that a 9S has been removed. There will be two other similar combinations giving you the names of the other two cards. Memorize the cards and after taking out the so-called detective card, touch each man's pocket, put the card to your ear, and name the card.

SUPER COUNT DOWN

Arrange the deck red, black, red, black, etc., the colors alternating throughout the pack.

After a false shuffle hand the deck to a spectator, asking which he prefers odd or even. If he says odd ask him to think of any odd number from 1 to 50. Turn your back instructing the spectator to first cut the deck several times, then count off on the table singly cards to the number thought of and to note the next card. Put this card on those dealt and drop the deck on top of all. Finally he is to cut again.

Take the pack and fan the faces towards yourself, note where two cards of the same color come together. Openly cut at this point so that one goes to the top, the other to the bottom. Run through the cards again and count as you do so until you reach two of the same color together. The first of these will be the noted card and the number that this card is from the bottom indicates the number thought of.

If the spectator has thought of an even number he is to note the top card of the heap on the table instead of the top card of the deck. In this case when you receive the cards instead of cutting when you reach the two cards of the same color, simply jog the second card slightly inwards with the left thumb and continue running over the faces until the second two of the same color is reached, cut at this point, between the two cards turn the deck face downwards and make a break below the jogged card. Lift the cards above the break, they correspond to the number mentally selected.

FATE AND THE JOKER

EFFECT:—A spectator selects a card by thrusting the Joker into a shuffled deck. Performer names the card by merely looking at the Joker.

METHOD:—Separate the red cards from the black. Put all the Hearts and Diamonds together in pairs whose value is 14, thus 7D, 7H, KH, AD and so on; J, Q, K, values being 11, 12, 13. In the same way arrange the Spades and Clubs in pairs of value 14. Put the two packets together making a bridge.

To begin, show the pack, cut at the bridge and riffle shuffle the halves slowly and openly calling attention to the genuineness of the shuffle. Remove the Joker, hand it to a spectator and invite him to thrust it into the deck wherever he pleases. This done let him take the card above or the card below the Joker.

Take the pack, turn it face up to remove the Joker and note the card near it which hasn't a mate near it of the same color but opposite suit to make up a total value of 14, then substract its value from 14 and name the other suit of the same color. For instance you find a 2H alone, the card drawn was the QD.

PSYCHOLIA

From two packs of cards take out all the low cards from 6 to 2 and discard one set of these entirely. Shuffle one of the 32 card packs thoroughly and then arrange the cards of the second deck in exactly the same order. Place this pack in your pocket. Put the low cards of the other pack on top, bridging the packets.

To begin, show the pack, cut at the bridge and riffle the two packets together slowly, calling attention to the thoroughness of the shuffle. Turn the pack face up and discard the low cards from 6 to 2 so that the cards will be in the same order as those of the pack in your pocket. Let a spectator cut the deck in about two equal piles and you hand the heaps to two persons, noting the bottom card of each as you do so. Now leave the room.

Take out the duplicate pack, cut it to make the face cards the same as those you noted in the spectators' packets. Spread the two packets face up some distance apart. Note which packet contains the AS. Now call to the spectators: "Have five cards chosen from whichever packet contains the AS and one card from the other packet, note the selected cards and shuffle them into the opposite heaps from which they were drawn. Now put the two heaps together with the AS heap on top. Kindly read aloud the names of the cards as they lie from the top." As each card is read discard its duplicate from your AS heap. One card will be read which is not in your AS heap. This is the one the spectator removed from his AS heap. Pick it out of your as yet unused heap and keep it separate. Let the reading continue until your AS is reduced to but 5 cards—these, and the one you have laid aside, are the selected cards.

Announce their names with dramatic effect.

THE WIZARD'S DREAM

Arrange the cards of each suit from Ace to King in sequence of value, A, 2, 3, 4, 5, 6, etc. The order of the suits being S, H, C, D. Cut a small card to the face.

Show the pack and put it on the table. Turn away and have a person cut the deck as often as he likes with complete cuts then give it a riffle shuffle and finally tell him to cut the deck about the middle. Invite him to take any card from one heap and put it in the other.

You turn around, take whichever packet he wishes and find the card. The principle is simple, a single dovetail shuffle does not destroy the arrangement it merely divides the sequence into two strings and by following each of them without regard to the interlying cards any strange card or any missing card can be detected at once.

DIABOLICAL TRANSPOSITION

EFFECT:—Two decks of cards are used, and four spectators join in the trick. The first two spectators are each given a pack of cards which they cut several times and then each deals off a packet of 26 cards. The first man pockets the lower half of the deck and hands the counted off 26 card packet to one of his neighbors; and the second man does the same. The two assisting neighbors both stand and each fans his packet of 26 cards, and proceeds to mentally select any one card. The magician causes these two mentally selected cards to leave the assistants' packets and fly back to the original halves of the decks still in the first two spectators' packets. Upon examination this amazing transposition is found to have taken place, and the decks may be examined without discovering the secret.

METHOD:—Using two complete packs of the same back patterns, you thoroughly shuffle one deck and remove 26 cards just as they come from the top. Take the duplicate 26 cards from the other pack, arrange them in the same order, and place these two duplicate half packs together. Do the same with the other two half packs. Each pack is therefore the complement of the other, i.e.; the 26 cards missing from the first arranged pack are in the second arranged pack, and vice versa, and the dealing of

26 cards will always leave their duplicates in the hands of the party originally holding them   It is now obvious that, when the procedure described in the first paragraph is followed, no matter what cards the assistants note their duplicates are already in the half packs held by the first two spectators. Before the audience realizes what is about to happen, however, the magician takes back the two (counted off) 26 card packets and boldly switches them, either by the pass or in laying them on the table —and the trick is done. Due to this little swindle the selected cards appear to vanish—on command of the magician—from their respective packets and are found to have returned to the original halves of the pack still pocketed by the first two spectators. Further examination of both complete packs will give no clue to the mystery.

CARD MEMORY

EFFECT:—Deck is shuffled, divided in half, one half is chosen by a spectator and read through once to the performer, who then leaves the room but remains within hearing distance. Spectator spreads the cards in a row face up and the performer names the cards in order both ways and names the cards at any numbers or the number of any card.

METHOD:—The cards are arranged but the arrangement can vary every time. Separate the black cards from the red, shuffle the reds and spread them face up from left to right. Take the black cards and arrange the values in the same order exactly, but where you have a Heart in the reds use a Club in the blacks and for Diamonds use Spades. Therefore supposing the 6th card in the red packet is the JH, you know that the 6th card in the black packet will be the JC and so on. Put the two packets together making a bridge between them.

To begin, show the pack, cut at the bridge and riffle the two packets together, calling attention to the fairness of the shuffle. Say that a full packet makes the effect too lengthy and that you will use half the cards only. Turn pack face up and deal one by one, the reds in one pile, the blacks in the other. Turn them face down and have a spectator choose one packet. Carelessly drop the other into your pocket. Have him cut the chosen pile several times and then call the names of the cards to you just once. Listen, pretending intense concentration, but remember the last card only. Leave the room, take the packet from your pocket, cut so that the card corresponding with the last card called by the spectator is at the face thus putting it in exactly the same order as the other packet.

Hold the packet face down and deal them face up and overlapping in a row from left to right, naming each card aloud as you turn it. After every fifth card jog the next 5 up and down alternately about an inch. After you have called all the cards you can locate any number instantly and call the card at any number named and vice versa.

SENSITIVE THOUGHTS

This is worked on the same principle as "Card Memory."

Arrange a pack exactly in the same way with a bridge between the two sets of reds and blacks.

Show the pack, divide it at the bridge, execute a riffle shuffle and then deal the packets, reds and blacks, just as in the preceding trick. Both packets are in the same order as set up.

Ask a spectator to choose a packet, to think of any number from 1 to 26 and name it. Address a second spectator and tell him he is to take the other packet, run over the faces of the cards and think of any card he may see. As you say this you have picked up the packet and run over the faces as if showing the second man what he is to do, really you locate the card at the number called by the first person. To do this quickly, subtract the number from 26, count as you fan from the face card, and when you reach the number note the next card, which tells you the card in the first packet at the number called. If it is the 7S for instance, you remember the 7D.

The second spectator names his card. Have the first person hold his packet to your forehead as he repeats his number. You name the card, and as he deals face up counting to that card note where the second person's card lies and remember the number. He, in his turn puts the pack to your forehead and you call the number at which his card lies in his packet. If the mate of card does not appear you must pick up the first packet and quickly continue the count as you show that all the cards are different.

RED AND BLUE BACK MIXUP

EFFECT:—The performer announces that a very peculiar affinity exists between cards of the same suit and value. To illustrate this he brings out two packs, one with a blue back, the other a red.

Each pack is shuffled by a member of the audience, then the performer puts the packs together and shuffles the double deck. He drops the cards into a borrowed hat and, holding it above his head, he has each of three people call any number up to ten. He brings out cards one by one, dropping them aside until he comes to the number given by the first party, this card is seen to have a red back and he stands it back outwards against a glass or displays it on an easel. He repeats the process with the second number called, that card proves to have a blue back, and lastly at the third number the card is a blue backed one.

The three persons are asked to call numbers again and bringing out cards accordingly the first card arrived at is blue. Continuing with the next two numbers the cards come out red and blue. Finally the six cards are turned faces outwards and they are seen to consist of three matched pairs.

METHOD:—The whole thing depends upon a mere arrangement of six cards, three taken from each deck. They are arranged 1, 2, 3; 1, 2, 3; red, blue, red, blue, red, blue. This packet is loaded into the hat secretly, ample opportunity for this is afforded while the two packs are being examined and shuffled by the audience.

TWO PERSON LOCATION

The pack used for this effect of pretended telepathy must be prearranged according to any system with which you and your assistant are familiar. Send your assistant out of the room. Give the deck a false shuffle and series of cuts and allow a spectator to make a free selection of one card. Casually cut the deck at the point from which the card was taken. Instructing him to concentrate his thoughts on his card, go to a second person and have him select any card. As you turn back to the first person secretly slip the card that was above the second chosen card to the bottom.

Have the first card pushed back into the deck at any point by the first spectator and square the deck perfectly. Do the same with the second person's card. The pack is taken to the assistant. All he has to do is to note the two bottom cards and take from the deck the two cards that follow these in the system and bring them into the room one in each hand.

Note. You can put the pack in an envelope and fasten the flap before sending the pack to your assistant. He has a duplicate envelope in his pocket. He simply tears the envelope open, takes out the pack notes the names of the two cards, writes them on the face of his duplicate envelope and puts the pack into it. He fastens the flap and returns to the room. The denouement follows.

DUAL SYMPATHY

Two packs are required one of which is set up according to any system for the whole deck that you many be familiar with.

By means of the usual equivoque force the unprepared pack on the spectator to shuffle while you false shuffle the setup deck. Change packs and instruct the spectator to do exactly as you do. Cut your pack several times. He does the same. Take off the top card, look at it, push it into the middle and square the pack. The spectator follows suit. Lift your deck and place it against his forehead, he puts his pack against your "aching brow" and in doing so gives you a flash of the bottom card. From this you know the card he looked at.

The packs are replaced on the table, cut, and the packs exchanged. The spectator takes his card out and puts it face down. You pretend to take out the card you looked at but really find the card that follows the one you sighted, according to the system. The cards are alike.

See also the section "Do as I do."

ANOTHER SYMPATHETIC MYSTERY

The effect is that the performer never approaches the spectator, yet he is able to pick out from his deck the duplicate of the card picked by the party himself.

You ask a spectator to hold a deck face down, cut it at any spot and note the card, then to replace the cut and square the deck. While he concentrates on his card, you run over the faces of your deck and finally take out one card. Spectator removes his card. The two cards are the same.

Two stacked decks, same system, are required. When the spectator cuts his pack, note the approximate position at which it is made. When the spectator replaces his cut, start running through your deck at a point as near as you can estimate that his cut was made, so you must come fairly close to the card selected. Because of the system of arrangement the suits rotate and the colors alternate, making the next part easier. You will have to ask a few leading questions as the person thinks of his card. You may say, for instance, "It's a red card, isn't it?" or, "You are thinking of a Heart, aren't you?" If the answer is "Yes," take the Heart nearest on either side, which includes a range of nine cards, and it is next to impossible that you would be that far wrong in making the location. With one query such as "High or low?," "Odd or even," "Spot or picture card?" you have the identity of the card fixed and take it out. Only one or two leads are necessary.

A QUAINT HAPPENING

Two decks of cards are provided. A spectator takes one and you take the other. Spectator shuffles his deck, cuts and notes the card cut at. You simply ask the value of the noted card and count off that many cards. The card at that number in your deck proves to be a duplicate of the one noted by the spectator in his deck which you have not even touched.

Both decks have to be arranged. In deck No. 1 take out all the Clubs and Hearts and assemble the deck thus: 6 indifferent cards, 13 H's and C's, in any order, 13 indifferent cards, 13 H's and C's, 7 indifferent cards. Put the deck back in its case.

Deck No. 2: Take the H's and the C's and arrange them from the ace to the King in sequence. Face the remainder of the cards and put the H's on one side, the C's on the other, replace this pack in its case also and remember on which side the suits are.

Show the two packs and have the spectator hand you one. If he gives you No. 2, let him take No. 1. If he selects No. 1, remove it from its case and give it to him. Tell him to cut the deck and riffle the halves together which will bring all the H's and C's to the middle of the pack. When he cuts about the middle he must get a H or a C. One question, "You are thinking of a red card," and the answer gives you all the information you need. You know how to remove your pack from its case so that the proper side is uppermost. Ask the spectator to tell you the value of his card. Suppose he says "Five." Count off the cards from the top of your deck and hold the fifth card face down. He names the card he looked at in his deck and you turn over the card you hold.

$1,000 TEST CARD LOCATION

You hand a deck of cards to a spectator and ask him to mix them well. He is then to square them up, make one complete cut, look at the top card of the deck and push this card into the pack so that it is lost. The deck is put on your outstretched hand and you name the selected card.

The method is not absolutely sure-fire but if it fails you repeat and it has never failed on the second trial so far. The deck is prearranged in the system you prefer. When you hand it to be shuffled and as soon as the spectator begins to shuffle say, "When you have them mixed, square the cards up on your left hand. Ready?" This is an innocent way of hurrying him and cutting the shuffle short. He cuts, completes the cut, looks at the top card and thrusts it into the pack.

What has happened is this, the complete chain of the stacked sequence has been broken but there are now a number of packets of cards that are still stacked and the shorter the shuffle the more cards there will be in each bunch. After the cut, which the chances are will be made in one of these bunches, you have simply to sight the bottom card and name the card that follows it in the sequence of the system.

You will be correct at least 80 per cent of the time but if it fails hand the pack back and try again. The odds are very big against a second failure.

SEEING WITH THE FINGER TIPS

NO. 1. *LIP READING TEST*

The deck in use must be a prearranged one, a switch being made with the ordinary deck of similar backs.

Allow a spectator to make a free selection of one card from the set up deck. Cut the deck and sight the bottom card. Proceed to name the chosen card from it by pretended lip-reading with the tips of the fingers. Patter about the facility with which deaf people, by simply placing their finger tips to a person's lips, can understand what is being said and continue with: "Please whisper softly under your breath the name of your card and I will attempt to tell what you are saying by feeling your lips." Place your finger tips to his lips and name the card.

NO. 2. *HERE'S YOUR CARD*

Continue with the same deck after making a false shuffle or at least several cuts. Invite someone to call the name of any card. Point out that no one can possibly know just where it lies in the pack. Glimpse the top and bottom cards and calculate its exact position by the system. Have someone blindfold you. Take the cards off the pack one by one pretending to read the index of each with your finger tips. When you reach the card announce it dramatically.

NO. 3 *THE MASTER'S TOUCH*

In gathering up the cards after the last trick, reset the deck and continue as follows:

After false shuffling the deck and having it cut several times with complete cuts, borrow an envelope and hand it with a pencil and a pad to a spectator. Approach another person, fan the deck behind your back and ask him to take out a group of cards, half a dozen or so in a bunch. Say, "Don't look at them yet, just have them put in the envelope without even counting them and seal the envelope." While this is being done, cut the cards so that the card just above the packet removed becomes the bottom card of the pack. This bottom card indicates where you are to start when naming the cards in the envelope, while the top card gives the clue for the card to stop it.

Have someone genuinely blindfold you this time since all the information necessary has already been acquired. Touch the envelope with your finger tips and ask the spectator holding the pad and pencil to be ready to jot down the names of the cards as you call them. When you call the last card ask how many you have named, say it is six. Pretend to weigh the envelope carefully and then declare the number is right.

Have the cards taken out, their names called and verified.

PERFECT CARD DIVINATION

The effect is that a spectator simply thinks of a card. He does not touch a card or write anything. The performer gets the very card thought of.

The deck is prearranged thus in groups of 6 and 7 cards:

AH.	7C.	5S.	JD.	9D.	3D.	
JH.	10C.	2S.	6S.	7D.	3C.	
6C.	4C.	7H.	5D.	6D.	QD.	
9H.	8S.	10S.	JC.	10D.	QS.	
6H.	2H.	8D.	5C.	5H.	AD.	KD.
9C.	2D.	8C.	JS.	KS.	AC.	4S.
QC.	9S.	QH.	KC.	3H.	2C.	3S.
8H.	KH.	4H.	7S.	4D.	AS.	10H.

In order to assist the spectator in making a mental picture of his card, take off the first group of six, show them and ask spectator to say "Yes" or "No," if he sees a card of the same value as his card. Do the same with the following three sets of six cards . Each of these groups has a value, 1 2 4 and 8. Add the value every time he says "Yes." Jack is 11, Queen 12 and if he says "No" four times his card must be a King.

The next four groups of seven cards are to determine the suit. They represent Spades, Hearts, Diamonds and Clubs. When he says "No" to a group then the suit that group represents is the suit of his card.

You don't look at the faces of any cards, just drop them aside after being looked at by the spectator. By switching the deck you can introduce the feat at any time.

UNIQUE TELEPHONE TEST

A spectator just thinks of a friend and mentally recalls his telephone number and name. In order to have several persons concentrate have him write it down and show it to them. From a shuffled deck placed in his pocket, the performer removes cards one at a time, placing certain cards aside face down. Spectator calls the phone number and the cards are turned one by one revealing it. Performer then announces the name.

The shuffled deck is switched for a prearranged deck by means of the pocket switch or by any other method you prefer while the phone number and name are obtained by using Baker's note book, or Annemann's Mental Masterpiece, or any other means at your disposal.

Knowing the number, you have simply to take the cards off the set up deck in your pocket and each time a card of the required number is reached lay it aside face down. By starting a new heap each time a card is reached the deck can be kept in order for other tricks with the arranged deck.

The name you simply pretend to get by telepathy.

PSYCHOLOGICAL DISCERNMENT

EFFECT:—Any card thought of revealed. A shuffled pack placed in performer's pocket, the cards brought out one by one, stopping on the card thought of.

METHOD:—Having divined the name of a thought of card by the method explained in "Perfect Card Divination," or in any other way at your disposal, switch the deck for a prearranged pack in putting it in your coat pocket. Then bring the cards out one by one and stop dramatically when you have the right card in your hand.

ANOTHER IMPOSSIBILITY

Two packs are required. In one, which we will call A, the top 10 cards are arranged in the Si Stebbins order as follows:

AD, 4C, 7H, 10S, KD, 3C, 6H, 9S, QD, 2C.

From pack B remove the corresponding 10 cards and place them at intervals of five cards throughout the deck. Thus the AD's will be the 5th card, 4C's the 10th card and so on. Put this pack on your table, hidden by a handkerchief.

Thus prepared, show pack A and spread the faces showing them all different, then execute the overhand jog shuffle, followed by a riffle shuffle and several false cuts, keeping the top 10 cards intact. Fan out the top ten cards widely and ask a spectator to mentally select a card. This done hand him the pack and let him shuffle it thoroughly. Take pack and apparently put it on table as you pick up the handkerchief, really dropping it into a well and bringing the prepared pack to light, or use any other switch you may prefer.

Have the handkerchief folded and tied over your eyes. Take the cards off the pack in batches of 5 and show the faces to the spectator, repeating to yourself the name of the special card in each set of five. When finally the spectator sees his card and removes it you know its name and you can name it in the usual hesitating way, as if the mental impressions were coming through by degrees.

COUNT THE CUT

The deck is arranged in the Si Stebbins order. In the right hand upper vest pocket place 8 cards of any suits from a pack with backs of the same pattern as the stacked deck, as follows: A, 2, 4, 8, K, 3, 10, K.

To begin, execute a false shuffle and have the pack cut several times with complete cuts. Finally ask a spectator to cut off a packet and put the cards in his pocket, doing it in such a way that no one can even make a rough estimate of the number of card taken. Pick up the lower part of the cut and, in putting it in your inside coat pocket you easily sight the bottom and top cards from which you calculate just how many cards were cut.

Announce that you will draw out cards haphazardly whose total spot values will indicate the number of cards cut. The cards you produce come from your vest pocket and with these you can make any total that is necessary. It is only necessary to remember the order in which they stand in your pocket.

A DISCARD TRICK

This trick is designed to follow the "Count the Cut" trick just explained.

Have the extra cards used for showing the total, in your left hand and with that hand remove the cards from your breast pocket leaving the extra ones behind. Put the deck together in its arranged order. Cut the pack, then have a spectator cut about one-third of the deck, note the next card, place it on the cut off portion and bury there by placing on it about half the remainder of the pack. He notes the next card also, putting it on top and the rest of pack on top of all.

Instruct him to deal 7 heaps, face down, a card at a time. Next to reassemble the pack by putting the last heap on the next to the left, these two on the next and so on. There will be three cards left over, glimpse the bottom one, it is the card that originally lay over the first card the spectator noted. That gives you the first card. To find the second card have him deal the deck into 6 heaps in the same way as before. There will be one card left over, sight it and since it is the card that originally lay below the second selected card, you are now able to reveal the cards as you please.

CREMO CARD RESTORATION

The trick depends on a subtle method of forcing a card. A duplicate card is required, suppose it is a 9D. Arrange the bottom 18 cards in the manner following, X representing an indifferent card, and D. any indifferent Diamond:

D, X, X, X, D, X, X, X D, X, X, 9D, X, 9C, X, 9H, X,X.
Place the duplicate 9D near the top of the pack.

Begin by making a false shuffle not disturbing the stacked cards. Hand the deck to a spectator, telling him to think of a number from 10 to 52 and then cut the pack into two piles. Force the selection of the packet that formed the bottom of the pack and have him count it, thereby reversing the order of the cards. On the pretense that his packet may not have a sufficient number of cards have him transfer four cards at random from the other packet to the top of the packet he has chosen. The choice of the packet, the counting and this transfer of cards makes it seem impossible there could be any prearrangement. Ask him now to name the number he has mentally selected. When he names it calculate the number of letters in its spelling.

If it is an odd number instruct him to deal a card for each letter, look at the card at the last letter and remember it value, then repeat the spelling and note the last letter card as the suit. If it spells with an even number of letters tell him to turn the next card. This process it will be seen, from the formula above, infallibly forces the 9D. Instruct him then to shuffle the whole deck and deal face up until he comes to the card, the 9D, then to put the pack in his pocket, tear the card into small pieces and hand them to you. Wrap them in a piece of tissue paper, vanish them by palming or switching for a packet of flash paper which you touch off with a lighted cigarette. He takes the pack from his pocket and in it he finds the 9D restored.

STRANGE COINCIDENCE

Arrange an ordinary deck thus:—any 4 court cards, 4 fives, 4 nines, 4 eights, 4 sevens, 4 sixes, 4 aces, 4 twos, 4 threes, 4 fours, 4 court cards, 4 tens, 4 court cards.

Ask two spectators to call two numbers, the first to name a number between 10 and 25. If it is divisible by 4 tell the second person to name a number between 12 and 17; if, however, there is a remainder of 1 after such division give him 13 and 18; if a remainder of 2, give him 14 and 19; if one of 3 give him 15 and 20. By this ruse no matter what number the first party chooses, the spots on the card there plus those on the card at the second person's number invariably total 10. Deal down to the numbers called and put the cards aside face down. Replace the dealt cards on the top and ask a third person to call any number over 4. If his number is 5, 6, 7, or 8 you have ten at each of them by dealing from the bottom. If he gives a larger number than 8, simply draw back one of the tens until the number is reached. Place the ten face up alongside the other two cards. Turn them over and show that the combined spots also total 10.

When drawing the cards from the bottom, deal them face down if you have to go beyond the first ten.

PREMIER BOOK TEST

Some preparation is necessary. First remove two aces, then set up all the other cards, regardless of suits, so that any two cards taken together from anywhere in the pack will have values totaling 14 or 15. For example—7, 8, 6, 9, 5, 10, 4, J, 3, Q, 2, K, A, K, and so on. The pack of course, can be cut indefinitely without upsetting the arrangement. Put the pack in its case with the two aces on the top. Open the book to be used in the experiment at pages 14-15. On the inside front cover of a small, end-opening note book write in two columns the first 13 words from pages 14 and 15, and put the book in your pocket.

To present the feat, remove the cards from the case and leave the two aces inside. Place the deck down beside the book and ask a spectator to step up. Ask him to cut the deck several times, then cut again, take the two cards cut at, and take them and the book to a far corner. Tell him to add the values of the two cards and open the book at the corresponding page.

Invite a second person to take the deck, thoroughly shuffle it, spread the cards face down on the table and turn up any one he wishes. He calls out the value of the card to the man with the book who is told to count to the word at that number on the selected page and memorize the word. You know the page as soon as he begins counting, the even numbered page being always on the left, odd on the right. Take out your notebook and a glance at the inside cover as you open it gives you the word. Write it on the first page, tear this out, fold it and give it to the second spectator to hold. The first man calls the word and the second man reads your writing.

BETWEEN THE LINES

This is considered to be one of the cleverest book tests with a pack of cards ever devised. It is simple yet effective.

An ordinary book novel is used, plus a pack of cards stacked in the Si Stebbins order of Ace, 4, 7, 10, K, 3, 6, 9, Q, 2, 5, 8, J, A, 4, 7 etc; with suits rotating.

Start by giving the deck a false shuffle or several straight cuts. Put the deck on the table with the book and walk away. While your back is turned you direct spectator. Tell him to give the deck a complete cut. Then say, "Better give it another." Continue, "Now hold the deck in your hand and deal three cards in a face up row from left to right from the top of the deck. These cards are going to indicate a page and word in the book. By the way, are there any picture cards among the three?"

If the spectator says, "YES," you say, "They're too confusing. Push those three cards away and deal three more the same way. Are there any picture cards there now?" Suppose he says "No."

You go on, "Look at the first two cards. If they are a six and a seven, open the book to page 67. If they are a five and a two, open the book to page 52."

"You have it? Now look at that last or third card. I want you to start at the top of the page you have and count across on the top line to the word at that number. If it is a 3, count to the third word. If an eight, count to the eighth word.

Now turn the cards on the table face down so I can't see them, and keep your finger on the word you have located." At this point you turn around, and proceed to reveal the word.

This effect can be gotten only through the use of a Si Stebbins' stack and no other. There are only four possible combinations of three cards without pictures A-4-7, 4-7-10, 2-5-8, 3-6-9.

Therefore you previously have looked up and memorized four words, the seventh word on page 14, the eighth word on page 25, the ninth word on page 36, the tenth word on page 47. A good method is to write the words on the left thumb nail. Two of these page numbers are even and two are odd. When you turn around and note spectator holding book with his finger on a word, you know it is an odd or even page because all even numbered pages of all books are on the left and all odd numbered pages of all books are on the right when book is opened before you. Therefore you are immediately down to two words. Start by giving the first letter of one of the two words. If right, continue. If wrong, say "Well, the last letter is ....." And you name the last letter of the OTHER word, and spell out the word backwards. When ever a spectator deals three times on table and has a picture card each time, the fourth or next deal of three will always be A-4-7. In such a case you don't even have to turn around, but can name the word immediately. If you get used to a book you can also judge which of the two words it is as the odd numbers are 22 pages apart and the evens 22 pages apart too. A book of 60 to 80 pages will be found perfect for this effect.

FATHOMED THOUGHT

EFFECT:—A spectator cuts off a portion of the deck and takes the next three cards for himself. He adds the values of these cards and opens a book at the page of the same number as the total arrived at. He notes the value of the highest card of the three and counts to the word at that number from the top of the page. The performer announces that very word.

METHOD:—Stack the deck in the Si Stebbins order. There are only 13 possible combinations of the values of three consecutive cards as shown by the following table. The card represents the card above the three removed by the spectator after he cuts, and you sight this as you assemble the deck following the cut.

Card	Page	Word	Card	Page	Word
Ace.	21.	10.	Eight.	16.	11.
Two.	24.	11.	Nine.	18.	12.
Three	27.	12.	Ten.	22.	13.
Four.	30.	13.	Jack.	12.	7.
Five.	20.	11.	Queen.	15.	8.'
Six.	23.	12.	King.	18.	9.
Seven.	26.	13.			

Use a small pad about 3 inches by 5. Along the top edge write as small as possible the 13 values and the words which you have taken from the book to be used. When the spectator cuts the deck and removes three cards, reassemble the deck and sight the bottom card. Take out the pad and pencil and note the word in the list. As soon as the page and the word have been found, write it on the lower half of the top sheet of pad, tear off the half sheet, fold it and give it to be held by a second spectator. Have the word read aloud by the first spectator, then the second man opens your slip and reads the same word.

WINNING THE CUT

Arrange a pack in two packets each containing 2 Aces, 2 twos, 2 threes, 2 fours, and so on, up to 2 Kings.

To begin, false shuffle and alse cut, then cut the pack at the 2 Kings which you can easily spot since you pretend to be anxious to cut the deck as near as possible into two equal portions. Have a spectator choose one heap, you take the other. Tell him to shuffle his packet while you shuffle yours, falsely of course.

The packets are placed on the table and you invite the spectator to cut and show the card cut at. Seeing this card, and knowing the arrangement of your cards, you can with a little judgment always cut a higher card than his.   Contrive if you can to beat him by one spot, or if he cuts an ace, you also cut an ace.

Finish by exchanging packs, each shuffling again.   In shuffling locate and Ace and hold a break, or jog a card.   You both cut once more and again you win.   Cards can now be examined and nothing suspicious can be found.

WIZARD'S WILL

Prearrange a pack of cards in any order that you are thoroughly familiar with.   False shuffle if you can, if not have a spectator cut as often as he pleases, each time completing the cut.   In taking the pack sight the bottom card, from which you know the top card.   Deal the cards face down in rows of irregular length, remembering the first card and, by going through the formula as you deal, memorize also the first card of each row.

Now name any card you please and tell the spectator that you will make him select that very card.   Invite him to touch a card.   Whatever card he touches you know what it is by its position in the arrangement. Pick up the card and lay it aside, not looking at it nor letting any one else see what it is.   Have him touch another card as you name the one just put aside.   Continue for three or four cards in just the same way, but if by chance the spectator happens to touch the card you called first, stop right there, turn the cards over and show that he has picked out the very cards you called for.

If, however, he does not touch that card, you do so yourself, calling it whatever the last card may have been.   With this card scoop up the packet of cards laid aside, turn the cards face up and they will be in the exact order called.

CARD DIVINATION

Arrange the top 26 cards of any deck thus:—KC, 9C, 5H, 4D, 3S, 2C, 6C, 2S, 4H, JS, AS, 9H, QH, 6S, 7C, 10C, AH, AC, 10H, 4S, 7S, JD, QD, 8S, 5D, 8D.

False shuffle keeping top stack intact.   Hand pack to spectator and instruct him to lift off about half the cards and return whichever portion he wishes.   If top half is returned, fan the cards for him to make a mental choice of one card.   If the lower half is returned use it to show spectator how he must fan his packet in order to mentally choose a card.   Selection is always from top packet.

Replace arranged packet on top and shuffle thus; under cut about one-third of cards, injog first card and shuffle on top. Under cut to injog, run seven cards, injog eighth and throw balance on top. Square up making break below jogged card. Cut the pack at break and put the packets on the palms of spectator's outstretched hands. For discription of in-jog see chapter on "Indispensible Sleights."

Ask spectator to name his card. The instant the card is named you are able to give instructions for him to find it in the most convincing way. There are 26 possible selections and each one is located in a different manner. A careful study of the table below and a few trials will show the simplicity of the proceedings.

Always place the top half on the spectator's left hand. The bottom card of this packet is 2S, top card 4H. Top card of the other heap 6C, and bottom card an indifferent one not used. These three cards are indicators to locate card spectator selects, except in case of a few which are spelled out. If either of these happens to be taken you force the heap and reveal it. For the 23 other cards proceed thus:

Seventeen cards are on spectator's left hand, they will be referred to as the right hand heap since they are on your right hand, the other 6 are on top of the other cards, call it the left hand pile.

Right hand heap. To locate card:—
JS.   Show the 2 spot on bottom of R. heap, count down 2.
KS.   do as above, but turn the next card.
9H.   Show 4 spot on R. heap, count down 4.
QH.   same, but show the next card.
6S.   Show 6 spot on top L. heap, count down 6.
7C.   do the same, but show next card.
10C.   Spell out TEN CLUBS.
AH.   Spell out ACE HEARTS.

The remaining cards of this heap spell out either on the final "S," or by turning the next card. For the last 3 spell THE.

Left hand heap. To locate card:—
2C.   Show 2 spot at bottom of R. heap, count down two.
3C.   do the same, but show next card.
4D.   Show 4 spot of R. heap, count down four.
5H.   do the same, but show the next card.
9C.   Show 6 spot top of L. heap, count down 6.
KC.   do the same, but turn next card.

The list is simple in practice. Do not attempt to memorize it, simply use it as a guide until the various combinations have become familiar. It is very effective to have two cards thought of by different persons and locate both at the same time, very often the spots on one card will locate the other.

DOUBLE DIVINO

Use two decks which have similar back patterns. From each you discard the same two cards of the same value, suit and color, as for instance, the 2S and the 2C. Shuffle one deck and then place the cards of the second pack in exactly the same order. Put the two together making one large pack of 100 cards. If you can false shuffle and false cut this enlarged pack it will strengthen the effect, but in any case a series of straight cuts should be made. Next deal the cards into four face down piles, one card at a time with the fifth card falling on No. 1; the sixth on No. 2; and so on until there are four piles of 25 cards each. Let the spectator choose a heap; if he takes No. 1, you pick up No. 3 and vice versa.

The same rules will then apply as in the preceding version but in this case you can actually produce the same card. After working one of the effects with two packets, put them aside and let the spectator take one of the remaining two, while you take the other. Place your packet behind your back and cut it to bring the cards in the exact order of the spectator's packet. Instruct him to lay his cards out in a face down row and then to push forward any two or three cards he pleases. From your packet, behind your back, you bring forward the same two cards placing them opposite the spectators cards. Each pair is then turned up and prove to be the same cards.

THE MISSING PAIR

For this a new unopened deck of Bicycle cards must be used. These come packed with the Joker at the face, followed by the court cards, then clubs, hearts, diamonds and spades. Open the case, take out the cards, discard the Joker and false shuffle. If you cannot do that, then make a series of quick cuts. Hand the pack to spectator who also cuts (complete cuts) as often as he pleases. Instruct him then to deal the cards into four face down piles, to choose one and shuffle it. Tell him to examine it and if it happens to contain any two spot cards of the same value, to pocket them, if not to take any one of the other packets until he finds a pair. This last is a bit of misdirection, there are pairs in every pile.

Pick up the pile from which he has removed a pair and note the clubs left, from these you at once know the value of the club taken and therefore the card taken with it. After the cards are dealt into piles, the A, 5, and 9 of C and D, will always be in one heap, the 2, 6, 10, in another, the 3, 7, in a third and the 4, 8, in the fourth. The C and D are the only spot cards that can be paired by the deal.

Note. Better run through the cards and see that the cards are stacked in the order given.

PREMIER CARD DISCOVERY

Arrange the pack beforehand thus, counting from the top: 14 odd cards, 12 even, 14 odd and the last 12 even cards. Count the Q's as even cards and the J's and K's odd, discard the Joker, and mix the suits in any order. Spread the cards and no set order will be noticeable. Invite a spectator to cut about the middle and riffle shuffle. Tell him to shuffle so that everyone can see it is thorough (the more evenly the cards fall the better). The central part of the upper half of the deck will consist of odd cards only and the central portion of the lower half will be made up of even cards.

Invite the spectator to divide the pack into two heaps about even, take one card from the center of either heap, note what it is and place it in the middle of the other heap. The cards are dealt face up and you simply have to watch for an odd card in a series of even cards, or an even card in a run of odd ones. Having spotted the card you can reveal it as you please.

LOCATION

During the course of other tricks an opportunity can easily be found to get four cards of the same value to the top. Say, for instance, you have gotten the four Jacks to that position. Riffle shuffle, leaving them there and have the pack cut. Complete the cut but keep the tip of your little finger between the two portions. Spread the pack, keeping the four Jacks in the most prominent position, and force one of them. Let it be replaced in another part of the deck, square it up and have the spectator shuffle. On running through the deck you find the Jack that is by itself and reveal the card in any way you please.

With the same set up you can allow any card to be drawn, then dividing the pack between the four Jacks have the card replaced at that point. Shuffle the cards yourself so that you do not disturb the middle cards and let the spectator cut as often as he wishes. You can locate the card at will.

A SIMPLE LOCATION

The necessary prearrangement in this case is very simple. Have all 13 cards of one suit together in the middle. Have a card selected from either the upper or the lower portion of the deck, and see that it is replaced amongst the center 13 cards of the one suit. The pack may be cut with complete cuts as often as desired, and you have only to run through the deck to find the odd card amongst the 13.

This can just as easily be worked by having a card drawn from amongst the arranged 13, and replaced amongst the other cards either above or below. After the cutting you have only to look for the single card of the set suit, or run through the remaining 12 to see which is missing.

OUT OF SIGHT

The deck used must be pre-arranged according to a system with which you are familiar. False shuffle and false cut, or if unable to do that, simply have the deck cut as often as desired, completing the cut each time. Turn your back and, holding the cards behind you, allow a spectator to remove one as you push the cards from the left hand to the right. Split the deck at the point at which the card is taken and, turning slightly towards the spectator say, "Please look at the card but give me no chance of seeing it." This action will take the cards behind your back momentarily out of range of the spectator's vision and you push off into the right hand the card that was above the chosen card, that is, the lowest of the cards now in your right hand.

As you again turn your back squarely to the spectator, bring your right hand in front of your body. A glance at the palmed card will tell you the name of the selected card, it being the next in the order. You may drop the palmed card into a vest pocket or add it to the top of the pack in taking the cards from your left hand. Take back the chosen card and slip it under the top card, the pack will again be in the set order ready for further tricks depending upon it.

PROPHESIED DISCOVERY

Beforehand separate the red and black suits of a deck. Sort 15 red cards in the following groups from the face towards the back:

10; 9, A; 3, A, 6; 4, K, 2, 4; J, 2, 5, Q, 3.

Ignoring the court cards, the spot cards in each group add to 10. Note the tenth card from the face of the packet of black cards, say it is the AC, and write that on a slip of paper. Place the two packets together and you are ready.

Show the slip with the prediction and put it face down on the table. Cut the pack at the color division and riffle shuffle very openly. Hand the pack to a spectator asking him to sort out the black cards from the red. He will naturally do this holding the pack face up and dealing the cards also face up, thus when the sorting is completed and the packets are turned face down, the AC will be the tenth card of the black pile; and the first

15 cards of the red pile will consist of the arranged cards. Let the spectator choose either heap. If he chooses the black, hand it to him to hold; if he takes the red, pick it up and deal one card by itself, then separate piles of two, three, four and five cards. Now have him choose any heap and add the values of the spot cards. Due to the pre-arrangement, he must arrive at 10. On dealing to that number from the top of the black pile he turns up the AC, which conforms with the prediction previously written on the slip you put on the table.

FROM ANOTHER PACK

Two pack are necessary. Pre-arrange one pack in four series of 13 cards running from the Ace to the King from the bottom upwards, without regard to suits. From the second pack take the four Kings, arrange them in order C. H. S. D., and put them in your right hand outside pocket. Thus prepared hand the ordinary deck to a spectator to shuffle while you false shuffle the arranged deck. Both decks are then placed on the table side by side and the spectator selects one. Interpret his choice so that he gets the arranged deck. The other is laid aside. Instruct the spectator that while your back is turned he is to cut the deck and complete the cut; then cut off a packet and turn it face up on the table, note the card on its face, take the remainder of the pack and deal cards face down on the table to the number denoted by its value and note that card. He is to count a J as 11, a Q as 12 and a K as 13. Thus if he cuts a 3, he must deal 3 cards, if a Q 12 cards and so on. This done his count will always end on a K. You will have to get the color and suit by leading questions, having these, you name the card in full. Have the other pack shuffled and then drop it into your pocket joining the 4 Kings. Knowing the order in which these are you can produce the right one instantly.

DIVINO

From any full pack of cards throw out two of the same color and value but of differing suits, say for instance the 6D and 6H. Put these aside, 50 cards only being used in the trick. Sort these into their suits in any order, and then place the Clubs and the Hearts together in one packet and shuffle them thoroughly. Spread the cards face up on the table and sort the Spades and the Diamonds into exactly the same order as the C-H packet and put the packets together.

To present the trick, let the spectators cut the deck as often as they please but see that each cut is completed. Then have a spectator deal the cards into two face down piles, a card at a time in each packet, and select either heap. If he takes the heap on the first card dealt, cut the other heap which you pick up at the 13th card and place these at the bottom. The cards of the same value and the same color will now lie in exactly the same order in each packet, that is, if the 6D is the top card of your packet, then the 6H is the top card of the spectator's pile. If, however, he takes the No. 2 packet you must cut off 12 cards and put them at the bottom of your pile to attain the same result. When the spectator names any number between 1 and 25 and looks at that card in his packet you have merely to look at the card occupying the same number in your packet and you instantly know the card he's looking at. (His card will be the same value and color but the other suit.) You can now reveal it in various ways, such as:

1. The spectator having called a number and noted his card, find the matching card and note it secretly. Have both packets shuffled, put together and the deck placed in your pocket. Draw the cards out one at a time until you reach the selected card, throw it face down on the table, have card named and turn it over.

2. After the number is called turn away and find the card in your packet. You may then reveal it simply as a mental feat.

3. A number having been called by the spectator and your packet cut to bring both in sequence, both deal cards face down in unison and stop at the chosen number . . . the cards are the same value and color.

4. The packet may also be left in the same order as dealt. In that case a very simple calculation will determine at what number the card he calls will lie in your packet, since you know that the 14th card of your packet will be of the same color and suit; if he chose the other packet your 13th card will match the top card of his packet. When he has found the card at the number he called, deal cards face up from your packet to show they are well mixed, until you have passed several cards beyond the matching card. Gather them up and name his card in any dramatic way you please.

5. Having sighted the matching card, have the two packets put together and the whole deck shuffled by the spectator. Afterwards run over the faces towards him to prove that the card is still in the deck, and so regain control of it, producing it as you desire.

If the spectator keeps his cards in the same order when counting to the number he chooses the trick can be repeated.

The value of this trick and all others depending on a set up is greatly enhanced if the deck which has been in use for several tricks, and which has been freely handled and shuffled by the spectators, is switched for the arranged deck.

WILLIAMS' CARD TRICK

Beforehand arrange a deck of cards so that every second card from the top is a Heart, thus; the second card, the fourth card, the sixth card and so on are all Hearts, running from the Ace up to the Ten. In your right hand coat pocket have a set of duplicate Heart cards in the same order. Ask a spectator to call a number between 1 and 21. If it is an even number ask him to count down and look at the card at that number, but if an odd number is called, tell him to deal to that number and look at the next card, and then shuffle the pack. In the meantime, standing at ease with both hands in your trousers pockets, you have ample time to count to the duplicate of the chosen card and palm it in your right hand.

Throw your handkerchief over your right hand, take the pack back in your left hand and lay it on the handkerchief just over the palmed card. Turn your hand so that the pack is upright and facing the front. Fold the back of the handkerchief over to the front, then fold it back on both sides of the pack so that the card at the back is securely held. Grasp the fabric by the four corners and the folds, letting the pack hang down in the improvised bag. With a little shaking the card will be freed from the folds and gradually appear, seeming to come through the fabric.

RED OR BLACK

For this trick it is best to use a new pack of Bicycle cards, preferably of the air cushion finish, with white border. Sort out the black and the red cards. Place a red card and a black card back to back and continue this arrangement with all of the cards, so that all the black cards are face upwards and the red cards face downwards. Show the pack fanned, it will appear to consist of all black cards, the backs of the red cards will not show, partly owing to the white borders and partly because the backs tend to stick together and do not slip as perfectly as the face surfaces.

Square the deck, covering the cards with the right hand and holding the face card only with it. Now drop the left hand about an inch carrying with it the rest of the cards, and slip the tip of the left thumb under the outer side of the pack and rapidly turn it over sideways. Take off the face card with the right hand, blow on it and put it on the bottom. Again spread the deck, this time the red cards only will show.

EXCELLO CARD DISCOVERY

Sort out the pack into its four suits, the cards in haphazard order, making one pile for each suit. Assemble the deck by picking one card from each packet in rotation. When you present the trick make a false shuffle and cuts if possible, if not, make a series of straight cuts. Have a card freely selected but keep the two parts of the pack separated at that point. Push four cards from the top of the bottom portion over to the right and hold the division at that point. Divide the pack here for the return of the chosen card. It will be, therefore, four cards lower in the deck than it was originally.

Let the spectator make as many complete cuts as he likes. To find the card, run over the faces and when you come to two cards of the same suit together, the one nearest the face of the deck will be the card. You can bring it to the top or bottom by cutting and then deal with it as you please.

NAMING CHOSEN CARD

Beforehand place all the even cards at the bottom of the pack, counting the Queens as even cards, Jacks and Kings as odd. Memorize the bottom card. You give a spectator the following instructions—he is to cut about one-third of the pack, note the card at the bottom of the cards so cut, riffle shuffle the cut cards into the remainder of the deck and then cut the deck with complete cuts several times.

When you return you have merely to run through the pack face up and find the card which is the first odd card above your key card, that is the original bottom card of the pack.

PSYCHIC CARD TEST

Two slates, two pieces of chalk and a stacked deck is required for this trick.

False shuffle and cut the deck if you can, if not simply make a series of quick cuts with the pack in your hands in position for shuffling. Spread the deck on the table in as long a row as you can manage. Have a spectator draw a card from the line and note the spot it is taken from. Tell him to take one of the slates and piece of chalk, go to a distant part of the room and draw a rough picture of his card. In the meantime you have casually picked up the cards, first the part of the row above the spot from which he took a card and then gathered up the rest using these as a scoop. A glimpse of the bottom card allows you to calculate what card the spectator took. Place the pack aside, pick up the other slate and also draw a rough picture of that card. The whole effect depends upon the presentation.

A CARD AND A NUMBER

Two packs are required and both must be arranged in the same order such as the Si Stebbins or the "Eight Kings, etc." Have both packs in their cases and allow a free choice of either. Hand the chosen pack to a spectator to place in his pocket. Ask another person to call any number from 1 to 52. Suppose 23 is called. Break the pack as near to that number as you can estimate, a glance at the bottom card at the break will at once give you the position of the 23rd card. You will rarely be more than 2 or

3 cards away from it. Proceed to force this 23rd card on a second spectator.

You announce that you will show a strange effect of sympathy between the two packs, by making the same card as that chosen to locate itself at the very number called in the pack which was placed in a spectator's pocket before the number was called. The spectator takes the pack from his pocket, counts down to the number called and finds there the duplicate of the chosen card.

The trick is very effective and the ideal system to use for it is Nicola's for two reasons, the cards are known by their numbers in the pack and the deck can be shown and handled freely since the cards are not in any recognizable order, that is to the layman.

MEDIUMISTIC STUNT NO. 1

Pack is handed to a spectator with a request to turn his back and cut wherever he pleases. He is then to deal as many cards as he pleases, stopping at any card whatsoever; he is to look at this card and note what it is, then put it face down on the table and deal four cards on it. These five cards he mixes together and then hands them to you.

To find the card you look for two cards of the same suit amongst the five and name the higher one. The pack has been set up in the Si Stebbins order, each card being three points higher than the preceding one and the suits being in rotation. The result given must follow.

MEDIUMISTIC NO. 2

The deck is set up in the Si Stebbins order. Make a false shuffle and execute several false cuts. Invite a spectator to take out a bunch of cards, all at once, from any part of the pack. He is now to take one and lay the rest aside. This card is sealed in the innermost of a nest of three envelopes which you hand to him. While this is being done you reassemble the pack by placing the remainder of the spectator's bunch of cards on the pack, which you had cut at the point at which he remvoed them. A glance at these will tell you what card is missing from the sequence.

Go to a second spectator and have him draw a card. By cutting at the point from which it was drawn and sighting the bottom card of the upper packet you know the card he holds and so proceed to read his mind. Replace his card on the top of the bottom packet and return to the first person. Let him place the nest of envelopes on your left hand and with the usual hesitation get the color, suit and value of his card.

Open the envelope, show the card and replace this card in its proper position—the deck will again be in order.

SYSTEM

Beforehand the pack is arranged in the "Eight Kings, etc." order, but each of the four suits is arranged separately. Put the pack in its case and hand it thus to a spectator when you are about to present the trick. Instruct him that he is to remove the pack from the case, cut it into two portions and riffle shuffle them carefully, once only, select one card from each heap and have their names noted. He is then to riffle shuffle the two packets together, square the pack and replace the two cards in it anywhere he pleases, either together or separately, and place the pack on the table. While this is being done you turn you back or leave the room. Be sure that the spectator thoroughly understands what he is to do.

When you turn around or re-enter the room, you take the pack, run over the faces of the cards and pick out the two chosen ones. You are enabled to do this infallibly because when the four suits are segregated the first riffle shuffle distributes the cards of each suit throughout half the pack in the same order and the second shuffle sends them throughout the pack still in the same order. Therefore if the intervening cards are removed each suit will be found in the original "Eight Kings, etc." order. To find the selected cards follow each suit through the deck, the two cards out of place will be the selected cards.

THE KNOCKOUT

EFFECT:—Two ordinary packs of cards are introduced and shuffled. One is temporarily placed upon the table, while the performer takes the other and has three cards freely selected by as many spectators, who immediately place the cards in their pockets without even looking at them. The performer's assistant is then introduced as the medium and is handed the other deck from the table. Without a word from anybody, she immediately locates the selected cards. The first deck is left in the hands of some disinterested party after the cards have been selected.

SECRET:—Two decks of cards with backs alike are essential. One deck is arranged in the well-known Si Stebbins style, or 8, K, 3, 10, 2, etc. —whichever is preferred. Come forward with the two decks and offer one to a spectator to shuffle, while you false shuffle the other (the prepared one). Place the deck that the spectator has shuffled on the table, in plain sight of all. Now for the under-handed business: Offer a card to be selected from your deck (the prepared one) in the same manner that you would in any other trick, but in closing the fan, slip out the card that was over the selected one, into the palm of the right hand. Then calmly place it on the top of the deck. This is the tell-tale card that furnishes the clue as to what the selected card is. The spectator places his card in his pocket without even looking at it, and particularly without letting those around him see it. Repeat these operations until you have three cards selected. Then you will have key cards on the pack. Step over to your table and pick up the other deck, placing the three key cards on it. You have previously palmed these off and given the deck to someone to hold. Hand the other deck to the medium and step into the audience without a word. The medium looks at the three top cards in running through the deck and figures back three cards according to the system, picking out the duplicates of those originally selected.

This effect should be played up strong, and the cards drawn out one by one with great "concentration." The wise ones will be fooled the most, for they are all looking for codes.

A PREARRANGED PACK OF CARDS THAT CAN BE SHUFFLED

Arrange your pack in the Si Stebbins order, then with the pack face up deal the first card face down and on top of this card place the next card and continue until you lay out 26 pairs. Now take each top card and trim it short and narrow. You now have the cards in pairs, assemble and you can now riffle shuffle pack with freedom. Each pair will fall separate. A card is removed while performer riffles the pack, by looking at the card below (long card) performer knows the value of the selected card, by adding 3 points and suit. Should the card be the 10 of clubs, the selected card must be the King of Hearts.

AMAZING MEMORY

To arrange a pack for this feat first sort out the cards of each suit, then take the Clubs and the Hearts and shuffle them thoroughly. Spread the cards and then sort the Spades and the Diamonds in exactly the same order with the Spades corresponding with Clubs set up and Diamonds with the Heart set up. Deal the Spades and Diamonds face down on the table, thus reversing their order, and then put the Club-Heart packet on top. Thus the top and bottom cards will be of the same color and value and, knowing one, you can at once name the other.

With a pack so arranged, execute a false shuffle and cut, and show the faces to prove the cards are well mixed. Next turn the faces towards you and run over the cards rather slowly pretending to memorize them. Offer the pack to a spectator asking him to make a free choice. Run the cards one by one counting them and note the number of the card chosen. Turn the pack and run over the cards from the bottom. To find the key to the card selected. For example: suppose the card drawn was the 16th from the top. You have merely to note the 16th card from the bottom to find the card of the same value as the other suit of the same color. Note the next card and continue running the cards until you reach the corresponding card of the same color, stop, call the name of the chosen card and have it returned at this location. The pack will then be in order for a repetition of the trick.

SIX PILES

For this trick you must make an impromptu set-up with 12 cards of any one suit, 6 at the top and 6 at the bottom. To do this run through the pack to take out the Joker and seize this opportunity to get several cards of one suit, say Hearts to the top and bottom of the deck. Remarking that you have also to eliminate four other cards, take out one card of the suit decided on, Hearts, and any three cards of other suits. The pretence of searching for special cards covers the placing of the remainder of the Hearts in the required positions. Lay the four discards and the Joker aside. Riffle shuffle without disturbing the 6 top and the 6 bottom cards. Hand the pack to a spectator telling him to deal 6 cards in a row and continue dealing one card at a time on these in rotation. The result is that each pile has a Heart at the top and bottom.

Instruct the spectator that, while your back is turned he is to take a card from the middle of any heap, note it, place it on top of any other heap and assemble the piles in any order he pleases. Finally he is to write the name of the card on a slip, fold it and put it on the table. Turn around and spread the pack face up on the table, run your hand over the line telling him to think "Stop" when you reach his card. Take a mental note of the card between two Hearts but do not stop. Gather the pack and lay it aside, then pretend to get the name of the card by putting your hand to his forehead. Name it in the usual piecemeal manner. The slip is opened and your mindreading is verified.

MEPHISTO'S MESSAGE

Beforehand arrange 16 cards of mixed suits on the top of the deck as follows: 3, 2, court card, 5; 2, court card, 5, 3; court card, 5, 3, 2; 5, 3, 2, court card. Note that these cards make up 4 groups of 4 cards the spots on which, counting court cards as 2, amount to 12. Count to the 12th card from the bottom and write its name on a slip of paper and seal it in an envelope.

Thus prepared, have a spectator cut the pack in half. Tell him to deal the cards in the lower packet face down and count them, and then snap a rubber band around them and put the packet in his pocket. Next instruct him to deal from the upper packet 4 hands of 4 cards each. It makes no difference whether he deals 4 cards at a time, or separately, but whichever method he adopts, remark that you meant him to deal the other way but let it go. Let him select any pile, and place his hand on it, while you pick up the other three and shuffle them back into the pack. The spectator counts the spots on the four chosen cards and gets the total 12. He then takes the packet from his pocket and counts down to the 12th card and finds we will suppose, the Ace of Clubs. On opening the envelope he finds this card named in your prediction.

NAME O' CARD

Prearrange the cards of a full deck with the Joker as follows—JC. 4S. AH. 4H. 3C. 8H. 10C. 5C. 9C. 9S. 9H. QC. QS. 6H. 5S. 5H. 7H. 6S. 3D. 6D. 5D, 9D. 8D. 3H. Joker. 2D. AS. 2S reversed. AD. 2H with an X on its face. 7D. 4D. 10D. 3S. QD. KD. JD. QH. KS. 10H. 7S. 7C. KC. JH. 10S. 2C. 6C. 8S. 8C. 4C. AC. JS. with an X on its back. KH.

With a pack in this order in hand, false shuffle and false cut, then ask someone to think of a card and then name it. Proceed to discover it either by spelling its name, and this applies to 42 cards, or in different ways applied to 10 special cards, these are:

JC. KH. 2S. AS. 2H. JS. JS. 2D. 2D. 3H and the Joker.

If one of them is called proceed as under:

JACK OF CLUBS. Snap the back of the deck ordering it to rise to the
   top. Show it.

KINK OF HEARTS. Same procedure cending card to bottom.

TWO OF SPADES. Reversed in the deck. Simply order it to do so.

ACE OF SPADES. This is the card above the reversed 2S. Order
   the card below it to reverse itself.

ACE OF DIAMONDS. Order card above it to reverse itself.

TWO OF HEARTS. Show that you have foretold the choice of this
   card by marking an X. on it.

JACK OF SPADES. Same as for 2H but mark is on the back.

TWO OF DIAMONDS. Order the Joker to locate the card.

THREE OF HEARTS. Same as for 2D.

THE JOKER. Take a card for each letter of the sentence, "You have
   called for the Joker" and turn next card.

DETAILED SPELLING TABLE FOR THE OTHER CARDS
Where an X appears turn the card after the last letter.

HEARTS

ACE. Spell "HEART" and hold the five cards face down and ask if
   "ACE" shall be spelt from top or bottom. Either fits.

TWO. THREE. See above.

FOUR. Spell "FOUR" remove the cards, snap on the back saying,
   "You want a Heart?" Show the 4H.

FIVE. Spell "THE FIVE OF HEARTS." X.
SIX. Spell "THE SIX OF HEARTS."
SEVEN. Spell "THE SEVEN OF HEARTS."
EIGHT. Spell "EIGHT" Take next card and say "HEART." Show it.
NINE. Spell "NINE HEARTS." X.
TEN. Spell "THE TEN OF HEARTS" from the bottom of pack.
JACK. Spell "JACK HEARTS" from the bottom.
QUEEN. Spell "THE QUEEN OF HEARTS" from the bottom.
KING. See above.

DIAMONDS

ACE. See above.
TWO. See above.
THREE. Spell "THE THREE OF DIAMONDS." X
FOUR. Spell "THE FOUR SPOT OF DIAMONDS" from bottom.
FIVE. Spell "THE FIVE SPOT OF DIAMONDS."
SIX. Spell "THE SIX SPOT OF DIAMONDS."
SEVEN. Spell "THE SEVEN SPOT OF DIAMONDS" from bottom.
EIGHT. Spell "THE EIGHT SPOT OF DIAMONDS." X.
NINE. Spell "THE NINE SPOT OF DIAMONDS." X.
TEN. Spell "THE TEN SPOT OF DIAMONDS" from bottom.
JACK. Spell "THE JACK OF DIAMONDS."
QUEEN. Spell "THE QUEEN OF DIAMONDS" from bottom.
KING. Spell "THE KING OF DIAMONDS" from bottom.

CLUBS

ACE. Spell "CLUBS" from bottom, then "ACE" from top or bottom
of these five cards.
TWO. Spell "TWO CLUBS."
THREE. Spell "THREE" then "CLUBS" with the same cards and
show.
FOUR. Spell "FOUR" from bottom, then "CLUB" with same cards
and show.
FIVE. Spell "FIVE CLUB."
SIX. Spell "SIX CLUB" from bottom.
SEVEN. Spell "SEVEN OF CLUBS" from bottom.
EIGHT. Spell "EIGHT" from bottom, then "CLUBS" with same
cards.
NINE. Spell "NINE CLUBS."
TEN. Spell "TEN CLUB."
JACK. See above.
QUEEN. Spell "QUEEN OF CLUBS.
KING. Spell "KING OF CLUBS."

SPADES

ACE. See above.

TWO. See above.

THREE. Spell "THE THREE SPOT OF SPADES."

FOUR. Order to top. Turn top card to show it is not there first then make a double lift.

FIVE. Spell "THE FIVE OF SPADES."

SIX. Spell "THE SIX SPOT OF SPADES."

SEVEN. Spell "SEVEN OF SPADES."

EIGHT. Spell "EIGHT" from bottom take off two cards on last letter and spell "SPADES" show card.

NINE. Spell "NINE SPADES."

TEN. Spell "TEN SPADES" from bottom.

JACK. See above.

QUEEN. Spell "QUEEN OF SPADES."

KING. Spell "THE KING OF SPADES" from bottom.

NEW PACK DETECTION

For this trick arrange to have a new unopened pack of Bicycle cards. Hand this to a spectator and ask him to break the seal, take out the cards, cut them several times and then deal two face down heaps, a card to each. Two persons each take one heap and each shuffles thoroughly. Then each draws a card from the other's packet and shuffles it into his own. You find both cards at will.

The trick depends on the fact that Bicycle cards are packed in one of two ways:—

1. A. to 10. S: 10 to A. D: 10 to A. H: 10 to A. C: J. to K. C: J. to K. S: J. to K. D: J. to K. H: Joker.

2. A. to 10. C: A. to 10. H: A. to 10. D: 10. to A. S: K. to J. S: K. to J. C: K. to J. H: K. to J. D: Joker.

Fan the pack and discard Joker. When the spectator cuts and deals into two packets each will consist of a certain easily learned set of 26 cards, so that when a strange card is introduced into either set it is readily recognizable.

FOUR-FOLD SYMPATHY

Two packs are used, one with blue backs, the other with red backs, and both having white borders around the back patterns. Remove from the blue deck the KS, AH, 10D, 3S, and put them on the top in that order followed by an indifferent card as the top card. Also take out the 7C, and put is on the bottom. From the red deck take out the same cards making a packet of them in the same order, with an indifferent card on the top and the 7C as the bottom card, and place this packet of red cards at the bottom of the blue deck.

To perform the trick, place the two packs on the table and force the red deck on a spectator using the usual equivoque. Ask him to shuffle his pack while you shuffle the blue deck. You can do this by a riffle shuffle without disturbing the top and bottom cards, but the cards must be well covered by the hands to avoid exposing the red backed cards on the bottom. Secretly make a break with your right thumb at the inner end of your deck separating the 6 red cards from the blue cards. Take the red deck from the spectator with your left hand and put the two packs together for a moment pretending to judge the thickness of the pile to decide how many packets you should make. Really you let the 6 red cards join the red deck at the top. Separate the two packs again and place them on the table. Cut the blue deck into two packets and invite the spectator to do the same with the red deck. Again cut each of your piles in half, the spectator follows suit. We will call the piles A, B, C, D. In making the cuts see that the spectator does exactly the same as you do so that the resulting packets are opposite one another. In each case the arranged cards are on top of pile D. Turn the top cards of your four piles face up, spectator does the same. Call attention to the fact that they are just any cards at all and have them all turned down again. Now move the top cards of your four piles from one heap to another apparently in a haphazard fashion, but in such a way that ultimately you have one of the four cards, KS, AH, 10D, 3S, on top of each heap. The spectator makes each move as you do, so that the four duplicates in his pack are brought to the same locations. The top cards are turned and shown to match, and are put aside.

The 7C, will be the bottom card of your packet A, while the red 7C is on the top of the spectator's heap D. Assemble the deck by placing D an C. DC on B and DCB on A, the spectator doing the same. Turn your pack face up showing the 7C, and tell the spectator to turn over the top card of his pack, and it also proves to be the 7C.

TELEPATHIC CONTROL

Under the pretence of taking the Joker out of a well shuffled pack. rapidly memorize the five bottom cards. The quickest and easiest way is to first take the values only, as for instance 7, 5, Q, 9, 4, then memorize the suits in the same fashion. Riffle shuffle several times, but do not disturb these five bottom cards.

Hand the pack to a spectator and have him make several complete cuts. He then fans the deck and hands you four cards as you call for them The first three cards called are just indifferent ones, but are not among the the four cards, name the bottom card of the five memorized and have the deck cut at this point, thus bringing the other four cards to the bottom of the pack. Tell the spectator to deal the cards into four face down heaps with the result that you have the four memorized cards one at the top of each heap. Spectator chooses a heap and looks at the top card. You tell him to cut the packet, look at the card cut and tell you if it is odd or even, then you name the top card. This odd or even business is for mis-direction only.

The other three cards can be read in the same way. *Note*: It is easier to have five cards set up in a formula you know by heart and add them to the bottom of the pack just before you do the trick.

CARDS AND POCKETS

EFFECT:—After shuffling and cutting the cards the performer in-stantly calls the number of cards in a packet cut off. After repeating this effect several times he divides the packet into four portions and puts each packet in a different pocket. Any card called for it then instantly produced.

METHOD:—The cards are arranged in four sections thus:—
No. 1. AH, 2H, 3S, 4S, 5S, 6D, 7D, 8D, 9C, 10C, JC, QH, KH.
No. 2. AC, 2C, 3H, 4H, 5H, 6S, 7S, 8S, 9D, 10D, JD, QC, KC.
No. 3. AD, 2D, 3C, 4C, 5C, 6H, 7H, 8H, 9S, 10S, JS, QD, KD.
No. 4. AS, 2S, 3D, 4D, 5D, 6C, 7C, 8C, 9H, 10H, JH, QS, KS.

Refer always to the first packet as the Heart packet; the second as the Club packet; the third the Diamond packet and the fourth the Spade packet. Having the packets so arranged face down, put No. 1 on No. 2. these two on No. 3, and these on No. 4. Thus assembled the top card will the the AH and the bottom card the KS. The packets being in numerical order (J counting 11, Q, 12 and K, 13), the value of the face card of the packet cut off will denote the number of cards in the packet. for instance, if the face card is a 7 and the packet contains a few cards only their number is 7; if however there are obviously more than 7 cards. simply add 13 and call 20 as the number of cards. Finally if you cut more than half the pack you must add 26 to the value of the face card of the cut.

For the second effect riffle the ends of the cards, locate the KH, (13th card) lift off packet No. 1 and put it in your left side coat pocket; riffle next to the KC and put packet No. 2 in your right side coat pocket; divide the remainder at the KD and put No. 3 in right trousers pocket and No. 4 in left trousers pocket. A very simple formula will enable you to find any card called for. Divide the numerical value of the card by three and the answer, ignoring the remainder if any. will designate the pocket contain-ing the card. For example the 7H is called for. Three ones into seven twice, so 2 therefore is the key number. The suit being Hearts refer to the Heart pocket (left side coat pocket) and count 2. counting the right coat pocket 1 and the right trousers pocket 2: the required card must therefore be in the right trousers pocket and as the packet is in numerical order it must be the 7th card.

Again suppose the JC is called for; 3 into 11 gives 3 for the answer.

The suit being Clubs, refer to the Club packet in the right coat pocket and count 3 from it in the same direction as given in the first example, bringing you to the left coat pocket in which the card lies. Since the Ace and the Two cannot be divided by 3, they will be found in the pocket of the suit called.

Place the packets in the pockets with the faces outwards. When a card is brought out do not remove it singly, count to the card, square the others behind it and bring them all out as one card, then replace them in the pocket so that the order of each packet is not disturbed.

COUNT DOWN DETECTION

Arrange thirteen cards (7 red and 6 black) in some well known order such as the "Eight Kings, etc." In presenting the trick make a false riffle leaving the packet on the top undisturbed. Hand the pack to a spectator telling him that, when you turn your back, he is to count off any small number of cards, look at the card counted to, remember it, replace it anywhere in the pack and shuffle the cards thoroughly. This done you turn around and take the pack. Ignore the first two cards of the arrangement, the count will always be more than two. Of the 11 cards remaining there are 6 black and 5 red. Ask whether the card was red or black as you run over the faces of the cards. If the answer is red, bring the five red to the top in their arranged order. Boldly announce that you have put the card on the top of the pack. The card is named and you show it as being the top one by turning two or more as one card. If the card is a black one do the same thing with the 6 black cards.

It has been suggested that after the color of the chosen card has been ascertained, one of the 5 or 6 cards be reversed in the middle, 1 or 2 brought to the bottom, 1 or 2 to the top and 1 palmed off and put in a pocket. When the card is named it can at once be shown in one of these positions and the necessity for the lifting of perhaps 5 or 6 cards is eliminated.

THE ADVENTURES OF DIAMOND JACK

A little story based on the deck of cards. First, let me introduce our hero, Diamond Jack (JD). No relation to Diamond Joe. Jack was just twenty-six (2S 6S), handsome, a regular King of Hearts (KH). He had been an Ace (AD) in the war, but now he was poor. In fact, he had not been flush (flush in Spades, K-Q-J-10-9) for a long time. He often felt blue (Show blue back of card) because he belonged to only one club (AC) while his friends belonged to two or three (2C and 3C). But Jack was proud; his hands (two fans of cards) had never turned a spade (AS).

One day at seven (7S) he had a date with a swell queen (QD). She was a 'pip' (snap spot of Q), but when he arrived she was not on *deck* (Look for Q on top of deck). "That is a nasty cut," (cut the cards) said Jack. So he picked up another blonde queen (Pick up QH from table) and ate (8S) with her. The head-waiter said he had a full-house (8H, 8D, 8C, 3H and 3D), but he seated them anyway, as head-waiters will. And say, she ate (8H) and ate (8D) and ate (8C). She ordered several club steaks (Throw down 8C) and everything on the card (Hold up 3H, back to them). The waiter brought tray (3H) after tray (3D) of food.

But finally as she was finishing off with a fancy, cherry-colored pear (7H and 7D), Jack realized he had only a ten and a five (10D and 5D). Luckily the bill was only thirteen spots (10C and 3S), but when the waiter added two more (Deal last two cards on table), Jack asked, "What for?" (4S).

"My tip," said the dirty knave (JC).

"The deuce (2D) you say," said Jack. "I don't mind forking (4C·KC) over ten per cent (10H), but this is outrageous."

Here is where the queen dropped out of sight (Drop QH on floor).

Then the waiter spotted the diamonds (6D) on Jack's cravat and snatched for them. Jack pasted a grand slam in his fifth rib near the heart (5H). "Nein, Nein, Nein," (9D, 9C, 9H) cry the German waiters excitedly. But the manager sicks (6H) the cops on them. In fact, he called out holf of the force (4H 4D). In the shuffle (Shuffle cards on table) that followed, Jack fanned a féw (fan), but he had the whole pack after him, and finally six or seven cubs (6C 7C) descended at once. His mind went blank (blank card).

When he awoke he was facing Judge King (KD). A lawyer was appointed to handle the case (Pick up card case from table). "Your name," said the Judge.

"Diamond Jack," (JD) shouted our hero.

"Not so much snap," (snap the cards) said the Judge.

Just then Jack saw his old sweetheart, Mary McClub (QC) from Oireland, who was acting as court stenographer.

"Your Honor, I was almost robbed by a knave (JH), a *highjacker* (Hold JH above your head), but this little girl will testify to my character."

"Let me get this *straight*" (K-Q-J-10-9) of S, same as used before) said Judge King.

"I love her with an aching heart," (AD, KD, AH) said Jack.

"So hearts (AH) are trumps?" asked the Judge.

"I'm no Joker," (Joker) said Jack.

"So you want to marry her?" "I do," said Jack, handing over a *solitaire* (AD).

"Accept my stamp of approval," (Snap revenue stamp on card-case) finished the Judge.

And so they became two of a kind (5S and 5C), two minds with but a single thought, two hearts (2H) that beat as one (AH). Finis.

Sequence

In the following pre-arrangement please note that the italic cards (*QH*, *JD*, *AD*, *KD*, *QC*, *AH* and the straight flush in Spades) are used two and three times. These are to be laid aside, so that they may be obtained later without hesitation:

QH on table, *JD*, 6S-2S, KH, *AD*, *K-Q-J-10-9 of S*, blue, AC, 2C, 3C, 2 fans, AS, 7S, QD, pip, deck, cut, pick up *QH*, 8S, full-house (3-8's, 2-3's), 8H-8D-8C, 8C, card, 3H-3D, 7H-7D, 10D-5D, 10C-3S, deal 2, 4S, JC, 2D, 4C-KC, 10H, *QH*, 6D, 5H, 9D-9C-9H, 6H, 4H-4D, shuffle, fan 3, 6C 7C,, blank, *KD*, case, *JD*, snap, *QC*, JH high, *QC*, *K-Q-J-10-9 of S* as used above, *AD-KD-AH*, *AH*, Joker, *AD*, stamp, 5S-5C, 2H, *AH*.

WRONG NUMBER

It is usually a source of irritation to both parties when a wrong telephone number is contacted. In this instance, however, it serves as a novel means of revealing information.

The magus casually remarkes that many times in his experience coincidences have made themselves evident in a very strange and unexpected manner. Before going into further detail, a local telephone directory is borrowed from the host or hostess and the book opened by a spectator to a selected page. The assisting spectator then concentrates on but one particular name on that page. Just about this time the telephone rings and the host, taking time out for the moment, answers it. That finished, the magus asks, if it is not too personal, who was that? He is informed that it was just a wrong number. "They wanted to know if this was Zilch's Exterminating Company!" "Zilch's Exterminating Company," muses the performer; then, turning to the concentrating spectator, "What is the name you are thinking of?" It is the same! Imagine the strange effect, if you will.

The method is quite simple. Proper timing and a good force are the essentials. For the latter, there are legions of methods to be used. Annemann had a very good, clean-cut force in his "One Man Mental and Psychic Routine." The second method of Telephone Telepathy in "You'd Be Surprised" may also be used. We recommend this variation on an old gag, however. Get a page with a name that you would want to use, somewhere near the middle of the telephone book. For complete simplicity, let the name be the first one on the page. Count-downs to a set number for names are sometimes confusing and the volunteer is likely to make a mistake. This is impossible if you tell him to look at the first name of the page, and the choice, so far as the effect goes, seems comparatively unlimited.

Into the telephone book at the force page you put a playing card. It is placed near the binding at about the middle. Close the book and have it handy. On top of your regulation deck of cards you have a duplicate of the card in the book.

Shuffle the pack and keep the top card in place. Now fan the cards and request someone to "remove a bunch of cards, say, from five to ten." These are taken from any part of the deck. Ask the spectator to hand you any one of the cards. Place it on top of the deck and then do the double lift, showing the face of the original top card to the audience. You tell them that this card is to be the indicator card. Turn the cards face down as one and then deal off the top card deliberately and insert it into the middle of the small packet of cards the spectator has taken from the deck. Have these cards mixed a bit "so that nobody will know the exact location of our indicator card."

Meanwhile, casually cut the remainder of the deck, bringing the top card to the center some place and out of the way. Bring forth the telephone book and lay it flatwise on the table. Tell the person who has the small bunch of cards that you want him to insert his cards into the book, one at a time, at random points, as the pages are riffled. To illustrate, you riffle the pages at the long side with the left thumb and fling two or three cards from the top of the deck into the book at different pages with the right hand.

While the spectator follows your instructions with his few cards, you explain that you could just as easily have one card inserted into the book for the page selection, but you have been ridiculously accused in the past of influencing the choice of where the book was opened, so you have devised this fairer procedure. Chance (?) is the only factor here that determines where the indicator card is put.

After the spectator's cards have all been put into the book, the book may be retained by him or given to another person to go through the pages and find out where the indicator card is. It won't take very long, because there aren't many cards and the book will open at those pages where there are cards. Having found the indicator card, the spectator is told to note the first name on the page. As a magician, you should easily get around the question of "right" or "left" side by the elimination gag or by any other preferred ruse.

Since the card itself is a force card, you can use its value for determining the column or a number of names to count down, in the event that you want to force a special name.

Of course, the person who calls up is none other than an unapplauded confederate who knows the 'phone number of the place where you are performing, the time when you will do the trick, and the person or company name you will force. All he does is call up at the particular time and inquire if it is ————, naming the person, company, etc., that the magus has forced.

Get a name to force that is unusual or funny-sounding, as that will be more easily remembered by the person answering the 'phone and also subsequently, by the other witnesses. Company names are usually better than individuals, so force one of the numerous company advertisements in telephone books. A classified telephone directory is preferable to the other one in this case, but both have ads in them. On certain occasions, a judicious choice of the force name will make for a more impressive effect. For instance, if your demonstration is at a Republican Club, force the Democratic Headquarters, and vice versa. If that doesn't make a laughable situation at the climax, what does?

The effect may be worked at any place and almost any time. Finding yourself in strange surroundings, you may have an opportunity to make a hurried 'phone call to your confederate beforehand, and give him the telephone number of the place and the time you expect to do the trick. Check your watches and also notify him of a change in the force name if you have decided on such a step.

Needless to state, the confederate must be dependable. The call should come through right on the minute you expect it, as you don't want to stall around after the name has been selected. In the event that the telephone doesn't ring right on the dot, however, the best thing to do is to have the person write the name down on a slip of paper, fold it, and put it in his pocket, telling him you'll come back to him later. Go on with another mystery, and then, when the call comes, all is in readiness for the revelation.

The confederate must also be coached to enunciate the name clearly and to repeat it at least once. Thus, his opening query may be, "Hello, is this ZILCH'S EXTERMINATING COMPANY?" Upon receiving a negative reply, apparently nonplussed, he again asks, "This is NOT ZILCH'S EXTERMINATING COMPANY?" After again being assured that it most certainly is not, he murmurs something about a wrong number, apologizes, and hangs up.

Try it just once when conditions warrant its use and you'll see how well it is received and remembered.

A PREDICTION TO END PREDICTIONS

The magician who uses this routine is not likely to have room for other prediction effects on his program.

In effect, the performer makes three direct predictions—the name of a selected (not forced) card, a word, and the date on a dollar bill. Each prediction is written on a slip of paper which is folded and dropped into a glass in full view before the selection. The three slips are held and read by spectators at the climax when all are verified. Never were more precautions taken to make all look absolutely fair and as genuine as such things can possibly be. How matters are handled from the standpoint of presentation will become evident in the explanation which follows.

Used are five or six papers, 2¼ by 3½ inches, folded once the long way, once the other way, and then once more the same way, as is usual in billet work, and then reopened. One folded billet is put in right coat pocket along with a lead pencil. The opened slips are placed in the same pocket. You also need two glass goblets, a tea cup, and an unprepared deck set up according to Si Stebbins or your favorite system. The glasses are arranged at opposite ends of the table with the cup in the middle.

Begin by announcing that you are going to make several outright predictions. The first one will be of a card which is going to be selected. Take out the opened slips and on the top one write a prediction, refold it, and drop it in full view in the right-hand glass. Ask them to remember that you placed the card prediction in this glass. What they do not know is that you actually wrote, "The date will be 1935." After folding the billet, write "Bill" on the outside. All of this is done openly, but they do not see what you write.

Now take out the deck, give it a false shuffle or at least some cuts, show the cards all different, and spread on the floor before a man for an absolutely free selection. When he starts to push out a card, gather up the cards from above that point and then note the bottom card, thereby giving you the name of the card he selected. Throw the rest on, give the deck a riffle shuffle, snap a rubber band around it, and toss it to someone to hold. You must make it known that a free choice was made for such is actually the case and every point is worth building up.

The next prediction will be that of a word. Pause a moment, look intently at one of the spectators, and then write a prediction as before, fold it, and drop in the left-hand goblet. Ask them to remember that you placed the word prediction in this glass. What you really wrote was, "The Seven of Spades will be selected" (or whatever card was selected) and on the outside of the folded billet you wrote "Card."

Now step out into the audience and hand a spectator a pencil and one of your pre-folded slips upon which to write any word of not more than six letters that occurs to him and then to fold the billet. Turn your back while he does this and ask him to tell you as soon as he is through. It doesn't take long. Meantime, you return the remaining slips to pocket and finger palm the folded billet. When he has finished, take his billet from him with right (which has the dummy palmed) and take back pencil in left. Turn to a spectator nearby and ask him to hold the man's billet above his head for safe keeping until needed. In the nonce, you make a straight one-handed switch and he gets the dummy. Ask him to mark it with pencil. Take pencil back in right hand which drops it in pocket along with the stolen billet.

(The switch is done as follows: Dummy is palmed by holding between first and last joint of the slightly curled-in second finger (Fig. 1). Take spectator's billet back between thumb and second finger, slide it back on palmed billet with thumb, pulling it back and pushing the under dummy forward in its place (Fig. 2). This leaves positions of billets reversed from

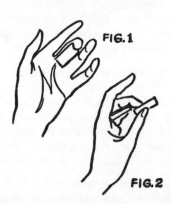

FIG. 1

FIG. 2

that at beginning of move. If you cannot do this, an alternative is to take back the slip in left hand and pretend to pass to right, but finger palm in left.

A better alternative is not to try the trick at all. The magus who wants to know more about billet work should read Annemann's "Complete One Man Mental and Psychic Routine.")

The last prediction will be the date on a bill. Again a prediction is written and it is dropped in the cup. What has actually been done is this: The right hand went to the coat pocket for the papers as before, but first secretly opened up the stolen billet and brought it out opened on top of the several blank slips. Now start to write something, but look at one of the spectators and appear to change your mind. Scratch it out and transfer the top slip to the bottom. Write your prediction on the clean slip, "The gentlemen will think of the word 'ROOK' (or whatever the word is)." Fold, write "Word" on the outside of the billet, and pretend to drop billet in cup, but really finger palm it out. Someone is asked to take a DOLLAR BILL from his own billfold, note the date on it, (it is down to the right of Washington's picture) then fold the bill and hold it above his head.

You are now set with the word "prediction" finger palmed in right hand, the card "prediction" in left-hand glass, the bill "prediction" in right-hand glass, and nothing in the cup. Audience thinks card prediction in right-hand glass, word in left, and date of bill in cup.

The three slips are now handed to three spectators to hold and read at the climax. You pick up the left-hand goblet by the stem with the left hand and step towards a spectator on the left. Say, "I want you to hold the word prediction." The right hand, with billet finger palmed, dips into the glass and apparently brings out the slip therein, but actually executes the switch as described and the spectator gets the previously palmed slip. (Simply grasp the billet in glass in your fingers and push the finger palmed billet into view at finger tips.) Another way is to turn the slip from the glass out into the right hand, which palms it and pushes the other one forward. Do whatever is natural for you. Goblet is momentarily passed to right hand which now contains palmed (card) slip.

Set down glass at back of table and pick up right goblet with left hand. Step up to a gentleman at right front and say, "I want you to hold the prediction I wrote before the card was selected," and switch for palmed billet as before. These switches are very easy to do and completely natural. Glass is passed to right hand which sets it back on table and picks up cup (but not by the handle) and lets finger palmed (date) slip fall therein. The cup is handed to a spectator who removes the slip and holds it. Cup is returned to table and you are all ready for the verification of the tests.

First you take the bill the man is holding, open it out and read off the date. It is an interesting fact that unless this is a very old bill (which you avoid), the date will be 1935! Time may change this, so take advantage of it while you can! Of course, a color or something else could be forced instead, but the bill idea is so clean and away from all trickery that it makes a nice item in the routine.

The owner of the bill verifies the date and you ask whoever is holding the prediction to open it and read it. Let us hope that it is correct.

Next the selector of the card is asked to hold up his card. You take it and hold it up for all to see, calling it out and reminding them that the card was selected with the deck out of your hands; in fact, the deck is still out of your hands, and will whoever is holding it please toss it back! Now ask who is holding the prediction and this man at once opens and reads his billet —it is right.

For the last test, take the marked (dummy) slip the spectator is holding, upon which the word was allegedly written. Open it and pretend to read off the word aloud, which you now know. Ask who wrote the word and, when he raises his hand, ask him if he was influenced in any way to write that particular word. Having completed the check-up, the prediction is read by the man holding the word slip. You meantime crumple the dummy and pocket it.

The explanation seems very long, but this is because something vital occurs at every move and attention to detail is absolutely necessary. When you get the idea, you will see how it all blends together logically. There is a certain amount of drag in all things of this nature and forceful presentation is naturally required, as the strength of the effect lies in the precautions taken to make the predictions seem fair in every way. There are no loop-holes and, while it is not the case, it seems as though the magus does not touch any prediction after it has been written or control the various selections in any way. It is no trick for a ten-minute turn, but a rather exceptional mental routine for the more intimate performance.

While the routine fits together nicely as it stands, it can be cut by omitting the card prediction. In this case, you start off by writing the word prediction (really the date) and actually dropping it in a cup, then proceed with the word business as described, working clear through to the point of "dropping" the "date" prediction in ANOTHER cup, really palming it out. The "word prediction" is handed to one man, handling the cup and switch just as in the routine with the goblets. Drop the now palmed date slip into the other cup and empty the cup into hand of another man. Everything is exactly as described before, but the card business is entirely omitted and the running time thus cut considerably. In any case, the only sleight is the billet switch and naturalness the important factor. All of the ideas have been used before in one form or another, so the combination into a routine of predictions is all that I can be held responsible for.

THE PAYOFF PREDICTION

Just when the previous routine was titled to spell finis to predictions for all time, this wrinkle slipped in that should meet favor with many who want a single effect of this nature that is strong and direct.

The magician writes a prediction on a slip of paper, folds it, and drops it in a cup. A man now writes any word of six letters or less on a slip and this is folded and held by a spectator. The prediction slip is turned out of the cup into another spectator's hands. When the word is read, the spectator verifies the magus' prediction of the identical word.

Never was a prediction more direct or a method a more barefaced swindle. It is all obviously an adaptation of the handling of the word billet as described in the previous routine. It will be seen in a moment that the performer never writes a prediction at all!

Used are a few slips, 2 by 3 inches, folded as described before. I shall explain the trick employing a thumb tip to make it possible for anyone to do the effect without sleights. A straight switch can, of course, be used instead. The folded slips just fit into the thumb tip and, at the beginning, the tip is loaded with a blank dummy and placed in the right coat pocket along with the rest of the papers which have been opened out. In the left coat pocket' is a pencil. An unprepared tea cup is all else that is required.

Begin by taking out the opened slips and apparently writing a prediction on one. You may write anything or nothing at all. The paper is folded and apparently placed in cup by right hand, but it is really palmed out and right hand takes the opened slips and drops them back in pocket along with the finger palmed billet.

Now step among the spectators and hand someone a pencil and a slip upon which to write any word. You have given him one of the opened slips and, in returning the others to the pocket, get the loaded thumb tip on right thumb. This is done while you are waiting for the spectator to finish writing. As soon as he is through, take back the pencil and drop in left pocket, then hold out left hand and he drops the folded billet therein. Right hand comes over and thumb is placed on top of billet, while left hand closes around it, and right thumb is pulled out, carrying dummy billet from tip between thumb and forefinger. Left drops to side and dummy is handed to another man. Left (with thumb tip and real word billet underneath) goes to left pocket and brings out pencil for spectator to mark dummy, which he does, and then holds it above his head. Tip and stolen billet are left in pocket. The thumb tip switch is due to Al Baker and part of the handling to Annemann.

Step to front, left hand having taken back pencil, which it drops in pocket again and gets billet there finger palmed. Left hand at once picks up the (empty) cup and secretly drops the finger palmed billet therein. Walk over to a spectator in another part of the room and tip the "prediction" out into his hand. Right hand immediately reaches over and opens out the billet before him as you say, "Don't tell what I've written, yet. I want to find out if it's right first!"

This is a mild gag, but it enables you to glimpse what word has actually been written. Needless to say, the spectator mistakes the word the spectator has written on the slip to be your writing—the "prediction" which you made at the start!

You now take the marked billet the other spectator is holding, open it, "read" the word aloud, ask the man who wrote it if he was influenced in any way, then turn to the spectator holding the (opened) "prediction" and ask him to read what you wrote before anything else was done and which you have not touched (?) since. It is right, as the spectator and the people around him will be able to verify. You meantime crumple and pocket the slip that you hold.

The only possible end that remains loose is that the spectator who wrote the word might see the "prediction" after the show. Unless the audience is quite small, this is nothing to worry about. If you like, you can take the "prediction" from the spectator after he reads it. The people around him will have looked at it and checked it, so there is no actual need to leave it out in the audience, just as the handling has been such that no one objects to the performer pocketing the "word" billet without showing it around.

Obviously, the only thing that is new here is the application of a known billet manipulation to a rather daring prediction, but the effect produced is something which has not been done before in so direct a manner.

. . . THINGS TO COME

We have here a test of the Swami order which is built up into quite a piece of prophecy.

Briefly, the performer gives a spectator written instructions which guide the latter to a sealed envelope wherein is found a prophecy, written, so the magician says, by a spirit medium friend. The predictions, which concern words, cards, numbers, etc., given by the audience, turn out to be quite correct.

The following preparation is necessary: Seal in an unprepared letter envelope a smaller envelope which is prepared by cutting a slit across the face about two thirds of the way up. Glue a card to the inside face of this envelope below the slit. The flap of this envelope is not stuck down but it is sealed with a bit of sealing wax. Thus, though sealed, it can be quickly opened by breaking the seal. This smaller envelope must be placed in the larger one flap side downward and to the face of the large envelope. On the outside of the flap of the large envelope, stick a small daub of wax or diachylon.

A stack of about eight blank cards, about playing card size or a little larger, is also needed. On one of these have a friend whose handwriting contrasts somewhat with your own write—

Instructions:

"Look in the corners of the room until you find a book with a green cover. Open book at page 172, where you will find a sealed envelope. Return with this envelope to the front of the room. Thank you."

Place this card, writing side up, second from the top of the packet and make a small mark on the top card so you will know which side of the stack is "up."

Also used are a slate, chalk, and a deck of cards set up according to your favorite system. Before the performance, slip the envelope in a book at the proper page and place wherever convenient in one corner of the room.

Begin by handing the slate and chalk to someone and asking for the name of some famous person to be called out, then any word of, say, six letters. These the man with the slate records. The deck of cards is produced and, after being briefly false shuffled, shown, and cut, is spread before another man, who very freely takes a card and pockets it. You gather up the deck and know at once, of course, what it is.

Now bring out the packet of blank cards and state that you are going to write a set of instructions which you wish some member of the audience to carry out. This you apparently proceed to do. Here is what you write:

"FRIDAY afternoon—

"This evening at 10:17 a GREY-haired GENTLEMAN in a BROWN suit will select the 7 OF SPADES. Someone will choose the word 'SYSTEM' and · the name 'EDISON.' The total of a column of figures given by spectators will be 43.—Roberta—Spirit Medium."

This message you have memorized so you can write it without hesitation, filling in with the proper data at the points capitalized.

Having written on the card, but still without showing what you have written, you turn to someone and say, "What is your name, please?" Do a double turnover with the two top cards and PRINT this person's name on the back of the present top card. Thumb this card off and the spectator actually gets the instruction card. Ask him to please do what is written on the card and return as quickly as possible. Note that this message is written in a handwriting other than your own.

As soon as the spectator, instructions in hand, has begun to look in the corners of the room for a book with a green cover, you, pencil and cards still in hand, go down among the spectators, asking a number of them to whisper single figures from 1 to 9 to you, which you deliberately put down in a column, taking care to let each see you actually record his number. You have turned over the packet, so you are writing on an unprepared card. As you write the numbers, add them mentally until you reach a sum between 34 and 43. Draw a line under the column rather below the last figure and, indicating that you want someone to add the numbers, add in the number you need to bring the total to 43. Leave the card with a spectator for adding. Later it will be remembered that the number addition took place AFTER the spectator was sent for the prediction.

By this time, the man to whom you gave the secret instructions has returned with the sealed envelope and it is time to proceed with the revelation. First ask the man to tell just what he did, then explain that the hidden envelope contains a message of prophecy which was written earlier in the day at your request by a friend who claims to be something of a medium. This is a test of this person's powers, with you taking no credit whatsoever, except for carrying out the conditions of the experiment.

Now you are still holding the little packet of cards and in coming front you have once more turned it over so that the real prediction card (writing side down) is now on top. Have the spectator satisfy himself that the envelope is sealed (he can feel something inside like another envelope and a card), then take it from him and transfer it to the hand holding the cards, placing it flap side down on top of the cards. This is apparently so your free hand can go to pocket for a small pair of scissors. Once the scissors are brought out, the envelope is taken and snipped open at the edge, but you will recall the little daub of wax which was placed on the envelope flap and understand that the top card of the packet is now stuck to the back of the envelope; this side we keep carefully away from sight.

Withdraw the smaller envelope from the larger one and lay it, flap side up, on the face of the large envelope, which is now held horizontally with the card underneath on the fingers of the left hand, which holds the envelopes. Call attention to the seal on the smaller envelope, then break it and open the flap. The flap edge is toward the audience. With the left thumb (which is

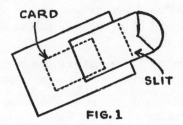

FIG. 1

(Right forefinger enters small envelope, goes through slit,
and withdraws card stuck at bottom of large envelope).

on top of the envelopes), push the smaller envelope forward a little so (Fig. 1), by reaching in with your right thumb and forefinger, you can get through the slit and grasp the card which is helped forward from under the large envelope by the left fingers. The card is deliberately withdrawn from the envelope, the subtlety of its secret introduction being completely deceptive.

Hand the card to the assisting spectator and ask him to read it aloud. Pocket the envelopes. As soon as he reads, "a grey-haired gentlemen in a brown suit will select the 7 of Spades," stop him and ask the selector of the card to stand so the description can be checked. He is asked to hold up the card and that is right, too. From this point on, each time the spectator reads one of the passages which is capitalized, stop him then and there for verification.

Later, when the "instructions" you gave the spectator and the "prediction" he found are passed around, the difference in handwriting will be noted and since you are assumed to have written the "instructions" in sight of all, it is apparent that you were not the author of the prophecy, Of course, you don't call attention to the point, but it is there to see.

One point about the handling of the instructions. Have things so arranged that the man sent after the envelope is in view all of the time and can not thus be suspected of any confederacy.

(Note): When working the effect before a rather large audience, take this suggestion for what it may be worth. Get one of those vari-colored lead pencils (pencils that write a different color by a simple twist) and write your "instructions"—really the prediction—with a lead that contrasts in color to the real instructions. After you turn the card(s) over and ask for the spectator's name, twist the pencil so that it writes the same color as that of the actual instructions and put down his name on the back. Continue as usual. The contrasting colors of the writings will be noted by the curious later on and should strengthen the assertion of different authorships. It is only a technical nicety, however; ordinarily, it isn't necessary to go to the extra bother.

THE "DIRECT" DIVINATION

This is the most direct method of obtaining secretly written information ever conceived.

In effect, a spectator writes something on a slip of paper and places it in his own pocket. He may use his own paper and pencil and is not approached by the magician during the writing.

Nevertheless, by establishing contact with the man, the performer quickly divines the information.

The secret is as straight to the point as the effect.

As soon as the person has written, step up to him and grasp him by the collar in such a way that the thumb presses on his jugular vein. Bring your head close to his, "to establish telepathic contact," and hiss, "Tell me what you wrote or I'll choke hell out of you!"

This you proceed to do unless he follows your instructions. In fact, it is best to kill the man anyway, thus leaving you clean at the finish.

The success of the trick depends upon selecting a man smaller than yourself.

THE PHANTOM PRESIDENT

This was worked out as a stunt for two people, but there is no reason it has to be done that way. It may also be a one-man proposition.

The effect is the important matter and is for a club or affair where most of the people know each other. We are going to elect an imaginary President. A number of spectators write secretly on slips of paper the names of any men present. These slips are folded and dropped into a handkerchief which has been formed into a little bag. Someone now freely selects one of the papers by simply reaching into the hank and removing one. Keeping it folded, he holds it in his hand. Another man takes a second paper and reads off the name written on it. Whoever answers to this name has to help find the "Phantom President." The medium is called in and, holding this man's hand, walks about with a top hat in her hand, which she, after some deliberation, places on the head of some surprised individual, asking him to stand.

"Just a minute, Prexy," says the performer, who has been standing out of the way for the moment—"What's your name?" The man gives it. Now the person holding the folded billet opens it and reads off the name, which is the same! The medium, among strangers, has successfully divined who was elected before anyone else knew.

Naturally, this is just a force of a name, but there are points in the handling which make it look otherwise. Beforehand, you must get the name of someone present whom you can spot in the crowd later on. You can always get a name and it won't be hard to arrange unless the audience is 'way too large. Of course, the medium knows all about this.

Write this name on about eight slips of paper. The handkerchief used is a Jap Hank, which is made up of two pocket handkerchiefs sewn together. See (Fig. 1). A whole quarter-corner remains unsewn and forms a pocket in

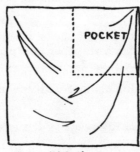

FIG. 1

the hank. It is into this pocket that the eight duplicate name slips are placed. This bit of preparation may have to be done just before the show, but it doesn't take long. The handkerchief is placed in a pocket.

Explain what is to be done and pass out slips to about eight spectators. They should not all be sitting together. While the writing is going on, you introduce the medium, who is then sent out of the room. You ask that the ballots be folded once each way. Now take out the Jap Hank and bring the four corners together, thus making a neat little bag. This is done without a word being said about the hank—it will be "ordinary" in the minds of the spectators as long as you don't mention it. Pass along and have the ballots dropped into the handkerchief proper.

When all are in, "mix" the slips, and in mixing, open the double pocket. Have a spectator—call him an unprejudiced person with non-political interests—reach in to the hank (really the pocket) and remove any one of the ballots. This is the way the President is to be elected. The selector holds the billet without opening it. You walk over to another man, meantime closing the pocket in the action of further mixing the slips. Have him reach in and take a second ballot. He does this and gets any one of the genuine slips. Ask the man to read this slip and whoever's name is called is asked to stand. He is asked if he knows who has been elected President. The man admits that he doesn't. "Well, you are going to help find the Phantom President just the same," says the magus.

You have meantime casually dropped the remaining genuine slips on the table and pocketed the faked hank. No one will want to know about these billets as they are obviously in the discard.

The sleuth (person selected) is asked to step out and bring in the medium, which he does. From here on, the little lady takes things in hand, the performer having retired discreetly to the side. The medium's walking around with the hat, hesitating as to who's head to place it upon, is interesting and amusing, as every man realizes that HE may be the President. As soon as the medium, still clutching the hand of her "guide," gets her man, the magus takes charge and winds things up as previously described with the verification of the name.

In working the effect without a mediumistic assistant, the performer himself sets out to find the President, using the "guide" as described. (Need it be explained that the object of using this second man is to kill the idea of a predetermined force in the selection of billets?) In this case, it is most effective to work blindfolded. This presents no difficulty, as you know where the man is located and can peek down your nose under the blindfold.

A changing bag (or any similar contrivance) may just as well be used for the selection of the slips. We suggest the Jap Hank because it appears freer of suspicion. The top hat doesn't have to be the real article. A cardboard imitation will serve just as well in most instances.

PICTURE PROJECTION

Probably the most effective demonstration of mentalism from the standpoint of an audience is the picture duplication test. In this routine, it is built up in dramatic form and makes an excellent climax for a series of mental effects.

A man is asked up front and is given a slate and chalk with which to draw any simple geometric design that he likes. While he is drawing, another man selects a card and pockets it. He, too, is given a slate and is asked to chalk down a picture of the card he selected.

The magician now takes a slate and, turning his back, offers to race the man who is going to draw the card. The first one through is to shout, "Ready!" Magus and man draw. As soon as the man says, "Ready," magician throws away his chalk. Back still turned, he asks the man to show his drawing. Magus then holds up his slate—both have drawn the same card!

The performer now turns to the other spectator who has been concentrating on his drawing. He asks the man to turn his slate around and show all for the first time what he has drawn. Immediately, magician turns his own slate around and the identical design is seen to be sketched thereon!

All of the ideas employed here are derived from several items in the book, "You'd Be Surprised," but the effect is something different and that is the important thing.

Three unprepared school slates, a supply of chalk, a damp cloth, and a forcing deck are all that are required. Scribble something on one of the slates. On another draw a picture of the force card. Picture should cover slate. It is well to have a straight deck in the right coat pocket so that after the selection you can drop the force deck in this pocket, later to bring out the straight deck instead and toss it on the table for anyone to look at afterwards.

Begin by asking a gentlemen up and giving him the clean slate and a piece of chalk with instructions to draw any simple geometric design that occurs to him, but not to show. He should stand well over to your left.

Now walk over to someone on the right. Take out the force deck, give it a good shuffle, and spread on the floor for a selection. As soon as the gentlemen gets a card, gather up the deck and pocket it. Ask the man to place the card in his pocket after he has looked at it. Step back to table, pick up slate upon which you have scribbled something, and, noting this, erase it with the damp cloth. Do not show wet side to audience. Hold slate in right hand. Turn to the man standing at the left, facing you, and say, "I want you to hold your slate before your eyes and concentrate on your drawing. Don't let anyone see it." He does so and you step directly in front of him, saying, "That's right. Up a little—hold it directly before your eyes." As you speak, grasp his wrists lightly, and the surface of the newly-washed slate held by the right hand gives you a perfect reflection of his drawing

FIG.1

(Fig. 1). Now walk directly away from him and hand the card selector the slate you hold. Ask him to step up front and draw a picture of the card he is thinking of. You do not give him chalk yet, however. Also, make it a point from here on not to approach the man who is concentrating on his slate drawing.

Step to table and pick up last slate, the drawing side toward you, and two pieces of chalk. Return to the card man (he should be well to your right) and hand him a piece of chalk, saying, "I am going to draw at the same time. Don't start until I say 'Draw,' and when you are through, say 'Ready.'"

You walk to middle and slightly behind both assistants, turning your back. Say, "Draw"—your left hand holding chalk and pointing toward the card man. Note that in this point of the game we are avoiding any attention toward the other assistant. You now begin to sketch on the clean side of your slate, drawing as well as possible the EXACT DESIGN YOU GLIMPSED FROM THE SLATE HELD BY THE FIRST MAN. You will undoubtedly get through first, but wait until the card man shouts, "Ready"—then throw away your chalk and hold your right hand above head.

Ask the assistant to show what he has just drawn. Ask him to name the card aloud. Back still turned, you hold up your slate—but you have REVERSED it, so that they see the drawing of the CARD. It's right! Climax.

Now turn to the man on your left and say, "Have you been concentrating on what you have drawn?" He declares that he has. "Please show us what it is." The man does so. You at once turn around the slate which you have been holding up high and there is seen the duplicate sketch. Surprise! The double climax makes an excellent effect.

(Note): A practical plan is to have a small sponge (about the size used in the Sponge Ball trick) saturated with odorless alcohol on hand. This is used in place of the damp cloth in wiping the slate. The surface of the slate will be wet for a long enough time to catch the reflection, but it will dry faster than it would if washed with a watered cloth, which is a desirable point.

TRANSPOSED MINDS

It is all very well for a magus to conjure with such objects as balls, silks, coins, glasses, etc., and to do such a customarily magical effect as making them change places, but when one begins toying with such intangibles as the minds of two volunteer committeemen, apparently causing the mental faculties of each to enter the body of the other, and showing supposed proof of this, well . . . . . ! It is all rather unique and eerie, to say the least.

Yet, that is exactly what seems to happen. The performer asks for two volunteers from the audience, preferably persons who have a good memory. Having secured them, both are asked to state their names. We will suppose they are Harry and John. Harry is requested to take a seat on one side of the stage and face the performer; John sits down on the other side.

The magus now shows each person a slate. Both John and Harry see some items on their slate, but they can not see what is on the other fellow's slate. On each of the slates are four items, which John and Harry are to remember. The first is the name of a color, the second is a number, the third is the name of an animal, and the last is the name of a city.

John's first name is written on the back of his slate, to identify what he has memorized. His slate is placed against a skeleton easel on his side of the stage, the items he has memorized facing the audience. The same procedure is gone through for Harry's slate.

The performer now goes into a short lecture on facts or supposed facts which he has gleaned from the latest findings of the occult. What will be attempted is an unusual experiment in hypnotism; the performer will try to bring Harry's mind into John's body and John's mind into Harry's body. After due spells are cast on each individual, the magus asks the person Harry if he can recall the first item—the name of a color—that he saw on his slate. He names a color, but it is not the one on his slate; the name of the color is the one on John's slate! John is asked for the name of the color he remembers and he names the color on Harry's slate! It is apparent that their minds have been transposed!

To further "prove" this, each spectator gives, in turn, the number, the name of the animal, and the name of the city that he saw on his slate—but in each instance, he invariably names the items that are on the other person's slate!

The performer now reverses the spell on each person, telling each that he has his own mind back again. The volunteers are thanked for being such willing subjects and dismissed with the admonition that they return to the performer for extra treatment if they should find themselves kissing strange women or doing unusual things.

All in all, the demonstration may be as droll or as serious as you like, but none the less mystifying.

Needed are two slates and a flap. On both slates, chalk down, in this order, "Red," "5," "Lion," and "Paris." On BOTH sides of the flap, put "Blue," "8," "Tiger," and "London." These items are written from top down, the long edges of the slate (and flap) being at the side. Put the flap on the writing side of one of the slates. The slate with the flap uppermost is put on top of the other; both visible writings are facing up. Cover the slates with a large envelope, silk, or piece of cardboard. This is only a precautionary measure to prevent an assisting spectator noting something that perhaps should not be seen by him.

In presenting, ask for two volunteer assistants. The success of the effect will depend a great deal on the type of individuals you select. They may be either men or women, or a combination of both, but they should be fairly intelligent and good-natured. Steer clear of the "loud-mouth" and the "smart-guy" who might attempt to spoil your trick; you can always spot them.

Have each assistant sit down on a chair at either side of the platform, facing you. Pick up the slates, holding them so the writing can not be seen, and place the top (flap covered) slate under your arm so the writing doesn't show. Show the other slate to the right hand man, holding it so that he alone can see its message surface. As soon as the man has seen and memorized the writing, ask his name and write this name on the blank side of his slate. Place this slate under your free arm, name side out, and go over to the left hand man and show him the other slate. As he is looking at it, bring out the other slate with your free hand, holding name side toward the man. When he has gotten the information, lay his slate, writing side down, on the writing side of the other slate, while you write his name.

There can be no question about the identifying of the slates. Lift off the top slate and put it against a glass or easel on the table on the left side, the slate being minus the flap, which has been dropped on the other slate. The four written items face the audience. The other slate, also message side towards audience, is stood on the right side of the stage.

Go to each spectator, in turn, and apparently put each into a hypnotic spell. A few whispered words to each to "play ball" will usually be heeded, inasmuch as you do not actually hypnotize them. All you want them to do is keep quiet.

Under the apparent hypnotic spell, you ask each person first for the color he has remembered. Harry names the color on John's slate and vice versa. The same goes for the number, the name of the animal, and the city. The poor, innocent victims of your trick will not be able to understand the reaction of the audience, but after you "readjust their minds" by more hypnotism, you state that you think they are "normal" again. A cigar, or some such offering, should recompense each man for missing the effect!

As a rule, it is not good to do tricks that everybody does not understand, but in this case, the effect on the audience proper is so thoroughly unusual that the two helpers may only be considered as a means to an end. In most cases, they will get as much of a kick out of what happened when they discuss it after the show as the audience does during the performance of the trick.

COMEDY "COLOR-CHANGING" SLATE

There's not so much mystery for magicians in this little number, but there is plenty of entertainment value, and, after all, entertaining audiences should be the primary aim of all magical workers.

A spectator is given a large envelope with a window cut in its face. In it is placed a slate, shown blank on both sides, and the whole is then set aside on the table in full view. Three folded slips of paper are shown, separately, and dropped into an empty bag. The performer explains that each slip has a description of a different scene or landscape, that one will be selected and, whatever scene it might describe, that picture will be magically (or "spiritually") produced on the slate. One of the slips is freely selected by a member of the audience and the performer returns to the front. The spectator is requested to open the slip and to read it aloud. He reads, "Two black cats in a coal bin at midnight." Magus removes the slate and there is the picture! Of course it is the picture—because the blank slate is all black!

Placing the slate in full view, the magus nonchalantly clears away the accumulated vegetables, and again bravely faces his audience. With that extraordinarily keen sense of hearing all magicians seem to have, he hears someone say that anybody could do that trick—but what would he have done if another slip had been taken? To prove to the skeptics that ANY picture would positively appear on the slate, the magus says he will repeat the trick. Another spectator freely selects one of the remaining slips in the bag and the performer returns to the platform, awaiting the reading of the second slip. Spectator opens slip and reads, "Two swans in a snowstorm." The magus turns the slate around and there's the picture—because the whole surface of the slate is white!

The slate is again placed in the envelope and given to a spectator to hold. The magus states that he has a vague idea that there are still a few persons present who may not believe that an authentic replica of any scene may be magically produced on the slate, down to the minutest detail. For the benefit of these "few" he will do the trick once again, and the scene produced will be that described on the last slip. A spectator takes the third paper, unfolds it, and reads: "An explosion in a paint factory." The performer says that such a scene would take the versatility of any artist, but let's see the result on the slate. The whole surface of the slate now shows a jumbled pattern of colors, all hues of the rainbow, in crazy-quilt design! Truly, it could be nothing less than "an explosion in a paint factory!"

Prepare a slate by painting as many contrasting colors on one side as you like. You needn't be careful about it, as the sloppier it appears, the more effective it is. Apply one color at a time and have it dry before applying another. No detailed outline is followed—just let the paint fall where it may, and when you're finished, you'll have a rhapsody of splotches that could compete with any surrealistic masterpiece.

A silicate flap that fits on the slate is also used. With mucilage or paste, attach a square of pasteboard or plain white paper, the same size as the flap, on one side, so that it is completely covered. Or, simply paint one surface of the flap white. Put the flap on the slate, the prepared portions facing each other, so that the slate appears blank. The window envelope is unprepared.

The bag used in the effect is a Changing Bag. However, any other similar contrivance, such as a Jap hank, will serve as well. In the secret compartment or side have three folded slips of paper, all of which have the writing, "Two black cats in a coal bin at midnight" on them. The arrangement of the bag at the outset is such that it may be shown empty.

Two of the slips of paper you show have the words, "Two Swans in a snowstorm," on them, and one has the words, "An explosion in a paint factory." You will have to keep track of the latter slip; mark it lightly to make sure you can't lose it. Needless to say, ALL of the slips, including the ones in the bag, are folded similarly, so that they have the same general appearance.

In presenting, hand out the envelope while you show the slate on both sides. Place the latter in the envelope and call attention to the fact that it remains in view through the window. Place it aside on the table. The bag, or what have you, is shown empty, the three slips of paper are shown and dropped into it, one at a time. The "Explosion in a paint factory" slip is placed in the bag last, or, rather, is only apparently placed therein, for it is immediately finger-palmed and when the hand comes out, the slip is concealed. Retain it in the hand for a while.

Go among the audience to have one of the slips selected and, as you do so, turn the handle of the bag so that the other compartment comes into place. Someone removes a slip and holds it until you return to the platform. Naturally, he has a "Black cats" slip.

As you go back to the front, turn the handle again, and then pocket the palmed "Paint factory" slip. Remove the slate after the person reads the inscription on the paper, turn it around, and show that the picture has substantially appeared on the slate!

At this point, you are facing the audience and the flap side of the slate is toward you. Holding the slate in both hands, right hand at top edge of frame, insert the right forefinger between the flap and the slate and grasp the top edge of the flap with right thumb and forefinger. Replace the slate in the envelope, but in doing so, separate the flap from the slate and slide the former BEHIND the envelope (Fig. 1). It is held in place there by the thumb of the left hand, which holds the envelope. At this point you change your mind—it works just as well without using the envelope, you say. With

FIG. 1

FIG. 2

the right hand remove the slate from the envelope. Hold slate and envelope in right and left hands respectively, before body, directly beside and touching each other. Turn the slate over flat, like a page, against the back of the envelope, over the flap (Fig. 2) and hold both slate and envelope in left hand, turning them horizontally, slate on top. With the right hand, pull out the envelope from under the slate, leaving the slate, flap down, in the left hand. Toss the envelope aside or hand it to somebody to hold. Place the slate in full view on the table, leaning it against a glass or some other object, flap ("picture") side away from audience, of course.

Go out to have another slip removed from the bag. Since you have already turned the handle, you can hold the bag with one hand at all times, and no matter which slip is taken this time, it is the one with the "Two Swans" scene.

When it is read out, you turn the slate around, and there's an entirely white surface! The flap side is toward audience and the fingers hold it in front securely. Take the envelope and, turning the slate about, replace it in the envelope, once again separating the flap and letting it slide BEHIND the envelope Ask one of the spectators for this initials and write them on the slate through the window. Keeping the flap side of the envelope away from audience, lay the envelope, flap down, on the table. If the table top is below the eye-level line of the audience, the envelope may be laid on a black-surfaced tray on the table.

Obtain possession of the pocketed slip in the right hand again at this time. Go into the audience, and say you will have the last slip read. Reach into the bag with the right hand, bring forth the palmed slip, and hand it to somebody. The spectators have no cause for suspicion here, since they believe only one slip remains in the bag and that, naturally, must be the one taken.

Before the slip is read, pick up the envelope, leaving the flap behind on the table, and toss it to the man who gave you his initials. At the close he removes the slate himself and holds it up to show the successful result.

TWO ROUTINES

We herewith propound two mental routines. The first is for rather close work:

1. Dual Impulsion.

2. Things to Come.

3. Wrong Number.

4. Phantom President.

5. Picture Projection.

"Dual Impulsion" utilizes cards and is described in the next section. It is performed as an experiment for psychic ability in the spectator and the performer. "Things to Come" illustrates how future events may be reliably predicted. "Wrong Number" is presented as an attempted divination, but turns out to be an unforeseen coincidence. "The Phantom President" shows how a mentalist may know beforehand who will be "elected" and is an especially entertaining bit. Finally, a clean-cut demonstration of telepathy is shown in "Picture Projection" and concludes the routine impressively. Routine takes about 30 minutes.

The second routine is for a somewhat larger audience:

1. Synchronism.

2. (a) Prediction to End Predictions.

   (b) Payoff Prediction.

3. Transposed Minds.

4. Picture Projection.

This act takes about 20 to 25 minutes. All that need be said here is that either prediction effect may be used for the second number, (a) lasting a little longer than (b).

Either act takes up very little room in packing and may almost be presented at a moment's notice.

THOUGHT ON THE LINE

A card trick that may be performed over the telephone is not a new idea. The ingenious Messrs. Al Baker and Audley Walsh put out "Number. Please," some years ago, where, in effect, the magus would call up some person he knew, tell him to pick up any deck of cards at hand and, after a few simple directions, eventually reveal a selected card.

The following effect is along the same line. A MENTALLY SELECTED card is divined over the telephone—an especially good point being that this is done without any "fishing" for information. You positively KNOW the card every time, although the person at the other end will not be able to understand how this is done.

Telephone your victim and, when you are ready for the trick, tell him to get a deck of cards, as you want to try out a mental experiment. Having the cards by the 'phone, instruct him to shuffle them well. Then request him to deal the cards face up on the table, one on top of the other, and name them to you as they are dealt off. The person is to merely THINK of one of these cards, but to give no outward indication, such as a slight hesitation or change of inflection in the voice. He is to continue reading and dealing off the cards after his mental choice.

Having read off a sufficient number of cards, you ask if the person has thought of one of them already. If not, he continues a bit further, but if he has, tell him to place the deck aside. Remind him that a card was just thought of and that you could not normally know what it is. What is more, he may change his mind, if he likes, and think of another card in the dealt-off packet.

Now instruct him to take the small packet of cards and deal them out into two face-up piles. That done, he is to remove the card he has thought of from whichever packet it is in and place it in the center of the other packet. This pile (now containing the thought-of card) is placed on top of the deck and the other packet on top of that. (Naturally, packets are placed on deck face down.)

The person now calls off the cards from the top of the deck, the idea being that he think of his card all the time, so that you will know it when he comes to it. A few cards are called off when you suddenly stop him. "Wait a moment," you say, "you haven't reached the card you are thinking of, yet, have you?" The reply is in the negative. "Good," you say, "I wanted you to SHUFFLE the deck first. Please give your pack a good mixing, will you? Go ahead."

The cards are shuffled and then called off again, as before, the person at the other end still concentrating on his card. When that particular card is reached, you instantly stop him, stating with certainty that he has reached the card he is thinking of. You are absolutely correct!

The foregoing are the exact details of the effect. Now for the explanation.

When you do the trick, you have on hand a pad, or piece of paper, on which you record the names of the cards when they are first called off. This is when the person first thinks of a card. The card names are, of course, written in abbreviated form, and in two columns, as shown. The first card named is put at the top of the first column (AS). The second card named is written right NEXT to the first (9S). The third card (10D) is put under the first and the fourth (KH) under the second. This alternate placing continues for the remainder of the cards named.

AS 9S   You may stop the person when about 10 or 12 cards have
10D KH   been called, asking him if he has already decided on one of
2S AH   them in his mind. It makes no difference when you stop him
JS 3S   —the number of cards dealt off may be odd or even. Having
4H 10C   thought of a card, tell the person to put the deck aside for the
KS   time being.

Then, as already described, the person deals the cards called off into two piles, transfers his thought-card to the center of the other packet, puts that on the deck, and finally puts the other packet on top, too.

As the person calls off the cards, at this point, there are three fundamental rules to keep in mind. Usually, the first will take care of the situation by itself, but the other two given will aid by finding out the chosen card in a shorter time.

RULE 1: The cards read off should follow one another from the bottom of one column to the top. When the person skips a recorded card in the order of that column, you know immediately that the omitted card is the selected one. In the example, say that the person names 10C, 3S, KH—you would see, as soon as this last card was named, that the AH was omitted and is, therefore, the chosen card. Consequently, you stop him, innocently inquiring if the card he is thinking of has been passed. Because of the handling of the packets, such could not be the case as yet, but ask, anyway; later on, after the trick is done, they will remember that point. Request a thorough shuffle of the pack.

Once in a while, you may run across a person who will give the order of one column from the top to the bottom. Do not let that worry you, as it makes no difference in the calculation of the chosen card. What has probably happened is that the person turned the small packet face down when it was picked up, so that he dealt out the two packets from the top.

RULE 2: If all the cards but the last in a column are called off in order (without omission), the last card there is the selected one. In the example, say that AS, 10D, 2S, JS and 4H are named. Stop the person right there, because the KS is, undoubtedly, the mentally selected card.

RULE 3: If the first card the person calls off is the SECOND card from either end, in either column, the first card at that end is the chosen card. In the example, if the person names 4H, the thought-card is the KS; if 3S, it is the 10C, etc. It is, therefore, possible to stop the person with the naming of only one card.

After the shuffle of the pack, the person reads off the cards again, constantly thinking of his card. Since you know what card it is, it's an easy matter to stop him when he reaches it. Or, if you prefer, you may reveal the card in some other effective manner.

You will find the principle of the "Rules" easy to grasp, so that you can do the trick with perfect assurance.

"PICTURE THIS —"

A deck of cards is used as the means for a "thought transmission" stunt. The performer announces that he will attempt a test of a psychic nature. He explains that in telepathy, a picture of an object is much easier to transmit and receive through the mind than letters or numbers. It is for this reason that the court or "picture" cards only will be used.

The deck is shuffled by the performer to everyone's satisfaction. Spectators may also cut the deck any number of times.

Magician now illustrates what's to be done. He holds up the deck with the face of the deck toward him. The cards are removed from the bottom until a picture card is reached. When a picture card is on the bottom, the spectator is to concentrate his attention on it—to form a mental picture of the card.

The spectator continues through the deck and does as instructed. The magician, now with back turned, correcty names each picture card as it is thought of. No confederates used.

Beforehand, remove all the picture cards from the deck and shuffle them. Write down the order of the cards from face to back on a small piece of paper. Place the picture cards on top of the deck and you are ready.

Do a couple of riffle-shuffles, retaining the 12 picture cards on top. Then call attention to the shuffle as you execute TWO genuine riffle-shufflles. The first shuffle distributes the picture cards through the top half of the deck and the next distributes them through the whole deck. This is most convincing from the spectators' point of view. However, the ORDER of the picture cards remains the same. Place the deck down and have a spectator cut the pack a few times.

When you illustrate what is to be done, you reach the first picture card and tell spectator to think of all these cards; REMEMBER the picture card.

Hand the deck to a spectator to carry out instructions. Meanwhile, you turn your back and move to a corner of the room. Remove the paper with the order of the picture cards from your pocket, but don't let anyone see this.

When the spectator reaches a picture card, he must tell you that he is thinking of it. He may either tell you this verbally, or, what seems to be effective, by one of those toy crickets children play with. Hand him this before you retire to your corner and have him click it every time he thinks of a court card.

All you have to do, when you are informed that a court card has been reached, is to look for the card you have remembered on your little list— and the card directly after it is the card the spectator is thinking of!

After you reveal this card as your "impression," have the spectator continue removing cards and stop when he comes to another picture card. You simply follow ahead in the order by glancing at the paper in hand and are correct every time.

It is not necessary to have the spectator go through the whole deck— you may stop at any point you like. Also, the pack may be handed to another person after a while.

NAME YOUR FAVORITE

This is a variation on "Picture This." Place the court cards on top of the deck in prearranged order as before. Give the deck several rifflé-shuffles, retaining the top stack of twelve cards. Give the deck a fair riffle-shuffle, lacing the cards as evenly as possible. Have a spectator cut the deck into halves, forcing him to cut a little below the center, and riffle them together himself.

Say, "What is your favorite court card? Do you like Queens, Kings, or Jacks?" Whichever he names, say, "What suit?" and, on reply, hand him the clicker and ask him to hold the deck faces toward him and take off the cards one by one, clicking the cricket each time he reaches a court card.

You turn your back and consult your list, unless you have the order of the cards memorized. Each time you hear a click, say, "Throw that card aside." When the card that has been named is reached, however, cry, "Stop! Hold that card up—it's the ONE YOU SELECTED, isn't it?" And so it is, since you knew what each court card was as it was clicked off and were thus in a position to stop the assistant at the proper one.

An only slightly more complex version enables you to have any card at all named, yet you stop the spectator when he reaches it in a shuffled deck.

In this case the whole deck is set up, the suits being separated and each arranged in some uniform order, say Eight King sequence, without reference to suits. Crimp the club packet concavely and place it on top of the heart packet, which you crimp convexly. Do the same with the spade and diamond packets respectively and put the club-heart pack on top of them. Make the crimp in each case across the width of the cards. Slip a rubber band lengthwise around the deck and place in your coat pocket.

To present, bring out the deck, squeezing it so the crimps do not show. Ask someone to name his favorite suit and, as soon as he has done this, cut at the proper place, facilitated by the crimps, to bring this suit to the top of the deck. Immediately give the deck a riffle-shuffle. From here on, handle the deck exactly as described above. Whatever the man's favorite card, he signals at each card of that suit and the magus correctly stops him at the favorite card.

Either arrangement is quite a little mystery, as the performer makes a point of at no time so much as glimpsing the face of a single card in the handling.

REMOTE REVERSO

This "You Do As I Do" effect has a slightly different and surprising finish.

Two decks of cards are used. A spectator takes one and the magician the other. Both deal off cards from the top of the deck in unison and whenever the spectator feels the inclination to stop, he does so. Performer and spectator both look at the card stopped at in their packs and then shuffle it among the cards counted off. This small packet of cards is placed on top of the respective decks and same given a complete cut.

The magician now names his card and asks the spectator for his. Performer snaps his deck and spreads it on the table. The card that the spectator names shows up reversed!

The performer asks the spectator to see if this will work in his own deck. Spectator snaps his pack and spreads the cards. The card that the magician had named is reversed therein!

METHOD: If you are working with two decks, both prearranged in some familiar set-up, such as the "Eight Kings" order, you need only see to it that the same card is on the bottom of each deck (so that each pack is in exact, identical order).

Assuming, however, that you have not been able to set up two whole decks in identical order, a minute's preparation is needed. Take one deck and arrange all the cards of one suit in order, from Ace to King, with the Ace on top. Place these cards on top of the deck and on top of this set-up put five indifferent cards. Follow the same procedure with the other deck of cards, using the same suit and order.

Whatever prearrangement you use, reverse the card that is about four cards from the bottom in ONE deck. REMEMBER THIS CARD.

When presenting the effect, give both decks a good false shuffle, leaving the cards in position. Hand a spectator the deck with the reversed card near the bottom. Ask him to deal off any number of cards from the top of the deck and to stop whenever he wishes. Tell him not to deal off too many cards, however, so as not to drag out the trick. The performer deals from his deck with the spectator.

The person will always stop somewhere in the set-up. If he should happen to stop at less than six cards, tell him to "deal a few more—for luck."

Naturally, since both the spectator and the performer have dealt off the cards simultaneously, they are at the same point in the arrangement. Ask spectator to look at the top card of the cards he dealt off and remember it, while you do the same in your deck. Now ask the spectator to shuffle his small packet of cards so that his card will be lost.

You apparently do the same thing, but during the course of your shuffle you reverse the top card, which you know to be the spectator's duplicate in your deck, by slipping it to the bottom, turning it over in the process, or by any favorite means. This is very easy, as it seems to be only a casual shuffle, and besides, people will usually watch the spectator's movements at this time. Be careful, however, that the reversed card does not show up.

When spectator is satisfied, tell him to place his packet on top of his deck, you doing the same. You both cut the deck once. When you cut the deck, cut it approximately two thirds down, so that the reversed card will be near the center. Spectator usually cuts at about the middle and this brings the reversed card in his deck to the center.

You now say, "My card was the ———. What was yours?" You name the card that is reversed in the spectator's deck as YOUR card. Spectator names his card.

As soon as it is made known, snap your deck and spread it across the table. The card just named shows up reversed. Ask the spectator to try his luck with his deck and, after he snaps his deck (rather incredulously, perhaps) and spreads his cards, it is seen that "your" card is also reversed.

The impressive effect gained completely overshadows the simple means used to bring it about.

SYNCHRONISM

This is a "You Do As I Do" in which the assisting spectator certainly does.

A red and blue backed deck are brought forward and one of these a spectator takes and shuffles thoroughly. We shall suppose he took the red deck. After the shuffle, this deck is spread face down on one side of the table and the blue deck is spread face up on the other side. The magician says that some people are more attracted to certain cards than to others and, therefore, he takes some pains in selecting from the face up deck a card which will work with the spectator involved. Let us say that the magician decides on the Two of Clubs. He removes this (blue backed) card and, holding it before the spectator, boldly states that he has synchronized the spectator's will with his own and has already determined which of the 52 cards in the face down red deck the spectator will finally decide to remove. Confronted with this challenge, the man makes a vain effort to prove his freedom of will—but the magician was right, for the card which he finally picks from the face down spread is—the Two of Clubs!

The idea is that you deliberately tell a person you are going to force him to select a certain card and then do it, despite the forewarning and the fact that you do not touch the cards while he makes the selection, from the deck which he himself shuffled.

All in all, it is quite a nightmare—and if the method seems a bit weird, consider it only in keeping with the effect.

Needed are TWO RED BACKED DECKS, one of them a forcing deck, the cards being all of one kind, and the other ordinary, but with the force card removed. We must also have a blue backed duplicate of the force card and two cases for the respective decks. The cases must not be the common flap type, but the kind consisting of a box and lid, which bridge decks are frequently put up in.

To set, the fair deck is placed in its case and the forcing deck, with an indifferent card on the bottom and the blue backed card on top, placed similarly in its case.

In the presentation, two switches are used, but, aside from a Hindu Shuffle, these two moves are the only ones in the trick and both are perfectly covered. The basic subtlety of employing two decks with the same colored backs, one tricked and one fair, under the guise of two differently colored decks, completely throws off any theory as to the solution of the mystery.

Presentation: The two decks are brought forward in their cases and a spectator asked to take one of them. If the red one, good. If he selects the "blue" deck, immediately take it from him and say, "Thank you. I shall use the one you have given me. Please take the other deck yourself and shuffle it." In any case, the spectator thoroughly shuffles the red deck and notes that it is all right. We must be sure that this is clear.

While the spectator is shuffling, remove the "blue" deck also from its case and hold the deck, back out, in the left hand without calling any especial attention to it. Simply say, "I shall use this deck, which is blue backed, while the gentleman will use the red backed deck." Toss your card case onto the table. Before taking the spectator's deck back, pocket the case from his deck.

When the spectator has finished shuffling his deck, transfer the "blue" deck, which you hold in the left hand, to the right hand, holding it in the latter hand thus: Backs of cards facing palm of the hand, the second, third and little fingers at the narrow end of the pack and thumb pressing against the

FIG. 1

opposite end. The forefinger is free. (See Figure). The red deck is taken in the left hand in normal dealing position.

Bring the hands close to each other and turn your right side to the audience as you return to the table. At the same time, push the top, blue backed card from the top of the deck held in the right hand forward with the right first finger, pushing it over so that the left thumb can square it on top of the deck in the left hand. This shifting of the top card of the right hand deck to the top of the left hand deck is a simple move and is entirely covered by the back of the right hand and the general misdirection of your returning to the table.

No sooner has the card been transferred than the right hand places its deck on the table and at once comes back, grasps the left's deck, and places it on the table alongside the first. This is all done rather quickly.

The spectator who shuffled the red deck is now asked to come up to the table. He stands at the left side and the performer at the side opposite him with his right side turned slightly toward the audience.

The deck which now shows red backed is picked up and spread face down in a ribbon before the spectator, who is reminded that he shuffled this deck and is, therefore, to use it in the experiment. As we know, this is actually the forcing deck.

You then pick up the "blue" deck and give it a brief shuffle. This is done as follows: The deck is placed face up in the left hand, then the right withdraws the lower three-fourths of the pack, holding it upright so the back of the blue card may be seen. Bring the right hand packet down on that in the left, not releasing it, however, and with left thumb and fingers (left hand palm up) strip off a packet from the top of the right packet, allowing it to drop on the cards in the left, bringing the hands apart and lifting the right again, showing the blue back again. This is repeated until a small packet remains in the right hand and this packet is then dropped on the rest. The face up deck is spread in a ribbon on your side of the table.

The adaptation of the Hindu Shuffle to apparently show the deck blue backed clear through is due to Jean Hugard and is extremely deceptive. It should be done casually, being a subtle touch which fits into the whole and makes the problem an insoluble one.

To recapitulate, the spectator has selected a pack and shuffled it, while the magus retained and shuffled the other pack of contrasting back. The spectator's pack is now spread face down before him, while the magician's is spread face up on the opposite side of the table.

With some deliberation, you now choose one of the face up cards; you choose the Two of Clubs. Take the card out and hold it up so all can see your choice. They get a glimpse of its blue back and this all goes to carry out the illusion of the actually mythical blue deck.

Drop this card on the table, gather up the rest of the face up cards and square them, face out, in the left hand, at the same time pattering to the spectator along the lines indicated in the description of the effect. Remind him that he alone shuffled the red cards, shuffled them so well that no one knows the location of a single one. This, you assure him, is really to his disadvantage, as it makes it easier for you to mentally force him to choose the card you wish him to.

While making these remarks, you pick up the case of the "blue" deck, which is needed no longer, and place the deck in the case, laying it aside on the table. What is not observed, however, is that in putting the cover on the box you turned the latter over, a la Okito coin box, actually placing the cover over the BOTTOM of the box and placing the whole, cover up, on the table. These inconspicuous actions are necessary to get us ready ahead of time for the final switch.

The spectator, after your harangue, touches any card at all in the face down spread and pushes it out. You sweep up the spread, square the cards, and drop the pack alongside the card case on the table, while you ask the man if he is sure his choice was a free one, etc. Once more you call attention to the fact that you first drew the Two of Clubs and again exhibit the blue backed card. Now the spectator looks at his card, holds it up for all to see, holds it up high because, sure enough, it, too, is the Two of Clubs!

At this point in the climax, you simply lift up the card case on the table and put it over the force deck, leaving the straight red deck in view. A moment later you pocket the card case (with forcing deck), which presumably contained the "blue" deck all along. The switch is indetectable.

The climax is now over, but before the spectator takes his seat, we pick up the red deck which alone remains on the table and, fanning it face out, ask the man to please return his card among the others. This gives us a complete deck with which we may now embark upon further mysteries.

DUAL IMPULSION

Simple and highly effective, this card experiment may be done before an audience of any size.

Both the magus and an assisting spectator remove a card at random from a shuffled deck. The magus writes the name of his card on a pad or slate and the spectator does the same, neither allowing the other, or the audience, to see what is written. Each replace the respective cards into the center of the deck, which rests on the table. After a thorough shuffle, obviously showing no control of the cards, the pack is spread out wide on the table, face down. Then, in illustration of what the spectator is to duplicate, the magus waves his hand slowly along the spread, saying that some impulse will command him to push out one card. The hand movement stops suddenly and a card at that point is removed and held in view by the performer. Now the assisting spectator does the same and holds his card.

Picking up his slate (or pad) with the free hand, the magus shows and reads aloud the name of the card he originally selected. The spectator shows the card he holds. It is the same! The spectator now exhibits what he wrote and names the card. Magus turns around the card he holds—it is the spectator's card! Each has "unconsciously" discovered the other's card!

As in all effects of a mental nature, a really serious presentation is essential here. Shown as a mere trick, you will not achieve the true effect, but offered as an earnest experiment and it will smack of real mentalism.

The instrument of trickery used to bring about the effect is one which some may disparage, but which is, nevertheless, one of the most useful ideas in magic—a one-kind forcing deck. From your straight deck, the backs of which match the force deck, remove the duplicate of the force card, which is, say, the Nine of Hearts and an indifferent card, say the Queen of Diamonds. The straight pack, minus the two cards, is placed ON END in your right coat pocket.

Mark the indifferent card with pencil dots on the back, at all four corners, so that you can detect it by sight anywhere in the deck. Put it—and the extra force card—in the forcing pack.

It is necessary, now, to force the INDIFFERENT card on the spectator. Such action may sound crazy, but there's a method to the madness.

Since the indifferent card is marked, it may be near the center of the deck and the regulation fan force made cleanly, as no break need be held. If you are not one to trust that force, use any other kind that you do well. If you like, try this: Have the indifferent card third from the top. Give the deck a few dovetail shuffles, retaining that card in position, and taking care that the faces of the cards are not seen. When ready, state that both you and your assistant are to remove a card; ask him to give a number—a rather low figure, as you do not want to take up too much time counting. Suppose he gives No. 6. Remark that you will take a number, too, taking one apparently at random, just like the spectator. Actually, you mentally count ahead 3 (or whatever number the indifferent card is from the top) and name No. 9. Immediately count off 9 cards, one at a time, taking the ninth for yourself, and replace the small packet on top of the deck. Then have the spectator count down to his number and take the card at that spot. He gets the indifferent card and that's that.

On your slate you now write the name of your card (Nine of Hearts) while the spectator does the same with his (Queen of Diamonds). The cards are then returned to the middle of the pack on the table and same given a few genuine shuffles. Then the deck is spread out wide so that you can sight the indifferent card by the marks.

Pass your hand over the spread once or twice and then, as you hover over the indifferent card, stop, and push it forward. Hold it in view, back out, and have the person go through the same business. Naturally, he gets a force card. As soon as he has it, scoop up the rest of the deck with the right hand and place it in the right coat pocket, on its SIDE. The name of the card on your slate coincides with the card the spectator holds, and vice versa, thus making the cross-discovery climax. Remove the straight deck (standing on end) from your pocket and add the two cards to it, after which it may be checked or used for any other effect requiring a regulation deck.

DUO PREDICTION

With any deck of cards, this impromptu effect will be found to be an effective interlude.

The trick makes use of the force suggested in the last trick. It is only necessary to know the second and third cards from the top. Any favorite means may be used to get this, the glimpse being about the most practical. Riffle-shuffle the pack, keeping the top three cards in place.

On a slip of paper, write the name of the card that is second from top, telling the spectators that it is the prediction for yourself. Fold the slip and put it on the table, slightly to your left. On another slip, write the name of the third card from the top, announcing that this is for the spectator. After folding it, place it on the table, slightly to your right.

Pick up the deck of cards and ask a spectator to give you a number, saying that you will take a number, too. We will suppose the number he gives is 14. You mentally add three to it and so you call out 17 for your number. Explain that you will count down to your number first, as you wrote the prediction for yourself first. Count off 17 cards and remove the last card, placing it next to the slip on your left, wnich is "your" prediction. Replace the cards counted off on top of the deck. Now recall the spectator's number—14— and count down to that number, removing that card and placing it next to the slip on your right, which is the spectator's paper. Put the deck ON TOP of the small packet (which was counted off) and leave it on the table a moment, as if you were all through with it.

Remind everybody that the predictions were made before the number and card selections. Then request the spectator to read what you wrote for his prediction. As he picks up the billet that is to your right, take the deck casually and place it in the left hand. The person reads the name of the card. Take the top card of the deck in the right hand and, VERY DELIBERATELY, flip over the card at the right. It is the same card you predicted!

Taking advantage of the momentary surprise, you now appear to flip over the card at your left with the card in hand. What you actually do is the MEXICAN TURNOVER sleight, which exchanges the cards. The Mexican Turnover is too well-known to require a detailed description here; suffice to say that it is a very deceptive sleight and will fool even when watched. In this case, you do it at the moment when people are off guard, so it materially decreases the chance of possible detection. The psychology of deliberately flipping over the first card also helps, as it will be supposed you did the same the second time. There's no reason to suspect otherwise.

Executing the Mexican Turnover, say, "Now, here is my card, the ——," and name it. All see it on the table face up. Put the card in right hand atop the deck and request someone to pick up "your" slip and read it aloud. It, too, checks!

THE TRIPLE ENIGMA

Here you bewilder by demonstrating par-optic vision, a telepathically receptive mind, and super-sensitive fingertips.

In effect, a regulation deck of cards is cut at some point designated by the spectator and one part of the deck is given to him. He shuffles these cards and the magus puts the remainder of the deck on the table. Turning his back, momentarily, the performer requests the assistant to put any number of cards he holds into some pocket. The actual number should not be known to the spectator. That done, the person may again mix what cards that remain, finally note the BOTTOM card, and then place all on top of the cards on the table. Deck is squared up.

The magus eventually tells the spectator the EXACT NUMBER of cards in his pocket—and correctly names the card that was noted! To finish, the wonder-worker states that he will attempt to find this card behind his back by the mere sense of touch. A card is brought out and shown. It is the one!

The deck used should be one with a border on the back. Otherwise, a key card is the only essential. Any kind may be utilized, but a short is about the most practical. Have it at a set number from the top—say, in 21st place, as that is about right. Wherever it is, however, you must know the number of cards above it. Set it in place before you begin or bring it there by sleight-of-hand.

Hold the deck in the left hand and riffle the front ends from bottom to top with the right fingers. Invite the spectator to stop you at any time. You can always time it or manipulate the riffle so that it stops at the short card. Hand the top part of the deck to the person and ask him to shuffle. Everything seems fair, but you KNOW the total number of cards he has. Put bottom part of the deck on the table.

Turn your back and tell the person to put a number of cards that he holds into a pocket. Specify that he, himself, should not know the exact number, as you do not want to get this part by telepathy. Then, tell him to remember the card at the BOTTOM of the remainder and place all on top of the deck on the table. Ask him to make sure the deck is squared up before you turn around again.

Pick up the pack and put it behind you. Say you will try to "get" the card he is thinking of. Riffle the ends softly to come to the short card. Hold the left little finger above it and then, with the right fingers, count the number of cards on top. (Do not count the short card). It doesn't take long. Mentally subtract this number from 20 (or whatever number of cards you know spectator originally had) and you have the number of cards in his pocket!

However, don't reveal it right away. You know that the card directly above the short card is the card that spectator has remembered. Take it out of the deck and put it second from the top, REVERSED. All this takes place behind your back.

Now say that you can't quite "get" the card as yet, but you will try for the number of cards in the pocket. Holding the deck squarely in your left hand, bring it forward casually, and announce that you "see"—par-optically—so-and-so many cards. When the man counts them, to verify, you have plenty of time to glimpse the noted card. You get a peek of the index very easily at the upper left corner by shifting the top card ever so slightly to the right with the left thumb and immediately bringing it back, square with the deck. It takes but an instant and the pack can then be put behind the back just as casually.

The cards having been counted and found to be of the same number you foretold, ask the person to concentrate on the particular card he noted. After appropriate build-up, announce the name of the card you glimpsed.

Finally, you will try to find that card behind your back by "feeling" for it with your finger tips. In time, take out the second card, bringing it forward face down. Show that it is the remembered card.

If your key card is not a short card, have it in position and hold a break with the left little finger above it. Riffle the front end of the deck with right fingers and request person to stop you at any time. Really stop at that point, but then close the break at the front end by lessening the grip with right fingers and lift off the part of the deck above the little finger at the back, and give to the spectator. The illusion is quite perfect that you hand out the cards from the point stopped at. This move will probably be recognized as one to force a card; in this instance, it forces a known number of cards on the spectator. Proceed as before.

If you are forced to work with an all-over back design, such as the majority of bridge cards, it will be necessary for you to bring the chosen card to the top or bottom, and when you casually bring forward the deck, you must sight it in some favorite way. Use the glimpse as detailed in the trick whenever possible.

NU-LOCATO

All that is necessary in this convincing location of a selected, or peeked-at card, is to know the TOP card of the deck.

We will assume that the now fairly well-known "peek at a card" idea is being utilized, this being especially good when used in conjunction with the dodge to follow. The left hand holds the deck with thumb held diagonally across the top card and the four fingers held firmly at the side. A spectator bends back the cards at the outside index corner, usually about the middle of the deck, thus "peeking" or glimpsing a card for identification. Since a fairly firm hold is exerted by the fingers, a "break" directly below the noted card becomes inevitable, and is held by the flesh of the finger tips. Deck is lowered at this point, as you direct the spectator not to forget the name of the card he saw.

The deck is now apparently cut a number of times to lose the card completely. Actually, this is so, but the first "cut" is not quite so innocent as it appears. The right thumb is held against the back end of the pack (nearest the body), the forefinger lifts up a part of the deck at the front end—about half-way between the point where the break is being held and the top of the deck—while the second finger cuts at the break. That is, a center portion of the deck is removed to the right (with thumb and second finger) with the noted card at its face. These cards are immediately placed on top of the deck. It should appear that you have taken some cards from the bottom and transferred them to the top.

Again the deck is cut; this time it is a genuine cut, but the method of cutting should appear to be the same as the first action. To make this so, the right thumb is held at the back end of the pack, the first finger lifts off half to two-thirds of the deck at the front end momentarily, while the second finger grips the bottom portion (at the front end), removes it to the right, and transfers it to the top. It is quite a natural way to cut a deck.

Through this manipulation (any number of similar additional cuts may be made), the noted card is brought right above the locator card! Thus, if the cards are spread on the table, the card may be discovered as person thinks of it. A good plan is to have a favorite key card (short, long, wide, etc.) as the top card so that you may eventually bring the selected card to the top, bottom, or veritably any position you like, with skillful cuts and shuffles. For a discovery, you can find the card behind your back.

The cards are handled easily and naturally at all times. Just watch your angles on the first (faked) cut.

In place of the peek, a card may be selected as usual and replaced in a spread of the deck. Close up the deck and merely hold a break BELOW the selected card with left little finger—then follow with the foregoing manipulation. You'll achieve the same result.

SIMPLEX CARD STABBING

Any deck may be used, but before presenting the trick, one card must be stolen and pierced in the center with a pen knife. The blade should pierce the card slightly flatwise. With this card placed on the bottom of the deck, the preparation is complete.

Advance on a spectator and force the prepared card on him. Here is the force best adapted for use in this trick: Fan the deck with both hands, the fingers under the cards, and with the finger tips run the bottom card along under the spread. The spectator touches any card and the deck is cut here, the bottom card being run to this point, and by the pressure of the right fingers it is slipped to the face of the top half of the deck as the cut is made. The spectator looks at this card (the card at the bottom of the top packet), but as the right fingers are naturally over the center of the face of the packet, the slit in the card is covered. Now turn right side to audience and sort of toss the packet back onto the deck. The face card, because of friction, will be found to remain naturally in the right hand, which completes the movement by throwing this card on top. Continuing directly with a shuffle covers this simple shift perfectly. Just do it all fast and it virtually works itself.

Hold the deck in your left hand, the cards face up, and the knife in the right hand lying across the fingers, the thumb on top of the handle. Place the deck in the right hand, face up, apparently on the knife, but really the knife blade is shoved through the slit. This is an easy, though bold, move and the audience has nothing to suspect. Extend the left hand now as though hitching up the sleeve—for misdirection.

With a sweeping, upward motion of the right hand, toss the deck several feet into the air and then, with a quick jab, stab the knife into the midst of the cards, scrattering them as they fall. With a gesture as dramatic as you like, exhibit the chosen card impaled on the knife.

That's all there is to it, but boldly done, it is exceedingly effective for use where you don't mind scattering the cards a bit.

THE IMPROMPTU FIFTEEN CARD TRICK

The "Fifteen Card Trick" has for a long time been a popular effect on magicians' programs, and deservedly so. The trick, in its regular form, requires a special deck of cards and care has to be exercised that the set-up of the cards is not disturbed. It is now possible (in this version) to do the effect with a BORROWED, SHUFFLED deck of cards and with two unprepared letter envelopes.

The effect is as follows: Two sets of fifteen cards are slowly and unmistakably counted on the table by a spectator from a shuffled deck. The magician picks up one set and has three cards selected by as many spectators. There is an absolutely free choice and, should the spectators desire, the respective cards may be initialled or otherwise marked for identification. The three selected cards are returned to the same packet and the cards are shuffled. One of the letter envelopes is examined by a spectator and the packet of cards is then openly placed into this envelope, which is immediately sealed. The remaining packet of cards is now counted again—15 cards. This packet is inserted into the other examined envelope and it is also sealed. Both envelopes are now initialled by two spectators and they are told to hold them in view. Under these stringent conditions, the selected cards are commanded to pass from one envelope to the other. The first envelope is opened and the cards counted by the spectator. There are only 12 cards and, by verification, the selected cards are not there! The other envelope is opened and cards counted. There are 18 cards—and, impossible as it may seem, the SAME chosen cards are among them!

PREPARATION: None. Just make certain, before you start the trick, that there are no pencils on the table.

METHOD: After the deck is shuffled, have a spectator count off 15 cards onto the table. This is done deliberately and either you or the dealer call the numbers aloud, so there can be no mistake about it. Pick up the cards and place them in the left hand, apparently for the purpose of squaring them up. Request the spectator to count off 15 more cards on the table, slowly. While he is doing this, quietly thumb count three cards from the top of the packet in left hand and hold a little break. When the second set has been counted off, pick them up with the right hand, thumb at one end, fingers at the other. Remark, "We will use this second set of 15." So saying, the left hand replaces its packet on the table, but as it does so, it passes beneath the right hand, and in that instant, the separate top three cards are neatly added to the bottom of the right-hand packet. If this is done CASUALLY—not deliberately—it will never be detected.

In your hands, you now hold 18 cards, the audience, of course thinking you have but 15.

Go to TWO spectators, in turn, and have each remove a card, marking it if they wish. Return to one of them and spread the cards, as if you wanted to have the card returned. Suddenly, close the spread and say that perhaps ANOTHER card should be selected. A third spectator now also removes a card. The procedure will psychologically impress the onlookers that it doesn't matter how many cards are taken.

Have the first card returned to the packet and immediately shuffle the cards. The shuffle is genuine and very deliberate. Do the same with the other two cards, shuffling the packet after each card is returned. Take one en-velope, which spectator has been examining, and insert the cards into it, in full view. Seal and drop it slightly to your left on the table, address side up.

Now pick up the other packet of cards and count them. Since there are really only 12 cards, the false count must be employed to count them as 15.

Take the other envelope, which has been examined also, and place the packet of (12) cards into it in the same open manner as before. This envelope is also sealed.

Here is where the crucial move of the trick enters. Hold the envelope you have just sealed between the FIRST and SECOND fingers of the right hand, address side up. Pick up the other envelope from the table with the left hand and hold it between the THUMB and FIRST finger of that hand.

Announce that you will want to have the envelopes initialled by dif-ferent persons. Turn to a spectator at your LEFT, gesturing slightly with the left hand, and ask, "Have you a pencil?" Before he has a chance to answer, turn to a spectator at your RIGHT and ask, "Have YOU a pencil?" Turn back to the spectator at the left and, as you do so, you switch the envelopes, as fol-lows: Both hands approach each other. The right-hand envelope goes un-derneath and is clipped between the LEFT first and second fingers, while the left-hand envelope is transferred to the right hand, between thumb and first finger. The switch is done in an instant and is not detected because of the misdirection. The envelopes are forgotten, momentarily, in the search for a pencil. Besides this, when the switch is made, you are turning toward the spectator at the LEFT; say to him, "You see, you are to initial this en-velope here." Give him the envelope in the left hand and point to a corner of the envelope. "And you, sir,"—here you go over to the spectator at your right—"you are to initial this envelope here." Give him the envelope in the right hand and have him initial it with a pencil, which has probably been forthcoming by this time. If neither person has a pencil, bring out one of your own from your pocket. Both spectators keep the envelopes in their hands.

Be assured that the switch of the envelopes, bold as it may sound, is never caught when executed with the misdirection provided. Attention is focused on the assisting spectators at the moment the switch takes place and when the audience looks at the envelopes again, the exchange has already been made. The switch was originally used for small slates by fraudulent spirit mediums and is not hard to learn. A few minutes' practice with envelopes in hand will make everything clear and simple.

As far as the mechanics of the trick is concerned, you are all through. All that remains is to build up the effect to a proper climax. Review what has happened and then command the selected cards to pass. Spectator at your left tears open his envelope, removes the cards, and counts them openly on the table. There are 12 cards. Have spectators who selected cards look through the packet to see if their cards are in it. Naturally, they are not. The spectator at your right opens his envelope and counts the cards. There are 18 cards—and each spectator who selected a card will find his card among them!

Because the trick can be done impromptu is no reason why it can not be used as a program item. Use Air Mail envelopes when you can—they are appropriate for the effect.

THE CHALLENGE BLINDFOLD CARD ROUTINE

In this impressive demonstration, the performer is GENUINELY BLIND-FOLDED. A newly-opened deck of cards, which the magus has never touched or even seen, is shuffled and the following tests are shown:

EFFECT No. 1: A mentally selected card is found by having the spectator think "That's my card!" when he sees it as the cards are passed before him one at a time. The magus succeeds in getting the "mental impression" as the card is reached.

EFFECT No. 2: Another selected card is found by dealing the cards on the table. At one particular card, the magus gets a certain "vibration," so the card is turned face up. It is the right card.

EFFECT No. 3: A selected card is found by having the spectator read off the cards. When he reaches his card and names it, the magus detects a note in the man's voice that tells him the name of the selected card has been called out.

EFFECT No. 4: Lastly, still another selected card is shuffled into the deck by the spectator himself. Cards are dealt onto the performer's hand until he calls "Stop—you now hold your card" and NAMES it. The card that is in the spectator's hand at this time is his selected card.

PRESENTATION: Allow yourself to be blindfolded or otherwise deprived of the use of your sight by any means a committee may impose upon you. Powder puffs, wads of cotton, adhesive tape, kneaded dough, or virtually anything may be placed over your eyes, if you go in for that sort of thing.

EFFECT No. 1: You actually know nothing of the cards that will be presented to you. A new deck is best to use, so, besides being more effective to ask for a deck of cards that is still sealed in its case, it helps materially in the handling.

A spectator shuffles the pack thoroughly. When it is handed you, tell someone to think of a card and remember its number from the top as you pick up the cards one at a time and show. Call out their numbers until about 12 have been shown and ask the spectator if he has memorized one of the cards. Make sure he knows its number from the top, too.

In picking up the top card, you nail-nick it indetectably on its face by the right second finger nail at the lower right-hand corner. The right thumb is on the back of the card in this action. The result is a small bump on the back of the card which may be felt by "feeling" for it with the thumb or finger tips.

The remainder of the cards shown are left alone and, when the person has indicated he has made a choice, replace the cards on top. Then, put the deck behind your back, saying you are going to change the positions of the cards. What you do is turn the top card around, end for end, and make ANOTHER nail-nick at the new lower right-hand corner. Then make still another nail-nick at the CENTER of the card.

Put the marked card on the bottom and bring the deck forward.

Ask the spectator at what number he saw the card he is thinking of. Count off the cards, one at a time, into the right hand—then turn over the card at the number he names. Naturally, it's not his card—the card is not at the same position any more. The packet of cards you have counted off (the spectator's selected card is on top of this packet) is placed on the bottom of the deck.

The person denies that the top face-up card is the one he originally remembered at the specified number. Turn it face down and push it somewhere into the middle of the deck.

Now give the deck two or more riffle-shuffles, keeping the bottom stack intact. Then have someone give the deck a single cut. This usually brings the spectator's thought-of card about 20 cards from the top.

Of course, the spectator's card is directly below the marked card, because of the method of handling. All you do is remove the cards one at a time from the top of the deck, show them to the person, and tell him to just think "That's my card!" when he sees it. When you have dealt about ten cards, start dealing the cards more deliberately. The right hand grasps each card, in turn, at the lower right-hand corner, so that the slight protuberance can be felt with the thumb. The left thumb pushes the cards out by the middle, so it can also feel the bump at that part of the card and serves as a sort of double-check. It will be almost impossible to miss the card, as one of the thumbs is sure to catch the feel of a bump. Even if the deck is turned around, it will make no difference, as you have another nail-nick at the other end.

Perceiving the card you have marked, put it down on top of the others dealt off. The next card is shown to the spectator. Act as if you were going to put it down, like the others, but bring it up again and hold it so that he sees it. Then announce dramatically that it is his mentally selected card. You are right, of course, so you go into . . . .

EFFECT No. 2: Replace the cards dealt off on top of the pack and also put the first chosen card somewhere in the center. The nail-nicked card is now on top of the deck.

Give the deck a shuffle, but keep the prepared card on top. Now fan the cards to have one selected. Make sure it will be remembered and then undercut the deck for its replacement. Have the onlookers give the deck a number of single cuts.

Now begin dealing off the cards, as before, only this time you don't show the faces, but deal them in a pile on the table. Your patter at this point can be to the effect that, since this second card was actually removed from the deck by someone, it will not be necessary to have him think of it—you will detect it by its foreign "vibration" from the other cards. Call it ESP, or what you will.

Continue dealing the cards—secretly, but quite naturally, feeling every card for the tell-tale bumps. When you feel it, stop. Replace it on top of the cards in hand and pick up the last card dealt off, as if you were undecided. Say, "I had a weak impression when I first dealt off this card, but it seems to be stronger now. Yes, I am quite sure that this card is your chosen card. will you please name it?" As you say this last, hold the card out in front of you and, when it is named, turn it around. Ask if it is right and go on.

EFFECT No. 3: Insert the left little finger under the nail-nicked card, which is the top card of the packet in left hand. After showing the selected card of Effect No. 2, place it on top of the marked card, then pick up the cards on the table and put them on top. Now make an open cut at the place where you have the little finger inserted. The bottom card becomes the nail-nicked card and the second card from the bottom is known to you, because it is the selected card of Effect No. 2 and was named before you showed it.

Hold the deck in the left hand and count off the cards from the top into the right, inviting a person to stop you at any time. When you are stopped, ask him to look at and remember the top card of either packet. If he looks at the top card on the right-hand packet, leave it there and put the other part of the deck on top. Should he note the top card of the packet in the left hand, have him transfer it to the top of the other packet, whereupon you put the left-hand packet on top of it.

Make a cut to bring his card nearer to the top, then hand the deck out to him and ask him to deal the cards face up on the table and to read them off to you. He is to continue the reading, even if he should pass the card he selected. You will try to get his card by a very slight change in his voice when he names it, you say.

As he reads the cards, listen for the name of the card that was selected in the previous effect. Pay attention to, and REMEMBER the next card that is named. This is the nail-nicked card. Then, the NEXT card he names is the selected card, so you stop him as soon as he names it, asking "What?"

He repeats its name. "Hmm-m," you contemplate, "that doesn't sound quite right. That must be the card you took, isn't it?" Spectator must admit that this is so.

EFFECT No. 4: Pick up the cards dealt on the table which are face up and, showing the face card, ask again, "Is that really the card you selected?" Your question is only to make sure he has dealt down his card. The card directly below it is the nail-nicked card. Turn the packet face down and riffle-shuffle the packet into the remainder of the deck, but keep the prepared card second from the bottom. Now give the pack an overhand shuffle. The bottom card is kept in place by the left fingers and the right hand shuffles the marked card to the top.

Request another person to name a "favorite" number from 1 to 10. Having given a number, run off the desired number (by an overhand shuffle), injog, shuffle off the rest of the deck, then cut at the injog and throw on top, which will bring the nail-nicked card into the position you want. This is a matter of indivdual preference and skill, so the reader will probably use his favorite means to the same end.

It is actually a force of the marked card when the person counts down to the number he called out. Any other simple force could be made, as long as you feel you can do it confidently and indetectably without your sight. The number force is bold, but good, as nobody should suspect you of knowing which card is which.

The spectator, having duly memorized the name of the card you have forced on him, now shuffles the deck as much as he likes. This is most convincing. Take the deck back from him and start dealing out the cards into two packs, one card at a time.

Your dealing is similar to the previous effects, i. e., your thumbs feel for the bumps on the back of what you know is the selected card. When you feel it, put it down in the packet where it belongs, just as usual, and continue your deal. However, you start a mental count, counting the nail-nicked card as "One." Deal the next card to the other packet and mentally count the next card you put on top of the selected one as "Two." The next card is dealt on the other packet as before, but every time you add another card on the packet with the selected card, you count ahead one in your mind. Thus, you always know HOW FAR DOWN THE SELECTED CARD IS!

If you have reached the marked card by the time you have dealt off two-thirds of the deck, put the remainder of the deck down, aside from the other two packets, saying that you think that you have divided the deck fairly evenly into three packets, which is what you wanted to do. Pick up one of the packets you know does NOT have the chosen card and spread it out with faces of cards toward the spectator who took the card, asking him if he sees his card therein. When he has denied seeing it, put the packet down and pick up the other packet that you know does NOT have his card and repeat your query. After he again denies seeing his card, put the second packet down and pick up the remaing one.

Say "Since you do not see your card in the other two packets of cards, it is evidently here. However, you don't know exactly which card is yours, do you? You don't even have an idea as to its approximate whereabouts in this packet, isn't that right?" Have him admit this. Then hand him the packet and state, "Perhaps I can help you locate it. Please deal the cards slowly on my hand, one at a time." Hold out your hand. As the spectator puts each card on your hand, mentally count up to a number one less than the number you know the selected card to be. Just time it so that he has the next card in his hand, then stop him and announce that he has his card. Name it and whip off your blindfold.

If the marked card is not reached when you have dealt off more than two-thirds of the deck, you continue to deal out the whole deck into two packets. You always start the mental count at the nail-nicked card and add one for each card you deal on top of it. Pick up the half that does not have the selected card and show it first, asking the spectator if he sees his card therein. When it is denied, give him the other packet and go on as before.

Obviously, there are many other stratagems that may be utilized if your own deck is used, or if you have seen the deck you will work with, or if you have opportunity beforehand for some preparation, but this routine was designed for practical use at any time, even when totally unprepared. The fact that you may use any deck which you never have seen or touched, is a strong point.

AN ALL-CARD ROUTINE

A complete act of card effects is more-or-less confined to the close-up worker. We advise that this routine not be done before a larger audience than that in an intimate club, as the effects will otherwise not be thoroughly appreciated.

1. (a) Picture This
   (b) Name Your Favorite
2. The Triple Enigma.
3. (a) Synchronism.
   (b) Dual Impulsion.
4. Impromptu Fifteen Card Trick.
5. Simplex Card Stabbing.

The opening trick makes use of a deck that is partly or wholly set-up, so it is a logical starter. After the deck has been shuffled and you conclude the first number, take it back, locate the short card, and shuffle it into its position for the "Triple Enigma." The short or key card, by the way, is the same as the force card in "Synchronism" or "Dual Impulsion." After the "Enigma" is done, palm off the key card, as the straight deck must be minus the force card in the next effect. If "Dual Impulsion" is to be done, the pack must first be switched for the forcing deck.

Whichever is performed, (Synchronism or Dual Impulsion) you are left with a complete, straight deck to work the "Fifteen Card" effect. It is possible to halt the routine right now. When you like, however, conclude with the unusual "Card Stabbing." Simply palm the slit-card into the deck (on the bottom) prior to performance of the effect. It is not necessary to palm away its unprepared duplicate in the deck as it is very unlikely to be discovered, especially after you scatter the cards around.

The routine lasts from 20 to 25 minutes and should prove interesting because of the variety of effects.

TWO SILK FOLDS

Methods of folding a silk for production purposes are common enough and it would seem that new ways are quite unnecessary. However, if you will try one or both of the silk folds to follow, you will use them constantly, because, in each case, they have advantages other types of folds have not.

SILK FOLD No. 1: When your routine calls for "plucking a silk from the air," this is just the thing to use. The silk, when produced, unfolds instantly and hangs by a corner at the finger tips.

We will suppose that the silk to be folded is about 18 inches square. Fold it in half, the diagonal way, to get (Fig. 1). The proximate corners ("C" in the sketches) are brought up, over the fold, so that another fold is made about an inch and a half from the first (Fig. 2). C is brought down over the newly-formed fold, thus making still another fold that is even with the top edge. Run C back and forth this way, always making the new folds even with the first top and bottom edges, until you reach the corners. When you are done, you have (Fig. 3).

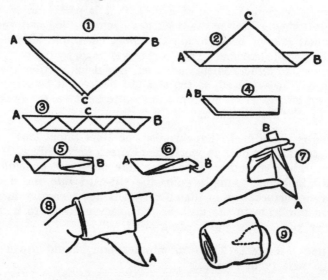

Pressing the corners C in place, fold corner B over to corner A (Fig. 4).
Fold corner B, alone, over to the center fold (Fig. 5).
Fold the silk in half again—the long way. See (Fig. 6).

Holding the part of the silk near corner B between the left thumb and forefinger, wind the silk strip around and around the left forefinger (Fig. 7).

When the corner A is reached (Fig. 8), tuck a good half-inch of it securely into the folds formed by the roll. Remove the silk from your forefinger.

The result is a compactly-rolled silk (Fig. 9), which may be vested, placed in a pocket, or loaded almost anywhere with perfect safety. You can obtain possession of it at anytime during your act and when you do, it may be palmed and further manipulated by "drop" moves, acquitments, etc., much the same as a billiard ball or any small object.

To produce the silk, all that is necessary is to unloose the tucked-in corner (A in the sketches), hold it between thumb and first or second finger, and "shake" out the silk proper. The silk appears in a flash and it is not creased or "ropey"-looking, as would be the case in such a fold as the "Finger Roll."

When using this fold in a trick, such as the one which follows, where there must be no fumbling before shaking out the silk, tie a piece of tape the color of the silk an inch or so from corner A. When the corner is tucked in, this bit of tape is left protruding so that it can be grasped between the thumb and forefinger, a simple shake, as before, producing the silk. If the silk is to be used later for some purpose which would make the attached bit of tape undesirable, simply twist the A end and tie a false knot in it, leaving a protruding loop long enough to easily grasp. The knot is pulled out by simply grasping the opposite ends and stretching the silk between the hands or, in laying the silk down, the fingers of either hand can pull out the knot.

SILK FOLD No. 2: The effect of producing a silk with this fold is the same as that obtained with a handkerchief ball. The latter serves its purpose well, but a silk kept in it for any length of time at all becomes creased and appears slovenly when produced, even though it may have been carefully pressed just prior to performance. Getting rid of the hank ball is another worry for the modern magus, so it is only natural to wonder if there could be a silk fold to take its place. Here is the answer that eliminates the faults while still retaining the basic silk production effect.

The start of the fold is the same as Silk Fold No. 1 until (Fig. 3) of that fold is reached. Then bring the bottom edge of the silk up to the top, thus forming (Fig. 1), for Silk Fold No. 2. Put some sort of weight, a deck of cards will do, on the silk, slightly to the left of the center. Fold corner B over at about two inches from its end and then fold a small tip of corner B up a little, so that it protudes above the top edge. See (Fig. 2).

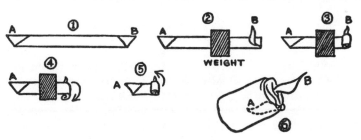

Start rolling the silk from the very end of the right side. When you have given it about four turns and have passed the corner B, stop, and then proceed to roll the silk THE OTHER WAY, giving it three or four similar turns. In other words, you neutralize the rolls, rolling it first over the top surface and then the bottom. Move the weight to the left as you go along so that you have room (Fig. 4).

Continue along the strip, giving three to four turns, first one way and then back the other, until three or four inches at the end A remain (Fig. 5). Make the final roll all one way and when corner A is reached, tuck it in among the folds, a la Fold No. 1.

The resultant small bundle (Fig. 6) may be manipulated exactly as the one you get with Silk Fold No. 1, previous to production.

When about to produce the silk, the bundle is concealed in the right hand, across the roots of the right fingers, with corner B protruding from the roll nearest the thumb. The hand is held somewhat at the side.

The left hand is shown empty as you gaze on it a moment. Reach out to your left, the left thumb and forefinger appearing to catch something. Holding the left hand PERFECTLY MOTIONLESS, bring up the right hand in a loose fist. Left thumb and forefinger grasp corner B of the silk and the right hand, holding the rolled silk rather loosely, moves downward. This is done quickly. The silk hangs down expanded from the left finger tips, from which point you may do with it what you like.

CONTINUOUS PRODUCTION OF SILKS AT THE FINGER TIPS

The simplicity of the effect and of the method makes this a very pleasing production. Though the hands are continually shown to be empty, silks successively appear in a flash at the finger tips. As many as eight 18-inch silks may be easily produced in this manner at any point in the program.

.The basic idea is made clear in (Fig. 1). The silk for production is rolled and secured inside the coat sleeve by a STRAIGHT, BLACK PIN which is run through the fabric from the outside and impaled in the rolled silk.

FIG.1

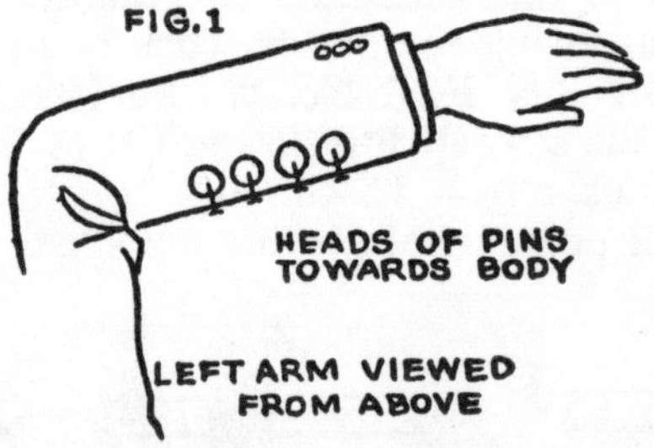

HEADS OF PINS
TOWARDS BODY

LEFT ARM VIEWED
FROM ABOVE

To obtain the silk, it is only necessary to pull out the pin (from the outside) and drop the arm, the little bundle dropping neatly into the fingers of the hand, ready for production as desired. Four, or even more, rolled silks may be loaded in each sleeve and may be safely carried for as long as you like. The first silk should be secured about four or five inches from the sleeve opening. The bundles are on the inside of the arm, toward the body. The best pins to use are those with spherical heads (used by most clothing stores), as these will not pull through the fabric as flat-headed ones may and they are much easier to grasp.

The moves employed in the productions ought probably to be left to the individual, but the following routine for the production of six handkerchiefs may prove helpful.

Five 18-inch silks are rolled by the First method as described in the preceding. A sixth one is rolled by the Second method. Three silks are loaded in each sleeve, the silk rolled by the Second method being between the other two in the left sleeve. At the start, the hands are empty.

I—With the left hand, pull up the right sleeve just a trifle, pulling out the pin nearest the sleeve opening. Right hand is seen empty. Similarly pull up the left sleeve a bit with the right hand, pulling the first pin from the left sleeve. Show left hand on both sides and drop the right hand at this time, getting the first silk. You need not worry about missing the silk. Reach with the right hand behind the left knee and produce the first silk. The left hand drops simultaneously and gets its first silk. The right hand displays its silk at finger tips, hand otherwise empty. Transfer the silk to the left hand and steal the balled silk from left hand into right—simply a change-over under cover of transferring the visible silk. Left hand is seen empty except for the visible silk. Drape this silk over the right forearm. At once, right hand, in front of body, produces the SECOND SILK at the finger tips. This silk is draped over left forearm—both hands shown empty.

The performer faces the audience while performing all of these moves. The pins are simply dropped to the floor.

II—The right takes the silk draped over the left forearm and lays it over the left shoulder. In taking the silk, it pulls out the second pin from the left sleeve. As the silk is thrown over the shoulder, the left hand drops and the next sleeved silk drops into the fingers. Keeping this balled silk concealed in the palm, the left hand repeats the move just made by the right hand; that is, it takes the first produced silk from the right forearm, pulling out the next pin, the right hand drops, gets its sleeved silk, and the left hand lays the just-removed silk over the right shoulder. The right hand now comes up and produces a THIRD SILK at the finger tips. This silk is at once transferred to the left hand, the change-over with the silk palmed in the left hand being made, the right hand stealing it. Left hand tosses the visible silk over the right forearm and then moves back left again, open palm to audience, and makes a grabbing gesture. Right hand comes up with silk (rolled by Silk Fold No. 2) palmed. The left thumb and forefinger grasp the corner of the rolled silk and this hand remains motionless while the right hand moves downward quickly, leaving the silk expanded at the left finger tips. This is the production of the FOURTH SILK and makes an effective variation. Right hand takes this silk and places it over left forearm. Both hands are empty.

III—The moves at the beginning of II are repeated, again giving you a silk palmed in each hand. The hands, backs to audience, are brought in front of body, a little more than waist high. Hold them motionless a moment, then quickly produce both silks simultaneously.

You now have six silks and may proceed to employ them to whatever mystical ends you please.

SILKS OF A COLOR FOLLOW EACH OTHER

The rather inane paraphrase on "Birds of a feather flock together" at least has the virtue of being descriptive of the trick.

Four 17-inch silks, two orange and two blue, are counted and dropped into an unprepared paper bag. A spectator pulls one out at random—let us say he chose the blue. This silk is freely shown and then most mysteriously multiplies into two. This is evidently because its mate has joined it, for the bag is found to contain only the two orange silks.

One of the orange silks is dropped back into the bag. The other is pushed into the left fist and vanishes. The vanished silk, which has been knotted one or more times for identification, appears in the sack with the other orange one.

The assisting spectator again holds the bag and the four silks are dropped in, one by one, and mixed by the spectator. The man holds the sack above his head and the magician, first showing hand empty, reaches in and pulls out three of the silks at random. Suppose an orange silk remains in the bag. Its mate is vanished as before and reappears with the silk in the bag, which is held by the spectator all the while!

The effect of the trick is simplicity itself and the repetitions serve to build up quite a mystery, as each one is done differently.

Employed are a medium-sized paper bag, obtainable at any grocer's, three thin orange silks and two blue silks, all 17 inches square, a false finger tip with a piece of orange silk glued inside at one end, as for the usual silk vanish, and two Ideal color-change gimmicks as commonly used for the change of a single silk through the hand (Fig. 1). These tubes are obtainable in a large size just suitable for a fine 17-inch silk. A tiny bead is sewn in each corner of each blue silk and one of the orange silks is loaded into one of the tubes, which is placed in the left coat pocket. The other tube is loaded with one of the blue silks and is placed in the left trouser's pocket. It is well to load the tubes just before the show so the silks will be fresh when expanded.

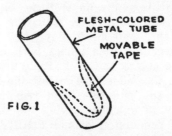

FLESH-COLORED
METAL TUBE

MOVABLE
TAPE

FIG. 1

The finger tip is placed in the little match and change pocket of the right coat pocket or in a little pocket formed by a strip of elastic tape sewn near the top of this coat pocket for the purpose of holding the tip until needed. One gimmick is used in each effect. A chair should be at hand to be placed at front left center at the outset.

Take the remaining blue silk and twist it very loosely ropewise, then double it in half, bringing the two opposite ends up together. Place this doubled silk on top of the first orange silk, which has been folded loosely diagonally, and on top of all lay the second orange silk, full length. These are carefully placed where they will not be disturbed until needed. This completes the preparation for the trick.

For clarity, the routine will be described in three parts.

PART ONE — A silk vanishes from sack held by spectator and appears in the magician's hand.

METHOD: Two orange silks and one blue silk are false counted as two orange and two blue silks and placed in a sack. The blue silk is forced on a spectator. The second blue silk is produced from an Ideal hank fake.

PRESENTATION: Shake open the paper bag and show it empty. Set it upright on the table and pick up the bunch of silks by the middle, allowing the four ends to fall over the back of the left hand and the two full length ends to hang down on the other side, between palm and thumb. The back of hand is held facing audience. The silks are held rather loosely. Count the silks as four—that is, take the first end hanging towards audience and fold it back of the thumb, saying "Orange," then the same with the next one, saying, "Blue," then "Blue" again, and finally, "Orange," each time taking each end separately and folding it back over the thumb. This is done quite deliberately and smoothly. As soon as you have finished the count, bundle the silks loosely together and drop them into the sack. This false count with silks is a slight variation on a method by Mr. William Larsen.

You now hold the bag with the left hand and place your right hand in the bag and appear to mix the silks thoroughly. What you actually do is swish them around so you can get the two orange silks and, with the same circular swishing movement, roll them up together into a rather small ball. As soon as this is done, and it takes but a jiffy, the left hand, from outside the bag, grasps the balled up silks tightly through a fold of the bag. The blue silk is left free.

Step forward and hold the bag above the head of a spectator, asking him to reach in and take out a silk. Of course, he gets the blue silk. You at once release the orange ones. You give him the bag to hold above his head and take the blue silk in your right hand. Left drops to pocket and gets tube fake. Hold it in palm by sticking tip of the second finger into the opening of the tube.

You ask the gentleman to come up front and have him stand directly behind the chair. Chair is at left center, remember. You step a little to right. Pull right sleeve up with left hand (containing tube). Right holds the blue silk at finger tips during this and the hand is seen otherwise empty. Turn left and pass silk to left hand, stealing tube with right by simply extending left second finger into right palm. The natural act of passing the silk covers the bringing the hands together for this change-over. Left holds silk at finger tips and right hand pulls up left sleeve.

Right hand strokes the silk several times. On the third time, the left fingers nip end of silk in tube. Left is held ABSOLUTELY STATIONARY while right moves downward, bringing the silk into view with pretty effect. Transfer the silks to right hand.

Ask the spectator to take the silks out of the bag one by one and drop them on the seat of the chair. He finds only the two orange silks, the "other" blue (which never was there) having made a clean getaway!

In this effect the handkerchief tube gimmick may be eliminated and Silk Fold No. 2 substituted. The folded silk is placed in the same pocket and handled as easily in manipulation as the tube.

PART TWO — A silk, knotted for identification, makes a clean vanish from the magician's hands and appears in the sack.

METHOD: The knotted silk (orange) is apparently placed in the left hand, but really palmed in the right by the End Roll palm. It is made to appear to still be in the left fist by the familiar finger tip method. While the piece of silk from the finger tip is still in view, the palmed silk is dropped into the sack along with the other orange silk. The Finger Tip Vanish is then executed.

PRESENTATION: Tuck the upper ends of the blue silks into the right coat pocket, allowing about two thirds of the silks to hang out, and letting the tube gimmick drop in pocket. Pick up the two orange silks and ask the spectator to take one of them and tie any number of knots in one corner— not too many, though, as he will have to untie them later. Place the other orange silk over left forearm. Take the sack from the man so his hands will be free to tie the knots and place it upright on the seat of the chair. Count each knot aloud as the man ties it. At the same time, you take the two blue silks and hang them over left arm alongside, but not on top of, the orange silk. In taking the blue silks out of pocket, you have gotten the finger tip gimmick onto right forefinger.

With the left hand, take the knotted silk from spectator. Transfer the silk to right hand, which holds it with knotted end between thumb and forefinger. Both hands are seen otherwise empty.

Now throw the silk over the back of left hand and place knotted corner on middle of left palm. Hold both palms tightly together and move the hands quickly in opposite directions with a rotary motion. This action draws the silk into the hand and rolls it into a compact ball around the knotted corner. The knots make this very easy. As soon as silk is in, turn left, contract right palm slightly to hold the tightly balled silk, and close left fingers loosely, as if around silk, moving left away and turning back of fist to audience. Right hand remains absolutely motionless for a moment, then goes up to left and inserts forefinger into fist, as if poking the silk in a little more, actually leaving finger tip in opening of left fist. Poke in the forefinger again and pull out the little corner of silk from the tip, letting this extend as much as possible from fist. It is allowed to remain thus during the next move, proving silk to be in left hand throughout.

Right hand (with silk palmed) takes the other orange silk by the corner with thumb and forefinger and pulls it deliberately off the arm, letting it fall free. This must be done slowly so they can see that you actually take only the one silk. If the preceding moves have done neatly, no one will ever suspect that there is a silk palmed in right hand. Make a short circular motion with the right hand, grasping silk at middle, which has the effect of loosely gathering the silk around the palmed one so it can be dropped in the sack along with the stolen silk. Hand sack to man to hold above his head as before.

Now deliberately poke the protruding orange corner back into left fist with right forefinger, actually poking it back into tip and getting the tip onto the right forefinger again. Left hand is slowly opened, after a throwing motion, and silk is gone—leaving both hands empty!

The assistant reaches into the sack and brings out the two silks. Take the unknotted one from him and ask him to untie the knots, counting each one aloud as he does so. The number is the same, in fact, it is the same silk! In the meantime, drop the finger tip into a pocket.

PART THREE — Repetition using variation.

METHOD: A silk in an Ideal hank fake is secretly added to those in the sack, so that two silks remain in the sack after three have been taken out. The extra silk is vanished with the hank fake.

PRESENTATION: The sack is again shown empty. Be sure to make the point clear. Hand the assistant the four silks, asking him to drop them in one by one and mix them around. He does this with the sack in his own hands.

The spectator holds the sack up above your eye-level line and you reach in and pull out a silk. This can be any silk that has a bead in its corner (i.e.— any blue silk). IT IS IMPORTANT THAT YOUR HAND BE SEEN EMPTY WHEN IT GOES INTO SACK TO PULL OUT THE SILK. While you reach in the bag and feel around a little, left hand drops into left coat pocket and remains there for a few moments. When it comes out, it brings out the tube gimmick (containing ORANGE silk) on the tip of the curled-in second finger. Right hand brings a silk out of bag at once and places this silk in left hand.

The empty right hand goes in sack again and brings out another blue silk, which it places in the left hand. You are apparently pulling these out at random, remember. Each time you bring a silk out, you call its color.

When you place this second silk in the left hand, extend the left second finger into right hand, which palms the tube. WITHOUT A MOMENT'S HESITATION, you reach into the bag again. Grasp the tube between the thumb and second finger with the open end down and the end closed by the tape upwards. Push the forefinger down on the tape, pushing it down to the other end of the tube and thus instantly popping the silk out (just what happens during a color-change, only your finger, rather than another silk, poked it out). Finger palm the fake and bring out the just-expanded silk. This move occupies a fraction of the time it takes to describe it.

As you bring out this third silk, say, "Orange. What color does that leave?" The answer is, of course, the other orange one. Tell the assistant to hold the sack up high. Take the two blue silks and lay them over the left arm. Pull the orange silk through left hand a couple of times and end by leaving the gimmick there as fist closes. Work fast here. Poke the orange silk into the top of the fist (into gimmick), beginning with one corner and pushing silk with right first and second fingers alternately. As soon as the silk is well in, give it an extra poke, insert tip of right second finger into gimmick, and bend this finger back into right palm with gimmick. Left fingers open just enough to let the tube pass. Rightside is slightly to audience, as the steal is covered by the back of the right hand. Give a couple more pokes with extended right forefinger, then bring left away and open to show empty, after the usual tossing movement. This is exactly the manipulation used in the familiar color-change, but we vanish the silk instead of changing it. Don't think I'm claiming originality for this. I just want you to know how it's done.

As soon as the silk has vanished, the assisting spectator inverts the sack over the chair seat and out fall the two orange silks!

Right hand takes the two blue silks off left arm, left picks up the two orange silks, and the colors are paired together again! Right hand stuffs the silks partially into right coat pocket and drops the gimmick therein. The sack is crumpled and tossed into the audience. The gentleman is dismissed, the silks laid aside, and we go into the next trick.

All this has taken a lot of explaining, for it is actually three separate tricks routined together. In things like this, every move is important, because it must dovetail with each succeeding move, and that is why I have gone into such detail to make everything clear. I think there is nothing here that anyone will find particularly difficult and the routine is not hard to learn, for, once you have gone through it a few times, you can forget all the minor details—they fit naturally into the logical sequence of things.

SILKS DO AS YOU DO

Three separate 18-inch silks, each of a different color, red, yellow and blue, are handed to a spectator. The magus retains another set of three of corresponding colors. Turning his back, the performer states that he will tie his three silks together in some unknown order and that the spectator is to tie his three silks together in ANY order he may care to. The magus predicts, however, that the order will be the same. Having finished his tieing the magus faces the audience and holds his set of silks folded in one hand. Spectator shows his silks in the order he has tied them. The performer displays his silks and they are in the exact same order!

Magus puts his set aside on a table and the spectator is directed to untie the knots on his own set, so that the silks are once again separate. That done, he states that the untieing resulted in a sympathetic reaction on the part of his own set of silks. The silks on the table are picked up, one at a time, thus showing THEM to be separate!

Finally, both spectator and magus tie their respective sets of silks in a similar order. The performer puts his set down on the table and says that a more difficult test of the silks' sympathy will be attempted. Spectator is told to free the center silk of his set—that is, untie the knots, put aside the center silk, and then tie the two end silks together. All these actions are being magically duplicated in his own set, the magus intimates. To prove, the silks on the table are picked up—the same center silk is loose and the other two are tied together!

There are only six silks required—three pairs of different colors. After dividing them into two sets, there is a little preparation for two of the silks in one set. The silk that remains unprepared in this set is preferably the silk of lightest color. Thus, if you have red, yellow and blue silks, it would be the yellow one.

One part of a snap fastener is sewn, about one inch diagonally inward from a corner, on one of the two other silks. The other part of the fastener

FIG 1

is similarly sewn on the second silk. Use Size 000 snap fasteners. Sew through a double thickness of the silk, as shown in the first illustration.

Replace the unprepared silk with the set and you are ready for your sympathetic effects at any time.

An obliging spectator from the audience is inveigled up to the stage or platform and given the set of unprepared silks. You take the other. Announce that you will turn your back and tie your set of three silks in some order, that the assisting spectator is to tie his three silks together in ANY order he pleases but, nevertheless, he will be "unconsciously" forced to tie them in the same order you do. Be sure to state this before you turn your back, else it will seem more like coincidence.

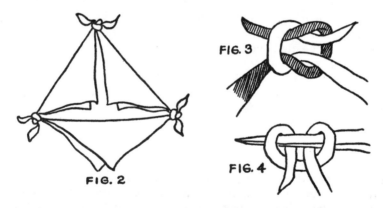

FIG. 3

FIG. 2

FIG. 4

When you turn your back, you tie the three silks together in an END-LESS CIRCLE (See Fig. 2). All the knots made are square knots, which are immediately upset by pulling the body and corner OF ONE OF THE SILKS ONLY. Figures 3 and 4 show the method very lucidly. The "knots" look genuine and will hold three silks tied together until such time when the silks may be pulled, thus dissolving the knots and freeing the silks.

The snap fasteners should not offer any difficulty if you tie a knot at these corners. If they do, though, simply use another corner. One may even snap the fasteners together, instead of tieing a knot at those corners. It is better to make knots, however, since you have the time and you might as well produce the real thing if you can.

Having tied the silks together in an endless circle, you must gather them up and hold them in the right hand as follows: Take one of the knots and "hook" it on the second finger. The knot isn't kept between the first and second finger, but is pulled down a bit, so that it is on the inside of the hand, resting at the root of the second finger. With the left hand, bring up the knot that connects the silk that hangs at the front with the one at the bottom, "hooking" it on the third finger. Again pull the knot down a little, so that it rests on the third finger. Bring up the remaining knot and hang it on the little finger—then pull it down a bit, as with the others. The knots' positions are shown in (Fig. 5).

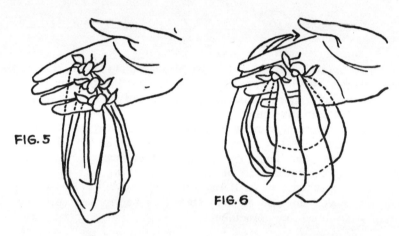

FIG. 5   FIG. 6

Face the audience as soon as you have the silks as described. Allow the spectator to finish his tieing if it is not already done. He then shows his silks in the order he tied them. You merely note the colors of the silks at the ENDS, then glance at the knots in your hand, and PULL OUT THE KNOT THAT TIES THESE TWO COLORS with the left hand. Grasp a corner of one of the loosened silks—it is better to take the silk that corresponds with the silk the spectator has on top of his set—and let the bunch drop. The order of the silks is the same as the spectator's. The principle of this effect is not new; it is only applied to silks.

Take the silks in the right hand, holding them as in (Fig 6). The two end silks are nearest the body. The knots rest against the second finger on the inside of the hand and the center silk is held between the first and second fingers. With the left hand, bring up the bottom corners of the end silks around the BACK of the hand (the side nearest the audience), putting them in the fork of the right thumb, the latter closing and holding them in place. In practically the same movement, the left hand pulls on the body of the end silks near the knots, thus making the silks separate. As soon as the end silks have been pulled free, place the unloosened corners on the right hand, the fingers closing up to hold them. The silks are laid on the table nearby.

Going over the foregoing with silks in hand, you will find it is not complicated. The whole action blends into one as you place the silks down and is completely covered.

Now request the assisting person to untie his set of three. In accordance with the presentation, your own set is subsequently shown—all three silks are also separate. This is a standard sympathetic silks effect, but it fills in well here.

At this point, you tell the spectator to tie his set in the same order that you do, for apparent "sympathetic" purposes. Take the silk that is unprepared and tie it to one of the other silks at a corner diagonally opposite the one with a snap fastener on it. Do the same at the other corner, thereby making the unprepared silk the center silk and the snap fasteners at the outermost corners of the end silks. The knots you make are similar to the first effect, i.e., you upset the real knots, so that the silks may be unloosened.

Display the silks in a string, the spectator doing the same. You now bring the silks again into position, as in (Fig. 6), and go through the same moves. When you bring the bottom corners of the end silks up and into the fork of the thumb, however, you SNAP THE FASTENERS TOGETHER. That done, you pull out the middle silk, exactly as detailed before, and lay the silks on the table.

Tell the assistant to untie his silks, so as to separate the center one, and then tie the end silks together. You can let the spectator take his time about it, as the audience will note the time it takes to bring about the result and when your own set is seen to be the same, it will be all the more puzzling. In showing your set, pick up the separate silk first and then the other two, which, thanks to the snap fasteners, appear to be tied together.

Take the silks from the spectator, thank and dismiss him, and go on with another mystery.

TWIN SYMPATHY

Another trick on the "Sympathetic Silks" order.

EFFECT: Two paper cones are shown and placed, points down, in glass tumblers on either side of the stage. Two silks of contrasting colors, red and white, are tied together at the corners and placed into the cone on the left-hand side. Another pair of silks, of the same colors as the first set, is similarly tied together and placed into the cone on the right side. After a brief interim, taken up by patter, the red silk is unloosened in one of the cones, removed to show it separate, and then replaced in its cone. Going over to the other cone, the magus turns it over and its two silks fall out—separately!

Taking these silks, the magus immediately reties them together at the corners and replaces them in the cone. Going over to the first cone, the silks are taken out—they are tied together!

Magus blows on the knot that ties the two silks and it dissolves, leaving the silks separate. The white silk is replaced in the cone alone and the red silk is draped over the performer's arm or shoulder. Now the cone on the other side is turned over and its silks fall out untied!

The separate silks are replaced in the cone. The red is taken out, thus giving the magus TWO red silks. Another paper cone is shown and the two red silks are stuffed into this, only to eventually disappear from it. Going to the respective cones in the glasses, the magus removes from each a white and a red silk!

PREPARATION: The cones used are really prepared sheets of newspaper or thick wrapping paper. Assuming you are using a newspaper, get a sheet, double it, and paste it together to from a sort of pocket with an opening at one end. Make three of these. Roll them up into cones with the opening on top. Fasten the paper with a pin or paper clip.

Into the fake compartment, or pocket, of two of the cones, put a duplicate red silk of the ones you will use in the effect. Do not pack it in. Rather, take a little care to put it in neatly, so that the silk will not widen the opening of the compartment because of its presence.

The glass tumblers, on their respective tables, are unprepared, as they are just to hold up the cones.

The silks are unprepared. Any size may be used, but 17 or 18-inch squares are about right.

SUGGESTED PATTER AND PRESENTATION: (The performer speaks). I should like to tell next, of a very unusual story. It concerns itself with two brothers who were twins. These brothers dressed, talked and even thought pretty much alike, so that it was really very hard to tell them apart. We will imagine that these two red silk handkerchiefs are the twin brothers. (Show the two red silks).

Being a couple of rising young business men with a comfortable nest egg on account at the local savings bank, the two brothers were somewhat desirous of getting married and settling down. Unfortunately, however, they didn't know any girls that would do, until one day, coincidence of coincidences, they met two sisters—twin sisters! Here they are. (Show the two white silks).

Yes, it was love at first sight, though which brother loved which sister is a bigger problem than I can solve. Anyway, they hied themselves to the nearest Justice of the Peace to get married. It wasn't very long before he "tied the knot" for the first couple. (Tie the corners of a red and white silk together in a square knot and immediately upset it, as described in the last trick). Then they went to their new home to set up housekeeping. (Cone on the left is shown, the fingers held over the pocket. The tied silks are then put into the cone, but they are separated, as soon as they are in, with a slight pull.)

The second couple were tied together just as quickly (second set of silks is tied and knot upset again) and they also went to their home—over here. (Place the silks in the other cone, after first showing it empty. The silks are NOT separated, however).

It wasn't long, though, before our friends, the second couple, had their first quarrel and it ended up by hubby storming out of the house in a rage. (Pretend to untie the silks in the right-hand cone. Actually, you only take out the silk that is in the compartment—apparently, the white is separate in the cone). He went back in a little while, but he was still mad. (Replace the red silk in the compartment of the cone).

Now the other brother, being of the same temperament, had exactly the same trouble at this time. He had an argument with his wife and left her for a while. (Red silk is taken out of the cone at the left, or the cone is turned over, showing the separation of the two silks).

But, before long, they decided to kiss and make up, and so they went back to their marital ties. (Retie these silks, but again upset the knot, as before). They were very happy as they went back to their little home. (Silks are replaced in the cone at the left and again they are separated by a pull).

By this time, the other brother was also of the same mind, so, as we look in on our other couple, we find them thoroughly knotted in the bonds of matrimony. (The two tied silks are taken from the other cone).

(Hold the outermost corner of the red silk in the left hand and the outermost corner of the white in the right.) It wasn't so very long before our young friends had ANOTHER argument—a more violent one, this time. Once again they parted. It seemed as if their romance had gone Phff-t! (Saying this last, blow on the knot. It dissolves—because you pull on the silks' ends).

The husband stayed out—the brute—leaving his poor wifey at home. (Put the red silk over your arm or shoulder and replace the white silk in its cone).

Yes, and the same situation happened at the house of the other brother. It seems that their troubles are as alike as their looks! (Turn over cone at the left and out pop the two separated silks. Then put the two silks back in the cone). The Missus stayed at home, just like her sister. (Remove the red silk from the COMPARTMENT).

While the two brothers were out, they happened to meet each other and, of course, told each other of their misadventures. They were apparently too proud to go back to their wives right away, so one of the brothers suggested that they rent an apartment for themselves. No sooner said than done—and here is the apartment they picked. (Show the third prepared cone, which has been kept at hand). "We'll show those wives of ours that they can't make fools of US!" said one brother. "We can cook our own food, clean our own dishes, and darn our own socks! We don't need a woman for THAT!" (As you talk, put your hand into the opening of the compartment, to make room for the silks. You are apparently rounding out the cone to a better form. Place the two red silks into the compartment. Remember, do not pack them in tightly; they should not show a big bulge).

I think the brothers were mistaken, though. Their attempts at housekeeping were pretty bad. They became so disgusted, they stayed away from their own apartment most of the time. In fact, if we should enter their house right now, I don't believe they would be at home! (Unfold the paper cone and show it on both sides. The fingers hold the top edge and close the pocket, so that it doesn't show. Crumple up the paper and toss it aside).

Where are they? Let us see if we can find them. Here at this house, there is still friend wife waiting patiently and—oh, do my eyes deceive me? Here is her husband back where he belongs—at home. (Take out the white silk from the cone at the right first and then the red silk from the compartment). In the other brother's house, we find the wife, of course, and—yes—the wandering mate has returned here, too. (Here you simply turn over the cone and the two silks drop out. Omega).

A ROUTINE WITH SILKS

Here the foregoing material has been combined with a couple of additional ideas to form a routine:

1. Color Transpo.

2. Silks of a Color Follow Each Other.

3. Silks Do As You Do (or Twin Sympathy).

4. Insto Knotting.

The first and last items require some explaining. In "Color Transpo" a silk handkerchief is produced from the air, then pushed into the closed left fist. The right hand removes a differently colored silk from the breast pocket and holds it at the finger tips. A shake and it visibly changes to the color of the silk in the fist. The left hand is then opened and out pops the silk—but now of the color of that which was originally held in the right hand. Evidently, the silks have changed places.

Three 13-inch silks are required, one each of the two colors used and a special silk that changes color by simply shaking it. The latter is obtainable from any dealer and is just the regular color-change silk without the ring. The unprepared silk of the color that the special silk shows at the start is pushed into an Ideal hank fake. Loaded fake is sleeved on the left side and a pin run through the sleeve and into the silk in the tube (from the tape side), as in the "Continuous Production of Silks." The other unprepared silk is rolled by the First method and secured for the Silk Production in the right sleeve. Prepared silk is tucked into the breast pocket.

To open, follow the routine at the beginning of the "Continuous Production of Silks," getting the silk in the right hand and, on producing it, getting the tube in the left, just as you would another silk in the Production routine. Show the right hand empty except for the just-produced silk, then spread the silk out between both hands, transferring the fake behind it into the right hand, where it is held by the closed second, third, and forth fingers. Left hand drops its end of the silk and hand is seen empty. Draw the silk several times through the left hand and end by leaving the fake in that hand, the hand at once closing into a fist. The visible silk is poked into the left fist, really into the tape end of the color-change tube, thus pushing the other silk out. Left third and little fingers close fist to prevent this silk from appearing. The tube, under cover of the visible silk, is at this point rather high in the fist—almost protruding from the top—but as soon as the loaded silk has been pushed out into the fist, the tube is pushed down and to one side of this silk. Visible silk is pushed into tube alternately by right first and second fingers and, when well in, the tube is stolen out into right palm on right second finger. This is the regular color change through hand, only the magus doesn't let the "change" silk show yet, but keeps it concealed in closed palm. Credit here to Ireland, we think.

Right hand, with gimmick palmed, goes to breast pocket and removes the special silk, gimmick being dropped into the pocket. All that remains to be done is to shake the right hand silk and open the left fist. The effect is quick and pleasing. Pocket the silks.

To avoid fumbling, we suggest putting a square of cardboard, of the same width as the pocket, in the breast pocket, thus dividing it into two compartments. The front side holds the color-change hank, leaving the back side for the tube getaway.

The silks set for "Silks of a Color" are clipped together at the "four" end with an ordinary spring paper clip and laid over the back of a chair on the table. If "Silks Do As You Do" is used to follow, a snap fastener is substituted for one of the beads on one of the blue silks. Its mate is sewn to one of the two extra silks necessary to complete the set of six required for this effect. These two extra silks (of a third color) are sleeved in the right and left sleeves above the silk and gimmick, respectively, used in the opening effect. After "Silks of a Color," the two silks are produced exactly as in I in the "Continuous Production" routine.

Of course, if "Twin Sympathy" is substituted, the same four silks used in the preceding effect may be employed, or, if desired, a different color scheme may be used and four more silks produced at the finger tips.

For the final effect, duplicates of all the silks used in the routine are required. These are tied together into one long string and a small metal weight sewn at one end of the string. Also needed is an especially prepared paper bag, a duplicate of the one used in "Silks of a Color." Obtain two paper sacks and cut two inches off the top of one. Push it inside the other, leaving the tops flush. Paste the tops together, leaving one wide side open. The tied silks are placed in the bag, weighted silk on top. Place this bag behind something (or on a chair, the back of which is turned to audience). At the close of "Silks of a Color," crush the sack used and toss it out, or, if the prepared bag is concealed from view, take it and place it alongside the prepared bag. In any case, at the close, pick up the special sack and the silks that you have been using. Stuff the silks into the secret compartment (held open by the left thumb), shake the bag, shaking the silks down into the double bottom, turn the bag toward the audience so they can see the (duplicate) silks lying in the sack, then make a throwing motion with the sack and the silks fly out tied together in a string, the mouth of the sack being turned at the same time towards audience to show empty.

A standard trick such as Blendo or Silk Dyeing could also be used for the finish.

THREE TO ONE

This method is unusually simple and direct in effect and I have consistently used it in preference to all others.

A nine-foot length of rope is shown and the ends tied together. The rope is held doubled and the section between the ends and the middle is drawn up and cut through, separating the rope into three pieces. But not for long, for the pieces become joined as in the beginning and the restored rope thrown to the audience.

You will understand the effectiveness of the procedure best by following through the method with rope in hand.

A piece of soft rope nine feet in length is used. Join the ends with rope cement or a short strip of adhesive tape, the latter being a quick and quite satisfactory method in most cases. Take a ten-inch piece of rope and tie it around the long piece making a false knot about two and a quarter feet from the joint. The joint, it will be seen, is centrally located on one SIDE of the circle, rather than OPPOSITE the false ends.

Plait the rope and place it in a pocket prior to preformance.

In presentation, bring out the rope, untie the knot in the short piece and hold the rope in the left hand with the ends protruding over the fist. Tie the ends together again around the rope. The knot is held in the left hand and the right hand holds the "center" of the rope opposite the knot, displaying the doubled piece to the audience. The joint of the two ends of the rope is halfway between the hands.

The left hand releases its hold and grasps the rope midway between the knot and "center"—holding it at the joint and seeing to it that the joined side is to the right. The joint is held tightly between the left thumb and second finger. You are assumed to be facing the audience up to this point.

Now drop the rope from the right hand. At this point the doubled rope is being held midway by the left hand with the "ends" and "center" hanging down on either side, respectively (Fig. 1).

Turn to the right so that the midportion of the doubled rope is completely concealed in the left hand, apparently grasp both sides of the rope in the right hand, and draw them up through the left hand as in (Fig. 4). Actually, the right hand grasps only the joined side of the rope, taking it on BOTH sides of the joint as it hangs from the left hand and, retaining hold of the joint with the left thumb and fingers, but letting it pivot slightly, this doubled section is drawn straight up and held between the left fingers as in (Fig. 2 and 3),

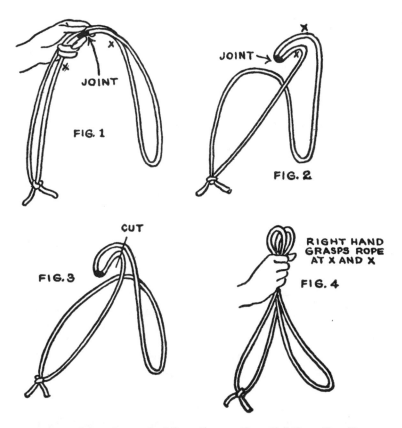

the left thumb and forefinger holding the section tightly. To all appearances, both pieces of rope have been drawn up. Back of the left hand is to audience throughout, of course. The move is just a bit difficult to explain, but is obvious in practice and completely deceptive. It need not be hurried. The figures show the actual state of things.

Hold the rope as in (Fig. 5), then drop the "center" again. The doubled portion is cut through. Pause a moment so all can note what has happened. Now let the actually cut ends drop and, at the same time, with the left fingers revolve one of the ends of the false pieces around the rope held in the left hand. These ends are tied around the rope just as with the false ends at

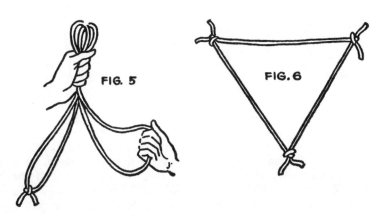

the beginning of the trick. The dropped ends are brought together and tied in a genuine but similar-appearing knot. There are now three knots in the rope, which appears to be in three pieces (Fig. 6). The handling is very convincing.

Gather up the rope in the left hand at the knots, trim off the ends, snipping off the fake knots and cutting off the real knot. Grasp one end and pull the rope slowly out of the left hand—in one solid length!

The tying and handling of the false knots will probably be varied by the individual performer.

THREE TO ONE

The manipulation in this version is very easy and clean. As the audience sees it, a length of rope is cut into three parts, which are knotted together. In a flash, in full view, the knots vanish and the rope is completely restored in a single piece. It is absolutely unprepared and may be tossed out immediately, if so desired.

The preparation of the rope is exactly similar to the previous method. Instead of cement or adhesive tape, I have usually found it good to SEW the ends together neatly. However, any means of attachment may be used. The rope is the same length, too—about nine feet—and half-way between the join and the true center of the rope, a short, eight-inch piece of rope is tied in a knot.

A simple overhand knot may be used to tie on the short piece, but it is likely to slide and get out of position. A better plan is to make the familiar knot commonly used to tie two pieces of string together (Fig. 1 and 2).

That done, the rope is fully prepared.

Display the rope casually in its "tied" condition and then untie the "ends." It is held in the right hand, at this point, with the false ends showing above it.

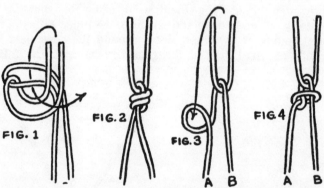

FIG. 1   FIG. 2   FIG. 3   FIG. 4
A B   A B

A special knot is now made. Learn and understand it clearly before going on. It is simple and natural to tie. With the left fingers, make a single loop on the rope, exactly as in (Fig. 3). Put the ends through the loop, as illustrated by the arrow. Make sure the whole short piece goes through, then hold the ends again with the right thumb and forefinger and pull on part A of the rope. This tightens the knot. Draw it up close to the short piece and the result will be (Fig. 4). BE SURE THAT NO PART OF THE SHORT PIECE IS BELOW THE KNOT.

Once the knot is made, the ends may be pulled to create the impression of tightening the knot still more, OR, parts A and B may be given several sound jerks. You need not worry about the knot unloosening, because it CAN'T. It is a genuine-appearing knot and can only be distinguished from the real thing upon very close inspection. In reality, it is a slip knot, merely held in place by the short length of rope. Thus, if the short piece is pulled out, a small knot remains, but if parts A and B of the rope are then pulled, it dissolves. We believe that credit for this knot should go to Bert Douglas.

The rope is again displayed, held with both hands, as in (Fig. 5). The joint is held in the right hand and the side of the rope with the false ends is nearest the body. Now bring both hands together and cross the part of

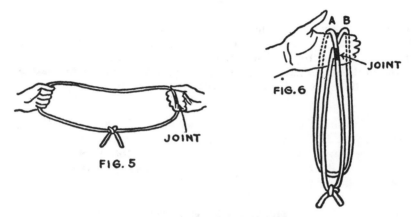

FIG. 5

FIG. 6

the rope in right hand over that in the left. See (Fig. 6). The part of the rope directly above the joint is clipped between the left second and third fingers.

Left thumb presses on part A of the rope, while right fingers grasp part B and slip it off the left forefinger (Fig. 7). Left third and fourth fingers close up, while the right hand slides out the jointed part of the rope and places it next to part A, over-lapping the left forefinger. (Fig. 8) shows this. The whole procedure takes only a moment.

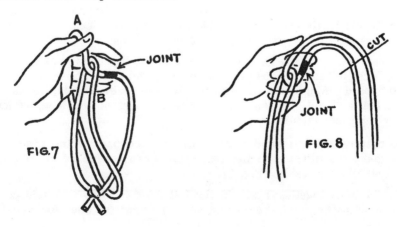

FIG. 7

FIG. 8

Holding the rope with the left hand, the scissors are taken in the right, and the doubled rope cut at the point shown—two inches, or so, from the joint. A spectator may do this, if desired. Rope is now seemingly in three parts.

In the complete series of moves, it should appear as if you simply cut the rope through at A-B, as in (Fig. 6). The whole secret manipulation can be done in turning over the hand and there should be NO HESITATION between this and snipping the rope—it is very deceptive that way.

Now you again tie the same special knot (Figs. 3 and 4) with the new false ends in the left hand. The rope then appears as in (Fig. 9).

FIG. 9

Scissors are again taken and the short ends at the knots are "trimmed" down to the knot. Snipping at these ends, you eventually cut away the short pieces entirely, leaving only the slip knots in place. Hold the rope outstretched with both hands at either end. To effect the visible restoration, pull outward at the ends and the knots will disappear, leaving the solid rope to to be seen.

Of course, ordinary overhand knots may be made instead of the special type of knot given, if preferred. In that case, the length of rope is wound around the one hand, while the other slides off the knots in the well-known manner. Utilizing the special knot, however, makes for a more open working and there is nothing to get rid of.

QUADRUPLE CUT

For the magus who believes that a greater effect is gained by restoring a rope after cutting it into FOUR pieces, the following method is a practical one to use.

The length of rope is nine feet and the ends are joined together by some means, as in previous versions. An eight-inch piece of rope (false ends) is tied opposite the joint—about three inches from the true center of the rope. Make the knot used to tie two pieces of string together.

In presenting, untie the knot and retie it in the "special" knot (described in the last Three to One version) or a simple overhand knot. Show the rope and find the supposed center. Hold the rope in left hand, as in (Fig. 1), the joint being concealed, and cut the rope at the topmost part of the loop, which is apparently the exact middle.

After cutting, the left hand retains the jointed part of the rope, while the right takes the other end; the hands are drawn wide apart to display the rope actually cut, as in (Fig. 2).

Bring the ends together again in the left hand. Grasp a double portion of the rope with the right thumb and second finger on one side and forefinger on the other at point half-way between the left hand and the knot at the bottom. This is brought up to the left hand, whereupon the right thumb

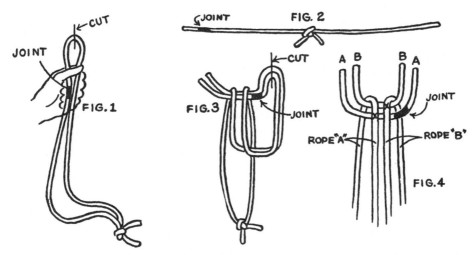

and second finger encircle around the double rope at the joint, the middle portion is released, and the new double part is pulled up above the left fist by right thumb and second finger. It is the common loop move, only done with a doubled rope. (Fig. 3) shows the position of the rope at this point. The new loops seen are apparently the doubled part of the rope brought up from the middle.

Cut both of the new loops at once, then let the two outermost ends drop. You have apparently severed the rope into four separate and equal parts.

Here is where an important move comes in: (Fig. 4) shows a close-up of the left hand holding the rope. The left hand grasps Rope "A," thumb held at the point marked X in the diagram and second finger on the opposite side at the same point, so that END A is held tightly between. Right hand holds Rope "B," with thumb and second finger holding END B tightly in place by a firm grip at its point, marked X. Be sure that each hand has its own end and that the respective remaining ends are NOT HELD, but are loose. On that the next move depends.

Holding on to the rope with the hands as described, PULL THE HANDS APART. The pull frees end A from Rope "B" and end B from Rope "A," so

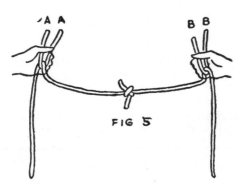

that the whole appears as in (Fig. 5). You could not show the rope more freely if you had actually cut it!

Bring the hands together again and clip the right-hand ends (B-B) between right first and second finger. The back of the hand hides the **true** condition of the rope at this place. A "special" knot (or an overhand **knot**) is made, tieing the A ends to the rope. Then drop the rope and tie ends **B** to the rope by the same knot.

For the restoration, either trim the ends away and dissolve the knots by pulling the real ends, or, if you have tied overhand knots, wind rope around one hand, slide the knots off, and get rid of them. In any case, the rope is completely solid and unprepared.

THE MAGIC LACES

John Goodrum worked out one of the prettiest of close-up pieces when he developed this real sleight-of-hand routine with laces. In effect, two laces of unequal length stretch several times until, at the end, you wind up with both laces the same length.

The laces employed may be of the shoe variety or otherwise. In the former case, a black and a white lace are used. For something a little more colorful, ladies' dress laces, obtainable at any five and ten cent store's Notions counter, are recommended. These laces are of rayon, braided, and tipped with metal. They are obtainable in colors and about two feet long. It will be found that they are slightly larger than shoe laces and offer much less resistance to each other.

In the diagrams, the shaded lace is blue—the other, red. Take a pair of laces in hand while following the moves given. These will be found to be both simple and direct. Remember that you are at all times handling perfectly ordinary laces. There is no need to call attention to the fact—simply do the moves naturally.

We promise you, however, that the description will be quite unintelligible unless you have some laces or string in your hands to follow with.

Both laces are the same length, but they are not shown so in the beginning. To prepare, take the red lace, double about three or four inches of it and tie this with red thread, as in (Fig. 1). Lay this lace, with the blue one, across the back of a chair, on your table, or fold them neatly and place in coat pocket. You will find that they can be handled quite freely.

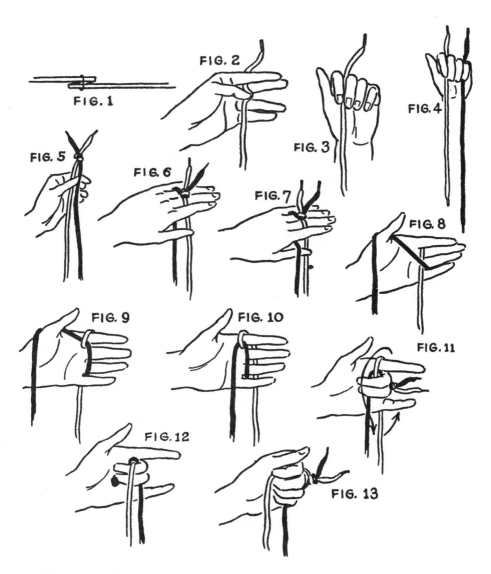

FIG. 1 FIG. 2 FIG. 3 FIG. 4 FIG. 5 FIG. 6 FIG. 7 FIG. 8 FIG. 9 FIG. 10 FIG. 11 FIG. 12 FIG. 13

To begin, pick up the red lace in the right hand and the blue in the left and compare their length, hiding the folded portion of the red one by the fingers of the right hand. Move the hands APART, breaking the strand of red thread with right fingers and let the red lace expand to its full length. This is unnoticeable. The laces are held at the finger tips and freely shown. Hold the blue lace in the left hand and lay the red one over the left forearm.

Now tie a single overhand knot in each end of the blue lace, about one inch inward. When you have done this, pick up the red lace and lay the blue one over the left forearm, then proceed to tie two similar knots in the red lace.

The red lace is in your left hand and in position for the beginning of the manipulative routine. It is held between the left first and second fingers, the knot against the back of the fingers (Fig. 2). Turn this hand back out to hide the move which follows while you reach with the right hand for the blue lace. Let the left thumb push the red lace into the crotch of the second and third fingers, where it is gripped by these fingers. Don't push it so far as to extend it on the back of the hand, however. Turn this hand back up and double the first two fingers down, the forefinger going on the upper side of the lace and the second finger below. (See Fig. 3). About three inches of lace have thus been taken up inside the hand.

Place the blue lace between the left third and little fingers and the result will appear to the audience as in (Fig. 4). Since the red lace was shown to be shorter in the beginning, there will be no suspicion of any trickery when it appears shorter here.

Notice how this simple series of moves subtly offsets any theory as to preparation. The laces were compared. The red one was shorter than the blue. Then they were held at the finger tips and it was plainly evident to all concerned that there was no preparation. The laces were then placed in the left hand—the red still shorter than the blue. All of these moves were direct and to the point; it is not necessary (or desirable) to emphasize them.

THE FIRST STRETCHING: Grasp BOTH laces at a point about five inches below the left hand and pull down on them, letting the right hand move down the two laces. As you do this, let the red one slip slightly until, at the end of the stretching movement, it is almost—but not quite—as long as the blue. Again stretch the red lace and this time tilt the left hand so that the thumb is down. Apparently, you have stretched the red one a little too far. Pull on the blue one and tilt the left hand back up to its former angle. The laces are now the same length.

THE SECOND STRETCHING: Grasp both laces together and tie them together at one end in a single overhand knot (Fig. 5). Turn the left hand back up, place the knot on the back of the hand, and thread the laces through the hand as before, the red lace between the first and second fingers and the blue between the third and little fingers (Fig. 6).

Grasp the blue lace with the right fingers and drape it over the left thumb as in (Fig. 7.)

Turn the left hand vertically, as in (Fig. 8), and bring the red lace up. Drop this one over the back of the left hand (Fig. 9) and, at the same time, release the blue one from the left thumb. The result is shown in (Fig. 10), back of hand to audience, of course.

Close the left second and third fingers over the looped laces and turn the left hand back upwards. (Fig. 11). Bring the red lace back to front of hand (Fig. 12) and close all fingers; hand assumes position as in (Fig. 4). At the same time, tilt the hand thumb up (Fig. 13) so that the laces appear even, despite the slack taken up by the doubling.

Without any hesitation, run the right hand down the laces, letting the left hand tip back normally and the red tape is seen actually longer. Run the right hand down the tapes, lightly grasping the blue tape with thumb and forefinger and pulling on it by degrees. As the blue lace is straightened out, the red one is pulled over and shortened (due to the looping arrangement), so that when the right hand reaches the bottom, the blue tape is now the longer. Once again the right hand travels down the tapes and this time the red one is grasped at the base of the right thumb and is stretched. The arrangement allows for stretching both ways and this effect may be repeated a number of times. Finally, the tapes are stretched even and, grasped by the knot on the back of the left hand, pulled free from the hand.

THE THIRD STRETCHING: If desired, the laces may now be untied, doubled together once, and an overhand knot tied at the looped part of the strand. The two red lengths are threaded through the first and second fingers and the two blue ones go through the third and fourth. The above moves are then repeated, the double lengths stretching as easily as the single ones did.

To finish, go to a spectator, still stretching the laces back and forth. Let him grasp one of the pairs of laces and pull until it is even with the other, then tell him to grasp the knot and pull the laces from the hand. This leaves the laces in the hands of the spectators and your own hands free of anything at all.

The third stretching may be omitted and this finish used at the close of the second part.

These manipulations are very easy to learn and the trick quite a bit out of the ordinary.

A CUT AND RESTORED SHOE LACE

John Goodrum also gave us this effective little item which is ideal for close work.

Two laces are required to prepare. From one lace clip off the two ends about two inches from the tips. Sew these tips together so that you have a short lace about five inches long with a tip on each end. Tie this around the center of another lace of the same color. From the piece of lace left, clip off a section four inches long. Insert one of the real tips of the whole lace in each end, this joining the lace in a continuous circle.

The small fake lace tied around the real lace now passes as the real ends of the lace.

As usual, untie the knot and show the two ends of the lace. Retie this knot and exhibit the lace tied in a circle. Get a pair of scissors from your pocket and clip the lace apparently in the center. You really clip the little fake piece of lace in half, this releasing the two ends. They are still covered with the cloth of the lace and pass as pieces of the MIDDLE.

Take one end (really a tip covered with a piece of lace) and place it between the left thumb and forefinger. Hold this lace at the finger tips. With scissors still in hand, grasp the lace at the knot and wind it around the left hand. At the same time, slide this knot along inside the right hand. When you get to the free end, remove the small tube and carry it along in your right hand, too. It is disposed of in the pocket along with the knot as the scissors are placed back. Remember that one end of the lace has its tip exposed and this must be kept out of sight for the present. The other end, still covered with the small cloth tube, is left in view and it appears that the cut ends are in sight until the very last moment.

Now grasp the free (tipped) end of the lace in the right hand and begin to unwind the lace. As you come around the hand for the first time and as you pass the other end of the lace, clip the cloth tube from the tip and palm it in the right hand. Continue to unwind the lace and then toss it out restored. The palmed piece of lace can be dropped on the floor or in a pocket.

While obviously no originality is claimed here, the presence of tips on the ends of the lace is a confusing point and makes this an effective trick.

THE CUT AND RESTORED LACE TIPS

This is a version of the Percival Shoe Lace Trick that at least has the advantage of being very easy to prepare. The effect is that of cutting off the tips of a lace and restoring them magically to the lace again.

Prepare a long black shoe lace by cutting the ends off another lace about one inch from the tips and inserting the tips of the complete lace into the double fabric of each of the cut-off ends, thus covering the real tips. The lace may be shown freely, even up close, with the fingers over the joints.

Hold the lace by one end in the left hand and bring the other end up and hold. Cut off the false tips and hand each to a spectator. Show the lace, keeping it slightly in motion.

Hold the lace in the left hand as before with the cut ends (false) just visible above the fist. Take the cut tips in right hand between first and second fingers in finger palm position and pretend to stick them in the opening of the left fist, but instead, right first finger and thumb simply nip the false ends and pull them clear off the lace, leaving the real tips visible above the fist.

Someone pokes the visible tips down into the left hand, which is then opened and the tips seen restored. The right hand gets rid of the false tips and ends in pocket when convenient, as there is no special hurry about this. The lace may be given to someone to examine and keep.

The trick is very easy to do.

TWIN SOULS

This effective trick can be done with any pack of cards. Begin by having the deck shuffled by a spectator. In taking it back sight the bottom card, make an overhand shuffle, bringing it to the top and note also the bottom card at the end of the shuffle. Go to a lady and say you will make a prediction foretelling exactly what she is about to do. Write on a slip of paper, "The gentleman will get the .... of .... " filling in with the name of the top card of the deck. Fold the slip and put it on the table under a glass or some other object. Hand the pack to the lady and ask her to think of a number, then when your back is turned, to deal that number of cards face down on the table, turn the top card of those dealt, note what it is, replace the packet on the pack and make one complete cut burying the chosen card in the middle. Turn away while the lady does this.

When she is ready, turn again and take the pack. Go to a gentleman and under pretence of fixing on a suitable card to impress on his mind, run over the faces of the cards, find the former bottom card and cut at that point. Note the card thus brought to the top. On a second slip write, "The lady will get the   of .... " fill in the name of this top card. Fold the slip and put it with the first. Ask the lady to whisper the number she chose to the gentleman. Hand the pack to him and tell him to deal the cards face down and note the card at that number. This done, reassemble the pack and shuffle it as you build up the effect by recapitulating what has been done. Hand out the slips in the reverse order to that in which you wrote them. Have the two cards named, then have the slips opened and read, proving that you predicted the choice of those very cards.

THE MAGIC BREATH

This is a good example of how the presentation can be made to transform a simple trick into a striking effect. The trick is that in which a card is sent to any number chosen by the spectator, the first time the cards are counted a wrong card appears but on a second count the right one turns up. The method is simplicity itself. The card is on the top so that the first count brings it to the number required so when the packet is replaced on the pack and again counted it is found at the correct number. In the older method the cards were replaced on the pretext of a miscount, a very weak procedure.

A card having been freely chosen, noted, replaced and brought to the top, execute several shuffles keeping it there. Addressing the spectator you say, "Have you a magic breath? Well I will show you how to find out. If you have you can send your card to whatever position you please merely by breathing gently on the cards. Will you choose a number? Nine? Then just blow on the pack and think intently of that number as you blow." Spectator blows, turn your head away with a slight grimace. "Your breath does not seem to be very magical, but I may be mistaken. Will you take the pack and count down to your number?"

He does this and turns a wrong card. Take the pack, put the packet counted on top and execute a false shuffle; take the card he turned up and push it in somewhere amongst the top eight cards. "I knew you would fail," you say, "instead of thinking while blowing, you blew while thinking, not the same thing at all. Let me show you a real magic breath. See, just a gentle zephyr, but it has sent your card to the number required. What was it you chose? Nine?" Deal 8 cards, have the spectator name his card and turn the ninth.

The testing of the spectator's breath can be done delicately or broadly according to the type of audience.

REVERSED COURT CARD

EFFECT:—Four cards are placed in a row, faces up. While performer's back is turned a card is turned end for end. He finds the one that has been reversed.

METHOD:—This is a development of the very old trick which was done by using cards the white margins of which were a little wider on one side than the other. In this method pick out of a pack of Bicycle cards the K. Q. and J. of S. Note the small white spades used in the body of the design. The J. has 5 small spades pointing up or down according to the way the card is turned. The Q. has 7 pointing to left or right and in the center of the K. design the large jewel is shaded at one end only.

Lay these cards in a row face up noting the way the designs point and invite a spectator to place any other Court card down with them. Turn your back while the spectator turns one card end for end. If he turns one of the S. you recognize it by the changed position of the design, but **if** these are unchanged then you know that the fourth card must have **been** turned.

THE SAGACIOUS JOKER

Using any deck, the Joker is first placed face up and a spectator is asked to shuffle the cards, then take out any face down card and without looking at it put it in his inside coat pocket with its back outwards. This done he passes the pack to a second person who does the same thing. The process is repeated with a third and fourth person. Thus four cards have been selected at random and even the spectators who have them in their pockets do not know what cards they are. You take the pack, remove the Joker and touching it to each person's pocket you call the names of the cards correctly.

To do this take the face down pack, spread it to find the face up Joker, cut to bring it to the top. Make a double lift taking the next face down card with the Joker and holding the two as one. Keep the Joker with its face squarely to the front and as you go to the first spectator sight the index of the card behind the Joker. Touch the Joker to his pocket and slowly tell the value of the card just sighted, then to get the suit insert the Joker in his pocket, drop the card from behind it and pick up in its place the card that was in the pocket. Take care to get it squarely behind before removing the Joker. Now name the suit. Spectator takes the card from his pocket and shows it. You sight the index of the new card behind the Joker and repeat the process. Always name either the suit or the color before inserting the Joker in the pocket.

NO. 2. In this method the rather awkward business of changing the cards in the pocket is avoided. After taking the pack to remove the Joker, run over the cards till you reach it, then reverse it and apparently take it out and put it face down on the table, really draw out the card next to it which may be any card at all. Cut the pack to bring the Joker to the top and keep the pack in your left hand. Pick up the card from the table sighting it. Insert it in the first person's pocket, calling its name and leave it there, bringing out the card originally placed in the pocket. Proceed in exactly the same way with all the others. Finally as the cards are being verified you have ample opportunity to put the last card left in your hand on the bottom of the pack and take off the Joker which you throw face up on the table.

NO. 3. This is an adaptation of "The Whispering Queen" (p. 24).

Using any pack that has a Joker, have it shuffled by a spectator. Take it and in removing the Joker sight and memorize the 2nd, 3rd, and 4th cards from the bottom. Invite a spectator to cut about the middle, put the packets on the table and place his hands on top of them. Tell him to lift one hand. If he lifts the hand from the original bottom half of the deck you say, "You want to use this packet? Very well." Hand it to him and put the other aside. But if he raises the other hand simply remove that packet and let him retain the one under his hand. Give any plausible reason that occurs to you and have him count the cards face down. Whatever the number may be you say, "That's fine. I think we'll succeed. Tell him to take off the top card and put it in the middle, do the same with the bottom card, and put the next card in his pocket without looking at it. The next two cards are put in the pockets of two other persons, also without being looked. Now since these three cards are the ones you memorized you have no difficulty in naming them, pretending, of course, to get the information from the Joker which you insert in the pockets and study carefully each time.

NO. 4. In this method four cards are freely selected and placed in spectator's pocket without being looked at as in the first method, but in putting the pack aside you must note the bottom card and really take the Joker only in your hand. Suppose the bottom card is the 7S. Advance to the first person, touch the Joker to the outside of his pocket and slowly name the color and value of the bottom card of the deck, in this case the 7S. To get the shape of the pips you say direct contact must be made. Insert the Joker, drop it and seize the card already in the pocket. Now name the suite, S., and bring out the card holding it face down. Tell the spectator to leave his card as it is till you come back to him. As you go to the second person tilt the card in your hand a little and sight the outer index. Go through exactly the same process, naming the card in your hand and exchanging it for the one in the pocket. Same with the third and fourth spectators. You will have to remember these cards and their order.

Finally put the supposed Joker, really the card from the fourth person's pocket, face down on the table and have the first person take out his card without looking at it and put it face down on the supposed Joker. Drop the rest of the pack on top. Lift the pack with your left hand by the sides as you say "Yours was the only card I am doubtful about." Bend your head down pretending to listen, then say "Yes I was right it is the 7. S." With the tip of the left 3rd finger draw back the bottom card and with the right hand pull out the next, the Joker, throwing it face up on the table, and next the 7. S. Pick up the Joker and with it touch the spectators' pockets, again name the three cards. They are taken out and verified.

THE TRIO

Allow a spectator to shuffle the cards (any deck). Take them back and under pretence of removing the Joker, memorize the 3 cards below the top card. Riffle shuffle, retaining the four top cards in the same position. Put the pack on the table and ask the spectator to cut it into two packets. Say that you will "take" one packet and invite him to touch one. If he touches the original lower portion of the pack, take it and put it aside: if he touches the original top portion tell him to take it. In any case that is the packet he must get.

Instruct him to take the top card of this packet and push it into the middle, the same with the bottom card, then to take the top card and put it face down on the table and hand the second and third cards to two other spectators. Now proceed to reveal the cards by mind reading, pulse reading or any other way that pleases your fancy.

CARDS OF CHANCE

In this trick a special move is necessary that is not at all difficult. It is to apparently show the faces of all the cards but to keep one hidden. You have the card on the top, turn pack face outwards and run the cards off one by one from the left hand into the right. When you are about two-thirds through separate the hands for a moment and spread the cards remaining in the left hand to show the indices at the same time pushing the lowest card, the top card of the deck and the one to be concealed, a little forward behind the others. Bring the hands together and as you take off the face card of the left hand packet pull off the top card behind those in the right hand with the right fingers. Then show all the rest of the cards.

You have a deck shuffled by a spectator and in taking it back sight the bottom card, then overhand shuffle it to the the top. Suppose it is the 10 spades. Cut, bringing it to the middle, keeping the tip of the little finger on the 10S. On a slip of paper write 10 S. and put it face down on the table without showing what you have written. Ask a spectator to point to a card and contrive to have the 10S. in position as he points Take the card out and put it face down on the table. Ask him to call the name of any card. Suppose he names the 2D. Hand him a slip of paper and have him write that and put the slip on the table. As he does so find the 2D. and slip it to the top. Run over the faces of the cards and show the card is not in the pack. Go to a second person and force the 2D just as you forced the 10S. He names we will say, the AH. Put the 2D down and as he writes AH on a third slip find that card, slip it to the top and show it is not in the pack, using the move explained. Finally force the AH. on a third person and place it on the table opposite your first slip, calling it the 10S. Have the pack examined, the three cards named are not in it. Gather up the three cards, mixing them, then match them with the three slips.

PUSH

Any deck is shuffled by a spectator and returned to you. With the blunt end of a pencil push out a packet of cards from the middle. Invite a spectator to note the top card of the projecting portion by lifting a corner and noting the index. You note the index of the bottom card of the top packet as you turn the cards edgewise to push the projecting packet flush with the deck. By running through the pack and noting the card below this one you learn what card the spectator looked at. Reveal it in as striking a manner as you can. There is little danger of the two cards being separated if you allow the spectator to make a short overhand shuffle. This strengthens the effect greatly.

CARD DETECTIVES

With any deck, after it has been well shuffled, secretly sight the two top cards. Riffle shuffle retaining these cards on the top. Put the pack down and have a spectator cut it at about the middle. Invite him to touch one packet. Whichever he touches interpret his choice so that he gets the one with the two cards you know on top. Tell him to do just as you do. Take the bottom card and put it in the center of your heap. He does the same. Put the top card in your right hand pocket. He does the same Put the bottom card in the middle and the top card in your left hand pocket. He does the same. Lastly put the top and bottom cards in the middle. He follows suit.

"It is a most peculiar thing," you say, "but through some strange sympathy that exists amongst the cards, the one in my right hand pocket will indicate to me what the card in your right hand pocket is, and the one in my left pocket will tell me what the one in your left hand pocket happens to be."

Take out the card from your right pocket, show it and then deducing from it any plausible or fanciful reason, name the card in his right hand pocket. Do the same with the other cards. The putting of the cards from the bottom to the middle is merely to confuse and misdirect the spectator.

THE "EASY" CARD IN WALLET

This method has several good points. The wallet is not prepared and the hand taking it from the pocket is empty.

Use a wallet that opens lengthwise and slip a heavy rubber band around one side. Open it so that the covers touch, back to back, and hang it over the edge of your inside coat pocket, the rubber band side in the pocket, the other side hanging out.

From any shuffled deck have a card freely selected, marked, returned, and bring it to the top. (Chapt. 19). Place both hands with the pack behind your back. Take the marked card in your left hand, reach up under your coat at the back and push the card under your right arm pit, retaining it with a slight pressure of the arm against the body. Bring the deck forward and throw out a card, any card, as you say, "Your card?" The answer will be "No."

Place the pack on the table, casually letting it be noted that your hands are empty. Take hold of the right edge of your coat with your right hand. With the left take the card from under your arm, slip it into the wallet, lift this from the pocket, flipping it over and closing it, and bring it out with the band side to the front. Put the right fingers under the band and pull it off as if it really encircled the wallet, open this and invite a spectator to take out the marked card.

PREDICTION

You have any deck freely shuffled by a spectator. Take it back face up and mentally note the face card. Secretly reverse the lowest card, as the pack lies and remember it also. Put the pack on the table, reversed card face down, pack face up. Invite a spectator to cut about 2/3 of the cards and put them face down beside the remainder of the pack. As he is doing this you write a prediction, (the names of the two sighted cards), on a slip of paper and hand it to a second spectator.

Now have the spectator cut the second pile about the middle and put the cut face up alongside. You now have three piles in a row, the middle one face down, the two outside ones face up. Place the first pile (reversed card at bottom) on top of the middle pile and both of these on the third pile. Invite the spectator to remove the face down section from the middle, put it on the table and cut it into two parts. Have your prediction slip placed on the top portion and the lower packet placed crosswise on that. The slip is thus between the two cards whose names you wrote on it. This way of placing the cut confuses the spectator into thinking the slip is placed at the place at which he cut.

A SMART LOCATION

Allow a spectator to make a free selection of a card from a freely shuffled pack. Let him replace it anywhere as you ruffle the outer ends of the deck. By keeping a tight hold of the inner ends you prevent the card from going right home. Tap the inner ends quite even and then give the protruding end of the selected card a sharp tap. This will send it through the pack and its inner end will protrude about the 1/8 of an inch.

With the right thumb on the inner end of the deck split the pack for a riffle shuffle at this protruding card but pick up one more card below it. The chosen card will thus be the second card from the bottom of the portion in the right hand. Riffle the two parts of the pack together but let the two bottom cards of the right hand part drop first then complete a genuine riffle. You can show the top and the bottom cards after the shuffle and then, with an overhand shuffle, bring the card from next the bottom to any desired position.

THE WHISPERING QUEEN

Any deck, borrowed if possible, may be used . Have the cards thoroughly shuffled by one or more spectators. Take it back and run through it to find and remove the QC., the most gossipy of all the Queens. In doing this spread the four top cards so that you can see and memorize their indices. Read the values to yourself thus for instance 47-36 (forty-seven-thirty-six) and then the suits, say C.D.H.S. After a little practice four cards can be memorized in this way at a glance. Have a spectator deal the cards into four face down heaps. Push the QC. face up below any chosen heap for a moment, then put the card to your ear. She whispers the name to you? and you call it. Repeat with the bottom cards of the other heaps.

THE CARD DOCTOR

EFFECT:—Using a borrowed deck, if so desired, the performer has a spectator call any number from 1 to 12. Dealing fairly to this number the card is shown and initialed by the spectator. Stating that the card is to represent a man who has met with an accident necessitating the removal of one leg, the performer tears a corner from the card and hands it to the spectator to hold. As the story goes, the man has a terrible dream in which he sees himself in many pieces. As he tells this, the performer tears the card into a number of pieces with the face of the card towards the audience. Then into the dream comes a great doctor who covers him with a white sheet, but before anything else can. happen, the man wakes up and finds himself still in the hospital, perfectly well except for the missing leg. The corner is then matched to the card by the spectator who identifies his initials.

METHOD:—Before starting take the 6, 7, and 8 spots of each suit and put them on the top in any order. Thus the selection must be from one of these cards. Take the card out and, while the spectator initials it, pick up the pack and the cards dealt, pick out a card of the same suit and put it on the bottom. If the chosen card is a 6. you pick a 7, if it is a 7.

pick a 6., and if an 8. take a 7. Suppose the 7 C. is the card selected, put the 6 C. on the face of the deck and cut same into two parts. Take back the 7 C., pick up the original bottom half of the deck and put the 7 C. at the bottom, i. e. over the 6 C., then slide the two cards together about an inch over the end of the deck that is opposite the odd spot of the 7 C. Hold the deck now with its face to the audience, the protruding card seemingly the 7 C. only. Place the remaining half of the deck in front, timing the patter about the man going into the hospital. Holding he deck firmly, deliberately tear off the index corner of both cards as one. Push out the 7 corner with the thumb and hand it to the spectator, then drop the other corner in your pocket as you take out a rubber band.

Turn the pack face down and apparently withdraw the 7 C. but with the left forefinger push this card back flush with the deck and draw out the 6 C. face down and put it on the table. Put the rubber band round the pack and hand it to the spectator. Pick up the card with the fingers covering the missing spot and index corner. As you continue relating the dream, tear it in half, placing the torn corner half in front. Now very openly tear the card several times. It is only necessary to vanish the pieces and the sheet in the dream is represented by your handkerchief which has a dummy packet in one corner. Throw the handkerchief over the pieces and give them to the spectator to hold. Really he gets the dummy packet and you pocket the pieces. Tell the ending of the dream, shake out the handkerchief, the pieces have gone. Riffle the deck at the corner, with the band still round it, stopping at the break and have the spectator remove the restored and marked card from the hospital for identification of the initials and the matching of the corner.

STAMPEDO

EFFECT:— A postage stamp is stuck to the face of a card to identify it. 10 cards are placed aside and the chosen card put amongst them. A spectator holds the rest of the pack. Chosen card returns to the pack, leaving 10 cards only.

METHOD:—Beforehand moisten one end of a 1c stamp and stick it over an end spot of the 3C., the end of the stamp adhering to the card near its end. Put this card on the bottom and the AC. at the top. Begin by forcing the AC, cut and bring the 3C. back to the bottom and put the pack on the table. Take the chosen card back, face down, show another 1c stamp, moisten it and, at the same time, the tip of the right middle finger; reach under the AC. and stick the stamp to its face in exactly the same position as the stamp on the 3C. Show the face of the card to the audience but do not look at it yourself, put it face down on the table and put pack on top of it.

Deal ten cards in a packet to one side from the top of the pack. Draw back the AC. on the bottom and draw out the 3C. Drop it on the packet of 10 cards. Cut the pack and hand it to be held. Pick up the packet, take the 3C. and push it into the middle far enough to hide the end spot, then raise the hands and show the face of the card, it appears to be the stamped AC. As you push it home wet the free end of the stamp and press it back, this will cause the card to stick to the card next above it so that the packet can again be counted as 10 and be shown or fanned with impunity.

The ace is found in the pack by the spectator.

COLOR DIVINATION

EFFECT:—From a face up borrowed deck a spectator deals the red cards face down on your left hand, the black cards face up on your right hand. Putting the black cards face up on the table, hand him the red ones to shuffle. Write something on a piece of paper, fold it and lay it down. The spectator picks any red card, face down, without looking at it and puts it in the pile of black cards. Fan the black pile and show the card, it is the card whose name you wrote on the slip. The card is replaced in the red packet and the feat is repeated.

METHOD:—Count the red cards as they are dealt on your left hand. the 26th is the one whose name you write on the slip, and as you receive it, slip the tip of your left third finger under it. As you turn to the left to put the black cards on the table, straighten the left fingers, levering the top card upwards, glimpse it, and slide it under the face up black packet as the hands pass: put that packet down, the added card at the bottom and hand the red cards to be shuffled. Write the name of the card you sighted, fold the slip and lay it down. Turn the black heap face down. The spectator pushes any red card into the black packet, face down without looking at it, as you fan the cards. Make the pass, bringing it to the top, then fan the cards. In the middle will be the card you secretly transferred, whose name is on the slip, but the spectator naturally believes it to be the one he just pushed in. Have the slip read, take the card out and replace it in the red packet. The feat can then be repeated.

THE VANISHING PAIR

In taking a pack from its case quickly note the top two cards and let them slip back into the case as you take out the remainder. On a slip of paper write the names of these two cards, fold it and hand it to someone to hold. Have the pack shuffled, then cut into two parts and one part handed to you. Pick up the case and slide this chosen packet into it: by making a break with the thumb at one corner and pushing this corner into the case first, the two cards in the case will be forced into its middle.

From the remaining packet deal four cards in a row face down. Look at the first, call its name as you deal it and give the spectators a glimpse of it; miscall the next two as the two cards you wrote on the slip and don't let their faces be seen as you deal them; name the last one correctly and again give the audience a glimpse of it as you lay it down. Allow a choice of the inside pair or the outside pair. Interpret reply that the inside cards are to be used and thrust them into the packet. Give it to be held. Order the two cards to fly to the packet in the case. The packets are examined and the deed has been done.

THE UNKNOWN LEAPER

Any deck, shuffled by any one may be used. Take it and pass the cards with their faces towards a spectator slowly, one at a time from the left hand to the right, counting them aloud and putting the second under the first so that the same order is retained. The person notes any card mentally and remembers its number from the top. A card must be selected before you reach the middle of the pack. This done, while the cards are upright, pull the top card of the right-hand lot on top of those in the left hand, square the deck and cut it as nearly as possible in half. Again run the faces of the cards in the top half before the spectator's eyes so that he can be sure his card is still in it. It is there but unknown to him it lies one card higher than he thinks owing to your having pushed off one card from his packet.

Hand the top packet to the spectator, you take the lower one. Deal one card face down on the table, the spectator deals his top card on yours, counting one; deal a second on this and he deals his second card on top, counting "Two" continue thus, dealing alternately until he arrives at one number less than the depth of his card in his packet. At this point pick up the pile of dealt cards (the top card is the selected card) with the right hand and as you ask him to name his card and deal it face down on the table, place the right hand packet over the cards in your left hand as if to square them but hold them upright and with the left thumb pull the top card of the right hand packet on top of the left hand pile. Put the right hand packet down, then deal the top card, the card just transferred, face down on the table. He names the card he thought of and turns his card, it is another card altogether: you turn yours, it is his card.

SELF CONTROL

EFFECT:—A spectator shuffles a pack of cards, which can be his own, and then spreads the cards face down on a table. He points to any card he pleases, and that card is removed from the pack and kept in full view. Next he is asked to think of a card. He names it and that card is missing from the deck. He himself turns over the card he pointed out, it is the card he thought of.

SECRET:—The trick is hardly as good as its sales talk but can be made effective. When the spectator points out a card you pick it up and place it in your outside coat pocket at the top, allowing about half the card to protrude, "in order to keep it in sight the whole time," as you say. As soon as he names the card he has mentally selected, pick up the pack, run through the faces quickly and on coming to that card transfer it to the top. Say that you cannot find it and ask the spectator to go through the pack to verify the fact that the card is missing. Palm the top card in your right hand and give him the pack. He also fails to find the "thought" card. With your right hand apparently take the card from your coat pocket and put it face down on the table, it is the card. What you really do is to push the card in the pocket right down out of sight and insert the palmed card, bringing it out in place of the other.

The following description of the effect of a trick by Robert Houdin in his book "Les Secrets," published in 1868 will be found interesting. "To place the first card that comes to hand on a table and to predict that whatever may be the card another spectator may please to think of such card shall be identical in suit and value with the card previously removed."

The modern inventor puts the card in his pocket instead of on the table and calls it a new trick.

IN HIS POCKET

Prepare for the trick by slipping two cards into your right hand trouser pocket. When ready to do the trick, you can show the pocket empty by pushing the cards to the top inner corner as you pull out the pocket. Have the deck shuffled, take it back and deal the three top cards face up. Memorize the values, ask a spectator to think of one of the three. Put them in your trousers pocket. Bring out the two previously hidden cards one by one and put them face down on the pack without showing the faces. Now have the card mentally selected and, remembering the values of the cards still in your pocket, and the order in which you placed them, you have no difficulty in bringing out the right card. It must be produced without hesitation or fumbling.

FIND THE QUEEN

The effect is that four aces and one Queen are sealed in separate envelopes. These are mixed thoroughly, yet when they are handed to you one by one you tell which contains the Queen.

The secret is very simple. The aces are placed in the envelopes on their sides, while the Queen is stood upright. Of course this is not done openly. Place the Queen in the envelope in exactly the same way as the others but under cover of the flap turn it upright.

By not announcing what you are going to do the Queen envelope may be handed to you first of all. In which case you say you "willed" the spectator to do that and open the envelope to see if you are right, turning the card lengthwise before bringing it out. The same effect can be obtained if the Queen envelope is handed to you last. In all other cases simply place the envelope to your forehead and announce which one holds the Queen. Camouflage the fact that you get your information by feel.

SUPER CARD PREDICTION

The trick depends upon a special move. Take any deck, hold it firmly at the inner left corner between the thumb and 1st and 2nd fingers. Press downward to the left forcibly with the thumb and the deck will break cleanly at some point. Close the pack and repeat the action, the deck will break at the same point. If the pack breaks at more than one spot, use greater pressure.

To apply this principle to a trick: borrow a deck after having had it well shuffled. Ask the spectator to take out a pencil and paper and under caver of his doing this, test the pack for the break as above; cut if necessary, to bring it at a point about one-third of the way from the top, after glimpsing the index of the card at the bottom of the portion that slides. Write this card on the paper, fold the slip and hand it to the spectator. Give him the top card and, holding the pack in position for the sliding move, call attention to its being squared perfectly and show all sides. Tell the spectator to thrust the card into the deck, face up, anywhere he pleases, but you take care it goes in under the natural break. Now move the inserted card so that it protrudes diagonally from the corner opposite your left thumb. Raise the pack with the left hand till it is upright, make the 'slide" motion, pushing the upper portion an inch to the right, at the same moment seize this packet and the inserted card with the right hand and draw them away. The bottom card of the packet is shown and your prediction read, they coincide.

THE FINGER POINTS

Any complete deck is handed to a spectator to shuffle: instruct him to merely think of a card as he shuffles. Take the pack and spread it widely on the table with the faces up. Tell the spectator to hold his right hand over the cards, with his forefinger pointing downwards, and move it slowly from one end of the row to the other and back again. When he comes to the card he thought of tell him he is to say mentally "That's it," but on no account to hesitae or stop. Before he does this take up your position a little distance away from the table.

It is a psychological fact that if the spectator carries out your instructions he will hesitate for a fraction of a second when he comes to his card. If you stood close to him this could not be detected but from a little distance it becomes quite noticeable and you learn the approximate position of the card, within 5 or 6 cards at the very most. Return to the table, glance at this group memorizing them, cut the deck to bring them to the top and put the pack behind your back. In memorizing the cards, disregard the suits and remember the values as you would a telephone number, thus 48-762. Ask the number of spots on the card and bring forward the correct one, putting it face down. The suit is named and you turn the card.

THE FIVE CARD MENTAL FORCE

The following five cards are placed face up in an even row on the table, K.H., 7C., A.D., 4H. and 9D. The performer addresses a spectator, somewhat as follows:—"I have picked out five cards at random and I want you to mentally select just one. You have an unrestricted choice and you must not think that I am trying to influence you in any way. For instance, here is an ace, occupying the central position; you may think of it, and again you may not. Perhaps you think I had a motive in placing just one black card among the cards. This might influence your choice, or again it might not. At any rate look over the five cards carefully, as long as you wish, but rest assured that whatever card you definitely decide upon I shall presently place face down upon your hand and, when you yourself are holding the card, I shall ask you to name your card. It will be your card. Even when the card is on your hand you have the privilege of changing your mind, still the card will be the one thought of."

When the spectator has made his mental choice, pick up the five cards, mix them, draw out the 4H. and put it on his hand face down. He names his card, it is almost inevitably the 4H. The trick is a purely psychological one. The spectator rejects the Ace and the King as being too conspicuous, the 7C. is the one black card and anyway 7 has become an overworked number in such tricks, the 9D. is never chosen being widely considered an unlucky card, and this reasoning leaves one card only, the 4H. Your patter must be directed towards making the spectator consider each card and form a reason for rejecting or choosing it; if you allow a snap choice the trick is almost certain to fail.

Until you have had some experience with the effect instead of putting the 4H. on the spectator's hand, simply lay 5 cards in a pile with the 4H. on the top and K.H. at the bottom. Then if the K.H. is named simply turn the packet over.

"JUST THINK" MENTAL MYSTERY

Ask someone to just think of a card as he shuffles the deck. He may change his mind as often as he pleases but, having fixed on one card he must keep to it. Next take a blank card about the size of a playing card, draw four lines across it, making five spaces, the first, third and fifth spaces somewhat larger than the second and fourth. Hand this with a pencil to the spectator asking him to fill in the spaces with the names of four indifferent cards and his card in any order he pleases. You address him somewhat after this manner: "You may write the cards in any order. Your mentally selected card can be written in any space you see fit. You may write your card in the first space, or the last or again in the middle, but don't let me influence your choice of space as this is entirely up to you." Almost invariably the thought card will be written in the second space, or, if not there, in the third space. However, you have a second string to your bow by watching his manner of writing. You should stand at some little distance from him since you need only watch his hand. There will always be a little hesitation in the writing of the four cards but, when he writes the name of his mentally selected card he writes it in rapidly.

This having been done, take back the pack and the list, glance at the name of the card in the space you have decided on and throw the list face down on the table. Run through the deck, take out the card and put it face down on the table. Give the spectator the list asking him to cross out the indifferent cards, then turn the card you put out. With very little experiences with the feat you should get the card every time. The impression left on the spectator's mind is that you picked the card from the whole pack.

MATCHING THE ACES

This is another trick of the psychological order, the mind of the spectator being influenced to follow your suggestions.

Take two sets of aces, hand one to the spectator and take the other yourself. Place the AH. face down on the table without showing it and say to the person, "I want you to select any one of your four aces and put it face down on mine. You may pick any ace you please, for instance the AS. but don't let me influence your mind or choice. Just put your card down here." Presuming you have chosen a man for the feat it is practically certain he will pick the AH, since he will eliminate the AS. through your having named it. If you are dealing with a lady mention the AC. and the probability is she will put down the AD.

Continue then by having the person deal the other three aces face up and you put your corresponding ace on each one. Finally turn the two face down aces showing they match.

If you have a magician to deal with always put down the AC as your first card. He will ignore the AH and the AD since they play an important part in mental selections of cards. Of the two black Aces he will choose the AC as being less prominent. Finish as above. Tricks like these are not certain to succeed but they are very interesting and, if presented as feats of mindreading, you lose no prestige in case of failure and score when successful.

SURPASSO

Any full deck and its case may be used. Allow a spectator to shuffle the cards, retaining one and hand the remainder to you. Square these carefully and insert them in the case. The spectator having noted his card, turn your back and hold out the case, open end towards him, asking him to insert his card somewhere in the middle. By pressing on the end of the case with your finger and thumb the card will be prevented from going exactly flush with the rest. Have the flap pushed in.

Keeping your back turned while the spectator writes the name of his card, quickly open the case, grip the pack tightly and pull all the cards halfway out of the case. Run your thumb lightly over the ends and pull out the one card that protrudes slightly, put it in a vest pocket, sighting it as you do so, close the flap again, turn and toss card case on the table. You not only know the card but you have possession of it and you can finish the trick as you wish.

Keep your elbows pressed closely to your sides as you extract the card from the case so that your movements are not betrayed to the spectators.

THE SVENGALI DECK

This special pack consists of 26 ordinary cards, all different, and 26 short cards all of the same suit and value. The latter may be narrower as well as shorter, but short duplicates only are generally used. The pack is set up by arranging the two sets alternately, thus every other card from the top of the pack is a card of the same suit and value. Burling Hull in his "Sealed Mysteries" claims its invention and that he copyrighted it in 1909. The Svengali deck soon leaped into wide popularity and into the hands of street peddlers. Many thousands of packs must have been sold, and are still selling, and yet its use must not be despised by magicians on that account. Like many other weapons in the magicians' armory it can be used even amongst people who know the principle without their suspicions being aroused.

VARIOUS METHODS OF HANDLING THE PACK

Briefly the pack is used thus: After giving the cards a riffle shuffle, which does not disturb the arrangement, square the deck and hold it face down with the outer end slightly raised towards the spectators. Slowly ruffle the cards by placing the tip of the right fore-finger on the outer edges of the cards, bend the pack slightly upwards and release the cards rather slowly, every card will be seen to be different. The short cards do

not appear since the cards fall in pairs. Lowering the pack, again ruffle the cards and invite a spectator to insert his finger tip, (or the blade of a knife) at any point he desires. No matter where he does this his finger will rest on the back of one of the short cards. Divide the pack at this point, let the spectator take out that card and the force is made.

It will be noted that the bottom card of the portion lifted off with the right hand is an indifferent card as is also the top card of the left hand portion after the card has been withdrawn, by showing these cards the apparent fairness of the choice is established.

From this simple principle many astonishing effects have been developed and it is safe to say that there are possibilities of further card miracles waiting to be evolved by ingenious minds.

The greatest effect is obtained by switching a deck that has been used for several tricks, in the course of which the spectators have freely handled and shuffled the cards, for a Svengali deck. Results can then be obtained which to the layman appear miraculous. In the following pages a method will be found for secretly exchanging the duplicate cards for 26 indifferent cards which, with the other 26 cards of the Svengali deck make up a complete deck that can be freely handled and examined by the spectators, thus leaving no clue to the feats performed.

Besides the ruffling method of showing all the cards different you may cut small packets from the top laying them down face up. Every face card will be different since you can only cut at a long card. Assemble the pack again and have it cut several times. This is a very convincing method.

In addition to the thrusting of a finger or knife blade into the pack for the choice of a card, you may cut the pack by the ends into several piles and have any one of them chosen. The top card of the heap chosen is lifted off by the spectator.

A second method of showing all the cards different is to hold the pack upright in the right hand, thumb at the top, fingers at the bottom, release the cards slowly from the thumb and they will fall forward in pairs, every card showing a different face. This is more convincing than the ruffle.

SIMPLE EFFECTS

Before explaining some of the special tricks that have been devised for the use of this pack and to enable the reader to become used to the proper handling of the pack, some of the simpler feats will be described first.

1. Show the cards all different by ruffling them, riffle shuffle and make a series of cuts each time showing a different card on the face of the right hand portion. Invite a spectator to insert his forefinger tip at any point he desires. Let him remove the card, note it and you read his mind by naming the card. Casually show the bottom card of those in your right

hand, that is the cards above the one he removed and also the top card of the portion in your left hand.

2. Have the card replaced in the same position and drop the right hand portion on top. Square the pack and cut several times to make the impression that the card is lost in the deck. Announce that you will place the cards, one by one, face down on the table and invite the spectator to call "Stop" at any time he wishes. Seeing that cutting the cards has left one of the shorts on the top, it follows that you have only to stop on any odd number to have a duplicate of the selected card in your hand. If, however, the spectator calls on an even card simply place it on top of the cards already on the table and say, "And the very next card will be your card." Turn the next card and show it, then place it on top of the pile on the table, pick up the pile, being careful not to expose the bottom card, and place it on top of the remainder in your left hand.

3. Hand the top card, the one already chosen and ask the spectator to place the tip of his forefinger on its back and hold it there for a few seconds, then placing your left hand with the pack behind your back, you take the card in your right hand and say you will push it into the pack behind your back so that no one can possibly know just what position it will occupy. Pretend to do this but simply put the card on the top of the pack. Bring the pack forward and again show that every card is different by making a series of cuts. Then ruffle the cards inviting the spectator to insert his finger tip anywhere he likes. He does this and you lift off the portion above his finger, while he names the card, (you have forgotten what it was?). Ask him to draw out the card and turn it over—and he finds it's his card. Again show that the card preceding it and the card following it are quite different cards.

4. The above effects may very well follow one another but, of course, you cannot keep on using the same forced card indefinitely.

A pretended prediction trick can be easily worked with the Svengali deck. After showing the cards all different and riffle shuffling the pack, you write the name of the force card on a slip of paper, fold it, and hand it to a spectator to hold. Have a spectator select a card as above with his finger tip, or a knife blade, as you ruffle the cards, or by his making a simple cut. Lay the card face down on the table, have the spectator read your prediction then let him turn the card over.

5. Naturally the use of this pack makes a sure-fire force. It can be used to force two cards by having two sets of 13 similar cards instead of the usual 26. However, you should be prepared to make a switch to an unprepared deck after the force. Various methods for effecting this will be explained here since they are indispensable if you wish to do a series of tricks with Svengali decks. It is hardly necessary to point out that the back patterns of all the packs must be the same.

SWITCHING PACKS

1. Pack in right hip pocket. Give some reason for putting the pack behind your back. Have it in your left hand, as the right hand goes to the back, pull out the pack from the hip pocket, change the decks and slip that just taken from the left hand into the right hip pocket. A slight turn to the right should be made to cover the right hand going to the pocket. The belt may be used in the same way.

2. Place duplicate pack in upper left vest pocket. When you turn away on some pretext, drop the pack in use from the left hand into your inside breast pocket while the right hand takes the duplicate pack from the vest pocket and put it into your left hand. Be careful to keep the elbows pressed to your sides as the change is made.

3. Duplicate pack is on your table covered with a handkerchief. Pretend to put down the pack in use as you pick up the handkerchief; in reality keep the pack in your hand, covered with the handkerchief, and the pack on the table appears to be the one put down. Use the handkerchief and put it and the pack in your pocket.

4. A bold method suitable for the smaller sized bridge decks is to have the duplicate pack in your right hand trousers pocket. Apparently put the pack in your left hand, palming it in the right. Toss the cards from the left hand to the spectators, thrust right hand into the trousers pocket, leave the palmed pack and bring out the duplicate.

5. On a chair seat have several sheets of paper and under them the duplicate pack. With the pack in your right hand lift up the sheets, drop the pack and take up the duplicate. This is a useful method in any trick such as the card stabbing in which the pack is wrapped in paper.

6. With the duplicate pack in its case in your right hand outside coat pocket, replace the pack in use in its case as if you had finished. Put it in your coat pocket, then decide to do one more trick and bring out the other case.

7. A standard method for a set performance is the use of a card servante on the back of a chair. The switch is simply done by dropping one pack into the bag of the servante and gripping the duplicate from its clip as you place a chair for a spectator to sit on facing the audience.

Other methods will be given in the special section devoted to sleights.

THE THREE HEAPS

To avoid repetition it will be taken for granted that you have shuffled and cut the pack and show all the cards to be different by one or other of the methods given above. This will be taken for granted in the description of each trick.

Cut the pack by the ends into four heaps and place one aside to be used later as an extra. Have a spectator choose one of the three remaining heaps after you have lifted the ends of the top cards to show them all different. You simply lift two as one, the lower long card making this an easy matter. Whichever packet the spectator chooses order the top card to change to whatever your force card may be, suppose it is the 8S. Lift the top card and show it. Drop the extra packet on top and at once show the faces of all the cards. The 8S has vanished. Turn the top card of one of the other two heaps, it is the 8S. Drop the extras on top of this pile and show the faces. Again the 8S has gone. Lift the top card of the third pile, it is the 8S. Drop all the rest of the cards on top and again the card has disappeared only to show up finally on the top of the pack.

CUTTING THE PACK WITH A KNIFE

When a knife blade is thrust into the ruffled pack it will, as has already been seen, rest on the back of the force card. If, however, you want to have the card appear as the bottom card of the upper portion, thrust the point of the knife in a downward direction which will bring it below the short card. If you wish to bring the knife above the short card without ruffling the deck, thrust the knife point into the pack in an upward direction. In both cases show the card preceding the force card and the one following it.

THE WRAPPED PACK

The card is selected, returned, and the pack wrapped in paper. A knife is thrust through the paper into the pack and the card will rest on the knife either above or below it.

ANY HEAP

After the return of a card cut the pack into six or seven heaps. Have one heap freely selected. Place a coin on top of that heap. Gather up the others, then show the chosen card under the coin.

REVERSED CARD

Surely this is the simplest of all reversed card effects. Reverse one of the force cards beforehand. Have the card returned, ruffle the pack and the card has vanished. Turn the pack over and let the card fall from the right thumb as already explained, and show all the backs. Then hold the pack upright, fan it with the backs to the onlookers, and the card shows up reversed.

THE UNSEEN CARD

A spectator takes a card (force card) and without looking at it, puts it in his pocket. Another person is invited to take a card, replace it and then names it. His card is ordered to leave the pack, fly to the first spectator's pocket and his card to return to the pack. Show the faces, the card has vanished and the first spectator finds that very card in his pocket.

THINK OF A CARD

Again a spectator takes a card (force card). It is returned and the pack shuffled and cut. Drop the faces of the cards before a second spectator asking him to merely think of one card that he sees. Square the pack and riffle to the card he names, draw it slightly out of the pack and ask the first person if he wants his card above or below the mentally selected card. Cut the pack and show his card accordingly.

CARD STABBING

Card chosen as usual and returned. Deal the pack into two heaps on the floor. One heap chosen, forcing the heap of duplicate cards by the usual method. Blindfolded you take a knife and stab any one of them. It will be the chosen card.

SVENGALI PREDICTION

In addition to the Svengali deck you must have 25 cards which added to the indifferent cards of the deck will make up, with one of the force cards, a complete and unprepared deck. Put these 25 cards in your left outside coat pocket.

Begin by writing a prediction, i.e. the name of the force card on a slip of paper, fold it and have it placed in a spectator's pocket. Shuffle the pack and have a spectator cut and look at the top card. He thus gets a force card. Replace the cut, again shuffle the deck, then deal the cards in two packets, a card to each alternately. Force the unprepared pile on the spectator and have him look through it to see if his card is there. It is not, so you have him pick any five cards from the other pile, without looking at them and put them face down on the table. Invite him to put his finger on the back of one of the five. Gather up the other four, add them to the rest of the force cards and hold the packet in your left hand. Now have your prediction read, the spectator turns his card, it is the card originally cut and the one named in your prediction.

Under cover of this surprise drop the force cards into your left coat pocket and bring out the unprepared cards there. You will now have a full pack of regular cards with the exception of the one force card which you can then use as a short.

Any small variation in the working, such as having the prediction already written and sealed in an envelope and having the card chosen by first shuffling and then spreading the force cards on the table, may be left to the reader's own fancy.

This trick and Jordan's "Mystery Problem" are two of the best that can be done with the Svengali principle.

THE MYSTERY PROBLEM

Some special preparation is necessary for this effective trick. The 26 long cards of the pack are Ivory finish Bicycle cards while the 26 force cards are Air Cushion finish. The remaining cards of the Ivory finish cards are placed in your right outside coat pocket with a rubber band around them. Suppose that the force cards are 4H, prepare a message reading "The Four of Hearts ———— 17th card," seal it in an envelope and you are ready.

Hand the envelope to one spectator to put in his pocket. After the usual preliminaries force a 4H on a second spectator and leave the card with him for the time being. Return to your table, say that you need only half the pack for the experiment and deal cards rapidly into two· heaps. When the card was drawn you cut the pack at that point so that after the deal all Ivory finish cards are in one heap and all the other force cards are in the other.

Snap a rubber band around the force cards and drop the packet into your right coat pocket, putting it behind the packet already there. Pick up the 26 ordinary cards, have the force card returned to it and let the spectator shuffle the cards thoroughly.

Take the packet back and to further mix the cards deal them into three piles. Detecting the chosen card by touch, it is the only air cushion card present, and note the packet into which it falls. Pick up the packets with this one in the middle and deal three piles again. This time pick the piles up with the chosen card packet on top, and at the end of the third and last deal place this packet second. The chosen card now stands 17th from the top. Have the prediction read and deal 16 cards turning up the 17th. Carelessly take out the packet of Ivory finish cards from your pocket and put it on the table. The pack is then complete and no clue is left to the mystery.

THE CARDS AND THE DICE

The card having been forced, returned and the pack cut freely, deal out six cards in a face down row, with each card slightly overlapping the preceding one. Continue in the same way until you have dealt six rows. It follows that the 1st, 3rd and 5th cards in each row will be force cards, that is if you start the count from the left end of a row, but if the count is begun from the right hand end they will lie 2nd, 4th and 6th. Hand the spectator a die, or borrow one if you can. Have it tested by trial throws and when all are satisfied that it is unprepared, ask the spectator to make a throw to determine which row shall be chosen. Whatever the result gather up the other five rows and replace the cards with the rest of the deck. Have a second throw made to indicate the position of the card in the row. If it is an odd number count from the left, if an even number from the right. Push the card out of the row and pick up the five remaining cards in such a way that the alternate set up will be completed when the last card is put on top.

Have the chosen card named and turn it over.

SVENGALI CLAIRVOYANCE

EFFECT:—The performer's assistant is genuinely blind-folded and seated with his back to the audience.

The performer shuffles a pack of cards and shows them to be well mixed. One of the spectators freely chooses a card, replaces it and the pack is again shuffled and cut. They are then dealt face down on the table. Suddenly the assistant calls "Stop." The spectator names the card he selected, the card stopped at is turned, it is the very card.

METHOD:— The trick is self explanatory once it is known that a Svengali pack is in use. After the usual preliminaries the assistant has merely to call "Stop" on an odd card. Well presented the trick will baffle any audience.

THE PRIZE WINNER

Two packs are required, one unprepared and one Svengali. Suppose the forcing cards of the latter deck are Tens of Spades. Remove the 10S from the ordinary deck and put it in your right hand trousers pocket.

To begin, show the two packs and put them on the table. Borrow a hat and while getting it palm the 10S from your pocket and secretly drop it into the hat as you lay it crown downwards on the table. Have a spectator choose one of the packs, interpreting the choice to suit yourself, i.e. if he points to the Svengali deck, then that is the pack to be used and you hand the other to him. If he chooses the ordinary deck just hand it to him to hold. Write "Ten of Spades" on a slip, fold it and give it to a second spectator to be held.

After the usual preliminaries with the prepared deck force a 10S and put the deck away. Instruct the spectator now to take from the other pack the card of the same value and suit as the one just freely selected. He searches for it and the card is not there. Tell him to count the cards, there are only 51, the card is missing. Invite the second spectator to take out your slip and read it aloud. You have predicted the card. Finally the borrowed hat is turned over and out falls the missing card.

THE MIRAGE PRINCIPLE

In addition to the Svengali principle of 26 force cards cut short, these cards are also cut a trifle narrower. The faces of all the indifferent cards and the backs of the force cards are prepared as for the slick card principle, while the faces of the force cards and the backs of the indifferent cards are slightly roughened. The result is that the cards tend to stick together in pairs and the deck can be handled almost in any fashion and the force cards will not show. They may be fanned, thumbed through, shuffled both by the riffle and the overhand method, sprung from hand to hand or spread with a sweep on the table and all with perfect safety. There would even be little risk in handing them to a spectator for a casual overhand shuffle. There are several ways of forcing a card with this deck.

1. Ruffle and let spectator insert his finger.
2. Have a knife blade inserted in the ruffle.
3. Have a number named and count down to it.
4. Deal the cards slowly and have a spectator call "Stop."
5. Spread the cards face downwards on the table and have a spectator point to any card.
7. Put the pack face downward on the table and have a spectator cut by the sides or ends anywhere he pleases.

The following tricks are good examples of what can be done with this improved Svengali deck.

MIRAGE DECK

After the usual shuffling and cutting have a card selected and have it placed on the face of the deck which you hold up towards the spectators. Suppose the card is the QH. Fan the deck show that there is no other QH in it. Hold the deck vertically, the sides parallel with the floor, ball of right thumb at the center of the upper side, the QH facing the audience. Patter about optical illusions and allow the cards to fall forward showing all the faces alike i.e. all Queens of Hearts. This results from the sides of the force cards being narrower. Square the deck and spread it face upwards on your right hand and every card shows a different face, thanks to the rough and smooth alternations keeping the cards in pairs.

THE EYE POPPER

Have the force card selected by one of the methods given, looked at and returned to the same position. Square up the pack, push off the two top cards as one and show the face of the indifferent card, turn the pack over and show the bottom card. Put the pack face down on your left hand, snap the pack and draw the top card off alone and the chosen card has apparently jumped to the top. Turn the card face down, push off two as one and bury them in the middle of the deck. This may be repeated several times quite safely. Owing to the preparation of the cards the moves are quite easy.

By riffling along the side edges the principle of narrow cards comes into play and you can cut a force card to the bottom at will.

SVENGALI MINDREADING

The deck is riffle shuffled, cut, shown all different, and then cut by the spectator.

Any number is then called by a spectator and you cut the deck into that number of piles. Turn up the index rear corners of the top cards and pretend to memorize them, then after much mental exertion write the name of the force card on a slip of paper (the top cards of the piles are all alike, of course). Fold the paper and put it on the table. Instruct the spectator that when you say "Ready," he is to seize the top card of any pile he feels impelled to take, and without looking at it, to put it face down under his hand. Stare intently at him, then suddenly call "Ready." The spectator does his part. You now gather up the piles, with the chosen packet on top.

Have the slip opened and the name of the card read aloud. The spectator turns up his card, it is the card you predicted.